SLOW COOKER
VEGETARIAN RECIPES 175

SLOW COOKER 175
VEGETARIAN RECIPES

DELICIOUS ONE-POT, NO-FUSS RECIPES FOR SOUPS, APPETIZERS, MAIN COURSES,
SIDE DISHES, DESSERTS, CAKES, PRESERVES AND DRINKS, WITH 150 PHOTOGRAPHS

CONSULTANT EDITORS:
CATHERINE ATKINSON & JENNI FLEETWOOD

HERMES
HOUSE

This edition is published by Hermes House,
an imprint of Anness Publishing Ltd,
Hermes House, 88–89 Blackfriars Road,
London SE1 8HA;
tel. 020 7401 2077; fax 020 7633 9499
www.hermeshouse.com; www.annesspublishing.com

If you like the images in this book and would like to investigate
using them for publishing, promotions or advertising, please visit
our website www.practicalpictures.com for more information.

Publisher: Joanna Lorenz
Senior Editor: Felicity Forster
Recipes: Catherine Atkinson, Jane Bamforth, Alex Barker,
    Valerie Barrett, Judy Bastyra, Jacqueline Clark, Carole Clements,
    Joanna Farrow, Christine France, Brian Glover, Nicola Graimes,
    Juliet Harbutt, Christine Ingram, Becky Johnson, Lucy Knox,
    Christine McFadden, Marlene Spieler, Kate Whiteman,
    Rosemary Wilkinson, Elizabeth Wolf-Cohen and Jeni Wright
Photography: Karl Adamson, Edward Allwright, Steve Baxter,
    Nicki Dowey, James Duncan, Ian Garlick, Michelle Garrett,
    Amanda Heywood, Janine Hosegood, David Jordan, Dave King,
    Don Last, William Lingwood, Patrick McLeavey, Thomas Odulate,
    Craig Robertson, Bridget Sargeson and Sam Stowell
Jacket Design: Nigel Partridge
Proofreading Manager: Lindsay Zamponi
Copy Editor: Jay Thundercliffe
Production Controller: Christine Ni

ETHICAL TRADING POLICY

At Anness Publishing we believe that business should be
conducted in an ethical and ecologically sustainable way, with
respect for the environment and a proper regard to the
replacement of the natural resources we employ.

As a publisher, we use a lot of wood pulp in high-quality paper
for printing, and that wood commonly comes from spruce trees.
We are therefore currently growing more than 750,000 trees
in three Scottish forest plantations: Berrymoss (130 hectares/
320 acres), West Touxhill (125 hectares/305 acres) and Deveron
Forest (75 hectares/185 acres). The forests we manage contain
more than 3.5 times the number of trees employed each year
in making paper for the books we manufacture.

Because of this ongoing ecological investment programme, you,
as our customer, can have the pleasure and reassurance of knowing
that a tree is being cultivated on your behalf to naturally replace
the materials used to make the book you are holding.

Our forestry programme is run in accordance with the UK
Woodland Assurance Scheme (UKWAS) and will be certified by
the internationally recognized Forest Stewardship Council (FSC).
The FSC is a non-government organization dedicated to
promoting responsible management of the world's forests.
Certification ensures forests are managed in an environmentally
sustainable and socially responsible way. For further information
about this scheme, go to www.annesspublishing.com/trees.

A CIP catalogue record for this book
is available from the British Library.

Previously published as part of a larger volume, *Slow Recipes: 500*

NOTES

Bracketed terms are intended for American readers.

For all recipes, quantities are given in both metric and imperial
measures and, where appropriate, in standard cups and spoons.
Follow one set of measures, but not a mixture, because they are
not interchangeable.

Standard spoon and cup measures are level.

1 tsp = 5ml, 1 tbsp = 15ml, 1 cup = 250ml/8fl oz.

Australian standard tablespoons are 20ml. Australian readers
should use 3 tsp in place of 1 tbsp for measuring small quantities.

American pints are 16fl oz/2 cups. American readers should use
20fl oz/2.5 cups in place of 1 pint when measuring liquids.

Electric oven temperatures in this book are for conventional ovens.
When using a fan oven, the temperature will probably need to be
reduced by about 10–20°C/20–40°F. Since ovens vary, you should
check with your manufacturer's instruction book for guidance.

The nutritional analysis given for each recipe is calculated per
portion (i.e. serving or item), unless otherwise stated. If the recipe
gives a range, such as Serves 4–6, then the nutritional analysis will
be for the smaller portion size, i.e. 6 servings. The analysis does
not include optional ingredients, such as salt added to taste.

Medium (US large) eggs are used unless otherwise stated.

Front cover shows Spiced Clay-pot Chickpeas –
for recipe, see page 32.

PUBLISHER'S NOTE

Although the advice and information in this book are believed to
be accurate and true at the time of going to press, neither the
authors nor the publisher can accept any legal responsibility or
liability for any errors or omissions that may have been made nor
for any inaccuracies nor for any loss, harm or injury that comes
about from following instructions or advice in this book.

Contents

Introduction

Slow cooking techniques have been used for hundreds of years, and the renewed demand for natural food that is packed with flavour and goodness, and free from artificial chemicals and

additives, means that many people are turning back to this wonderful method of cooking. Slow cooking works really well for vegetarian dishes, bringing out the full flavours of vegetables, nuts, beans, peas, rice, lentils and fruit.

Slow-cooked recipes are perfectly suited to the modern world, where people often find that they do not have time to create complex or labour-intensive meals. The beauty of many of the vegetarian recipes here is that they are prepared with an absolute minimum of fuss. For many dishes the fresh ingredients can be chopped and put straight in a casserole in the oven, a large pan on the stove or in a specially designed slow cooker and then left to simmer away gently to make a fantastically tasty meal with very little effort. Slow cooking is also ideal for dinner parties, freeing up the host to spend more time with their guests while a delicious meal is cooking away in the kitchen. As a bonus, after everybody has eaten, there will be less washing up than usual because many slow-cooked recipes require only a single pot.

Finished meals will rarely spoil if not eaten the moment they are ready. Many can be cooked and then kept warm in the oven, slow cooker or pan, or quickly reheated on the stove or in a microwave. In fact, many dishes such as curries and casseroles will actually improve if they are made the day before, so that all the flavours can fully develop and blend together. Some dishes, such as those including rice or pasta, need some last-minute attention, but when the majority of the meal has been prepared in advance, the effort is minimal.

Many recipes in this vegetarian collection call for a slow cooker, an appliance that is becoming an essential addition to many kitchens. It is a superb way to experience the pleasures of leisurely cooking as it creates such a low, gentle heat that ingredients can be added to it many hours before the food is required. Its reputation for creating soups, succulent stews and casseroles is well known, but there are many other recipes that highlight its extraordinary versatility.

The 175 deliciously tempting vegetarian recipes included here are clearly explained in steps and feature a shot of the finished dish. They are divided into sections so that you can find all the recipes you want, when you need them – Soups and Appetizers; Main Courses; Side Dishes; Desserts; Cakes; and Preserves and Drinks.

The huge appeal of slow cooking means that there are recipes from a rich heritage of worldwide cuisines, so you can be certain to find one that is perfect for any occasion. There is a wide variety of classic vegetarian dishes throughout the book, as well as delectable new creations. Start your meal with a sustaining soup, such as Minestrone with Pesto, or try an appetizer such as Mushroom and Bean Pâté. The choice of main courses offers something for everybody, such as Savoury Nut Loaf, Baked Aubergines with Cheese, and Tagine of Yam, Carrots and Prunes. Many traditional and enticing desserts are well suited to slow cooking, such as Frosted Carrot and Parsnip Cake or Steamed Chocolate Puddings, and preserves and chutneys are also featured, including Mango Chutney, Whiskey Marmalade and the classic Lemon Curd.

So why not relax, make life easier for yourself and experience the simple and delicious pleasures of slow cooking with this fantastic collection of recipes aimed at the leisurely cook.

French Onion Soup with Cheese Croûtes

Probably the most famous of all onion soups, this is a hearty and warming dish, perfect for the slow cooker.

Serves 4

40g/1½oz/3 tbsp butter
10ml/2 tsp olive oil
1.2kg/2½lb onions, sliced
5ml/1 tsp caster (superfine) sugar
15ml/1 tbsp plain (all-purpose) flour
15ml/1 tbsp sherry vinegar
30ml/2 tbsp brandy
120ml/4fl oz/½ cup dry white wine

1 litre/1¾ pints/4 cups boiling vegetable stock
5ml/1 tsp chopped fresh thyme
salt and ground black pepper

For the croûtes

4 slices day-old French stick or baguette, about 2.5cm/1in thick
1 garlic clove, halved
5ml/1 tsp French mustard
50g/2oz/½ cup grated Gruyère cheese

1 Put the butter and olive oil in the ceramic cooking pot and heat on high for about 15 minutes until melted. Add the onions and stir to coat in the butter and oil. Cover with the lid, then place a folded dish towel over the top to retain the heat and cook for 2 hours, stirring halfway through the cooking time.

2 Add the sugar and stir well. Cover again with the lid and dish towel and cook on high for 4 hours, stirring occasionally so the onions colour evenly. They should turn a dark golden colour.

3 Sprinkle the flour over the onions and stir. Next, stir in the vinegar followed by the brandy, then slowly blend in the wine. Stir in the stock and thyme and season with salt and pepper. Cook on high for 2 hours, or until the onions are very tender.

4 For the croûtes, place the bread slices under a low grill (broiler) and cook until lightly browned. Rub with the cut surface of the garlic and spread with mustard. Sprinkle the cheese over the top.

5 Turn the grill to high and cook the croûtes for 2–3 minutes, until the cheese is bubbling and brown. Ladle the soup into warmed bowls and float a croûte on top. Serve immediately.

Carrot and Coriander Soup

Root vegetables, such as carrots, are great for slow-cooker soups. Their earthy flavour becomes rich and sweet when cooked gently over a low heat.

Serves 4

450g/1lb carrots, preferably young and tender
15ml/1 tbsp sunflower oil

40g/1½oz/3 tbsp butter
1 onion, chopped
1 stick celery, plus 2–3 leafy tops
2 small potatoes, peeled
900ml/1½ pints/3¾ cups boiling vegetable stock
10ml/2 tsp ground coriander
15ml/1 tbsp chopped fresh coriander (cilantro)
150ml/¼ pint/⅔ cup milk
salt and ground black pepper

1 Trim and peel the carrots and cut into chunks. Heat the oil and 25g/1oz/2 tbsp of the butter in a pan and fry the onion over a gentle heat for 3–4 minutes until slightly softened. Do not let it brown.

2 Slice the celery and chop the potatoes, and add them to the onion in the pan. Cook for 2 minutes, then add the carrots and cook for a further minute. Transfer the fried vegetables to the ceramic cooking pot.

3 Pour the boiling stock over the vegetables, then season with salt and ground black pepper. Cover the pot with the lid and cook on low for 4–5 hours until the vegetables are tender.

4 Reserve 6–8 tiny celery leaves from the leafy tops for the garnish, then chop the remaining celery tops. Melt the remaining butter in a large pan and add the ground coriander. Fry for 1–2 minutes, stirring constantly, until the aromas are released.

5 Reduce the heat under the pan and add the chopped celery tops and fresh coriander. Fry for about 30 seconds, then remove the pan from the heat.

6 Ladle the soup into a food processor or blender and process until smooth, then pour into the pan with the celery tops and coriander. Stir in the milk and heat gently until piping hot. Adjust the seasoning and serve garnished with the reserved celery leaves.

French Onion Soup Energy 418kcal/1747kJ; Protein 11.5g; Carbohydrate 51.8g, of which sugars 19.4g; Fat 15.9g, of which saturates 8.2g; Cholesterol 33mg; Calcium 209mg; Fibre 5.3g; Sodium 1195mg.
Carrot and Coriander Soup Energy 168kcal/697kJ; Protein 3g; Carbohydrate 11.9g, of which sugars 9.2g; Fat 12.4g, of which saturates 6g; Cholesterol 24mg; Calcium 94mg; Fibre 3.1g; Sodium 758mg.

Tomato and Fresh Basil Soup

Peppery, aromatic basil is the perfect partner for sweet, ripe tomatoes – and it is easy to grow at home in a pot on a sunny kitchen windowsill. This slow-cooker soup is perfect in the late summer when fresh tomatoes are at their best and most flavoursome.

Serves 4
15ml/1 tbsp olive oil
25g/1oz/2 tbsp butter
1 onion, finely chopped
900g/2lb ripe tomatoes, roughly chopped
1 garlic clove, roughly chopped
about 600ml/1 pint/2½ cups vegetable stock
120ml/4fl oz/½ cup dry white wine
30ml/2 tbsp sun-dried tomato paste
30ml/2 tbsp shredded fresh basil
150ml/¼ pint/⅔ cup double (heavy) cream
salt and ground black pepper
whole basil leaves, to garnish

1 Heat the oil and butter in a large pan until foaming. Add the chopped onion and cook gently for about 5–7 minutes, stirring, until the onion is softened but not brown, then add the chopped tomatoes and garlic.

2 Add the vegetable stock, white wine and sun-dried tomato paste to the pan and stir to combine. Heat the mixture until just below boiling point, then carefully pour the mixture into the ceramic cooking pot.

3 Switch the slow cooker to the high or auto setting, cover with the lid and cook for 1 hour. Leave the slow cooker on automatic or switch to low and cook for a further 4–6 hours, until tender.

4 Leave the soup to cool for a few minutes, then ladle into a food processor or blender and process until smooth. Press the puréed soup through a sieve (strainer) into a clean pan.

5 Add the shredded basil and the cream to the soup and heat through, stirring. Do not allow the soup to reach boiling point. Check the consistency and add a little more stock if necessary. Season, then pour into warmed bowls and garnish with basil. Serve immediately.

Chilled Tomato and Sweet Pepper Soup

This delicious soup is made in the slow cooker before being chilled. Grilling the peppers gives a mild smoky flavour, but you can leave out this step, if you like.

Serves 4
2 red (bell) peppers
30ml/2 tbsp olive oil
1 onion, finely chopped
2 garlic cloves, crushed
675g/1½lb ripe tomatoes
120ml/4fl oz/½ cup red wine
450ml/¾ pint/scant 2 cups vegetable stock
2.5ml/½ tsp caster (superfine) sugar
salt and ground black pepper
chopped fresh chives, to garnish

For the croûtons
2 slices white bread, crusts removed
45ml/3 tbsp olive oil

1 Cut each pepper into quarters and remove the core and seeds. Place each quarter, skin side up, on a grill (broiler) rack. Grill (broil) until the skins are blistered and charred, then transfer to a bowl and cover with a plate.

2 Heat the oil in a frying pan. Add the onion and garlic and cook gently for about 10 minutes until soft, stirring occasionally. Meanwhile, remove the skin from the peppers and roughly chop the flesh. Cut the tomatoes into chunks.

3 Transfer the onions to the ceramic cooking pot and add the peppers, tomatoes, wine, stock and sugar. Cover and cook on high for 3–4 hours, or until the vegetables are very tender. Leave the soup to stand for about 10 minutes to cool slightly.

4 Ladle the soup into a food processor or blender and process until smooth. Press through a sieve (strainer) into a bowl. Leave to cool before chilling in the refrigerator for at least 3 hours.

5 Make the croûtons. Cut the bread into cubes. Heat the oil in a frying pan and fry the bread until golden. Drain on kitchen paper.

6 Season the soup to taste with salt and pepper, then ladle into chilled bowls. Top with croûtons and chopped chives and serve.

Tomato and Basil Soup Energy 335kcal/1387kJ; Protein 3.1g; Carbohydrate 11.7g, of which sugars 10.8g; Fat 28.9g, of which saturates 16.4g; Cholesterol 65mg; Calcium 50mg; Fibre 3g; Sodium 168mg.
Chilled Tomato Soup Energy 262kcal/1090kJ; Protein 3.5g; Carbohydrate 17.6g, of which sugars 11.5g; Fat 18g, of which saturates 2.6g; Cholesterol 0mg; Calcium 47mg; Fibre 3.4g; Sodium 499mg.

Wild Mushroom Soup

This robust, creamy soup is ideal for the slow cooker. The rich flavour and colour of the soup are enhanced by adding dried wild mushrooms and a dash of Madeira.

Serves 4
15g/¹/₂oz/¹/₄ cup dried wild
  mushrooms, such as morels,
  ceps or porcini
600ml/1 pint/2¹/₂ cups hot
  vegetable stock
25g/1oz/2 tbsp butter

1 onion, finely chopped
1 garlic clove, crushed
450g/1lb button (white) or other
  cultivated mushrooms, trimmed
  and sliced
15ml/1 tbsp plain (all-purpose) flour
fresh nutmeg
1.5ml/¹/₄ tsp dried thyme
60ml/4 tbsp Madeira or dry sherry
60ml/4 tbsp crème fraîche or
  sour cream
salt and ground black pepper
chopped fresh chives, to garnish

1 Put the dried mushrooms in a sieve (strainer) and rinse under cold running water to remove any grit, then place in the ceramic cooking pot. Pour over half of the hot vegetable stock and cover with the lid. Switch the slow cooker to the auto or high setting.

2 Melt the butter in a large pan. Add the onion and cook for 5–7 minutes until softened. Add the garlic and fresh mushrooms to the pan and cook for 5 minutes. Sprinkle over the flour, grate in some nutmeg and add the thyme. Cook for 3 minutes more, stirring all the time, until blended.

3 Stir in the Madeira or sherry and the remaining stock, and season with salt and pepper. Bring to the boil, then transfer to the ceramic cooking pot. Cook for 1 hour, then switch to low or leave on auto and cook for 3–4 hours.

4 Ladle the soup into a food processor or blender and process until smooth. Strain it back into the pan, pressing it with the back of a spoon to force the purée through the sieve.

5 Reheat the soup until piping hot. Stir in half the crème fraîche or sour cream. Ladle into bowls, swirl a little of the remaining crème fraîche or sour cream on top and sprinkle with chives.

Spicy Pumpkin Soup

This stunning golden-orange soup has a smooth velvety texture and a delicate taste, which is subtly spiced with cumin and garlic. Gentle simmering in the slow cooker really gives the flavours time to develop to make a wonderful autumnal dish.

Serves 4
900g/2lb pumpkin, peeled
  and seeds removed

30ml/2 tbsp olive oil
2 leeks, trimmed and sliced
1 garlic clove, crushed
5ml/1 tsp ground ginger
5ml/1 tsp ground cumin
750ml/1¹/₄ pints/3 cups
  near-boiling vegetable stock
salt and ground black pepper
60ml/4 tbsp natural (plain)
  yogurt, to serve
coriander (cilantro) leaves,
  to garnish

1 Using a sharp knife, cut the pumpkin into large chunks. Place the chunks in the ceramic cooking pot.

2 Heat the oil in a large pan and add the leeks and garlic. Cook gently until softened but not coloured.

3 Add the ginger and cumin to the pan and cook, stirring, for a further minute. Transfer the mixture into the ceramic cooking pot, pour over the stock and season with salt and black pepper.

4 Cover the slow cooker with the lid, switch to the low setting and leave to cook for 6–8 hours, or until the pumpkin pieces are very tender.

5 Ladle the soup, in batches if necessary, into a food processor or blender and process until smooth. Return the soup to the rinsed out cooking pot, cover and cook on high for 1 hour, or until piping hot. Serve in warmed individual bowls, with a swirl of natural yogurt and a few coriander leaves.

> **Cook's Tip**
> To save time, reheat the soup on the stove rather than in the slow cooker.

Spicy Pumpkin Soup Energy 89kcal/372kJ; Protein 2.3g; Carbohydrate 6.2g, of which sugars 4.7g; Fat 6.3g, of which saturates 1.1g; Cholesterol 0mg; Calcium 75mg; Fibre 3.1g; Sodium 127mg.
Wild Mushroom Soup Energy 143kcal/592kJ; Protein 3.7g; Carbohydrate 8.2g, of which sugars 3.2g; Fat 9g, of which saturates 5.3g; Cholesterol 22mg; Calcium 41mg; Fibre 2g; Sodium 174mg.

White Cabbage, Beetroot and Tomato Borscht

There are many versions of this classic soup, which originated in eastern Europe. Beetroot and sour cream are the traditional ingredients in every borscht, but other ingredients tend to be many and varied. This slow-cooker version has a sweet and sour taste and can be served piping hot or refreshingly chilled on a summer's day.

Serves 6
1 onion, chopped
1 carrot, chopped
6 raw or vacuum-packed (cooked, not pickled) beetroot (beets), 4 diced and 2 coarsely grated
400g/14oz can chopped tomatoes
6 new potatoes, cut into bitesize pieces
1 small white cabbage, thinly sliced
600ml/1 pint/2½ cups hot vegetable stock
45ml/3 tbsp sugar
30–45ml/2–3 tbsp white wine vinegar or cider vinegar
45ml/3 tbsp chopped fresh dill
salt and ground black pepper
sour cream and dill, to garnish
buttered rye bread, to serve

1 Put the onion, carrot, diced beetroot, tomatoes, new potatoes and cabbage into the ceramic cooking pot and pour over the hot vegetable stock. Cover the cooking pot with the lid and cook on the high setting for about 4 hours, or until the vegetables are just tender.

2 Add the grated beetroot, sugar and vinegar to the pot and stir until well combined. Cook for a further hour until the beetroot is cooked.

3 Taste the soup, checking for a good sweet and sour balance, and add a little more sugar and/or vinegar if necessary, tasting after each addition to check the balance. Season to taste with plenty of salt and ground black pepper.

4 Just before serving, stir the chopped dill into the soup and ladle into warmed soup bowls. Garnish each serving with a generous spoonful of sour cream and plenty more fresh dill, then serve with thick slices of buttered rye bread.

Spinach and Root Vegetable Soup

This is a deliciously rustic soup, traditionally prepared when the first vegetables of spring appear and the winter vegetables are still widely available. The slow cooker really helps to bring out the rich flavours of the root vegetables. You will need to use a large slow cooker to accommodate the spinach.

Serves 4
1 small turnip, cut into chunks
2 carrots, diced
1 small parsnip, cut into large dice
1 potato, diced
1 onion, chopped
1 garlic clove, finely chopped
¼ celeriac bulb, diced
750ml/1¼ pints/3 cups hot vegetable stock
175g/6oz fresh spinach, roughly chopped
1 small bunch fresh dill, chopped
salt and ground black pepper

For the garnish
2 hard-boiled eggs, sliced lengthways
1 lemon, sliced
30ml/2 tbsp chopped fresh parsley and dill

1 Put the turnip, carrots, parsnip, potato, onion, garlic, celeriac and vegetable stock into the ceramic cooking pot. Cook on the high or auto setting for about 1 hour, then either leave the cooker on auto or switch it to the low setting and cook for a further 5–6 hours, until all the vegetables are very soft and tender.

2 Stir the chopped spinach into the cooking pot and cook on the high setting for about 45 minutes, or until the spinach is tender but still green and leafy. Season with salt and plenty of ground black pepper.

3 Stir in the dill, then ladle the soup into warmed bowls and serve garnished with egg, lemon and a sprinkling of fresh parsley and dill.

Cook's Tip
For best results, use a really good-quality vegetable stock, preferably home-made, if possible.

White Cabbage Borscht Energy 125kcal/531kJ; Protein 3.5g; Carbohydrate 27.8g, of which sugars 7g; Fat 0.7g, of which saturates 0.1g; Cholesterol 0mg; Calcium 58mg; Fibre 3.2g; Sodium 357mg.
Spinach and Vegetable Soup Energy 67kcal/280kJ; Protein 3g; Carbohydrate 11.5g, of which sugars 7g; Fat 1.3g, of which saturates 0.1g; Cholesterol 0mg; Calcium 121mg; Fibre 3.9g; Sodium 499mg.

Spicy Red Lentil Soup with Onion

This wholesome soup is light and refreshing, and the slow cooking on top of the stove helps to bring out the subtly spiced flavour. It is delicious served as an appetizer or as a light lunch with chunks of fresh bread.

Serves 4
30–45ml/2–3 tbsp olive or
  vegetable oil
1 large onion, finely chopped
2 garlic cloves, finely chopped
1 fresh red chilli, seeded
  and chopped
5–10ml/1–2 tsp cumin seeds
5–10ml/1–2 tsp coriander seeds
1 carrot, finely chopped
scant 5ml/1 tsp ground fenugreek
5ml/1 tsp sugar
15ml/1 tbsp tomato purée (paste)
250g/9oz/generous 1 cup split
  red lentils
1.75 litres/3 pints/7½ cups
  vegetable stock
salt and ground black pepper

To serve
1 small red onion,
  finely chopped
1 large bunch of fresh flat leaf
  parsley, finely chopped
4–6 lemon wedges

1 Heat the oil in a heavy pan and stir in the onion, garlic, chilli, cumin and coriander seeds. When the onion begins to colour slightly, toss in the carrot and cook for 2–3 minutes.

2 Add the ground fenugreek, sugar and tomato purée and stir in the lentils, until all the ingredients are well combined.

3 Pour in the stock, stir well and bring to the boil. Lower the heat, partially cover the pan with a lid and simmer for 35–45 minutes, until the lentils have broken up.

4 If the soup is too thick for your preference, thin it down to the desired consistency with a little water. Season with plenty of salt and ground black pepper.

5 Serve the soup as it is or, if you prefer a smooth texture, leave it to cool slightly, then pour it into a food processor or blender and process to the desired consistency. Reheat if necessary.

6 Ladle the soup into bowls and sprinkle with the chopped onion and parsley. Serve with lemon wedges to squeeze over.

Lentil and Pasta Soup

This rustic vegetarian soup makes a warming winter meal and goes especially well with Granary or crusty Italian bread.

Serves 4–6
175g/6oz/¾ cup brown lentils
3 garlic cloves, unpeeled
1 litre/1¾ pints/4 cups water
45ml/3 tbsp olive oil
25g/1oz/2 tbsp butter
1 onion, finely chopped
2 celery sticks, finely chopped
30ml/2 tbsp sun-dried tomato
  purée (paste)
1.75 litres/3 pints/7½ cups
  vegetable stock
a few fresh marjoram leaves
a few fresh basil leaves
leaves from 1 fresh thyme sprig
50g/2oz/½ cup dried small pasta
  shapes, such as macaroni
  or tubetti
salt and ground black pepper
fresh herb leaves, to garnish

1 Put the lentils in a large pan. Smash one of the garlic cloves using the blade of a large knife (there's no need to peel it first), then add it to the lentils.

2 Pour the water into the pan and bring to the boil. Simmer for about 20–25 minutes, or until the lentils are tender. Transfer the lentils into a sieve (strainer), remove the garlic and set it aside. Rinse the lentils under the cold tap and leave to drain.

3 Heat 30ml/2 tbsp of the oil with half the butter in the pan. Add the onion and celery and cook gently for 5 minutes until the onions have softened slightly.

4 Crush the remaining garlic, then peel and mash the reserved garlic. Add to the pan with the remaining oil, the sun-dried tomato purée and the lentils. Stir, then add in the stock, herbs and salt and pepper. Bring to the boil, stirring. Simmer for about 30–35 minutes, stirring occasionally.

5 Add the pasta and bring the soup back to the boil. Reduce the heat and simmer until the pasta is tender, for about 15 minutes. Add the remaining butter and stir until melted.

6 Taste the soup for seasoning, adjusting if necessary, then serve hot in warmed bowls, sprinkled with herb leaves.

Spicy Red Lentil Soup Energy 203kcal/856kJ; Protein 11.1g; Carbohydrate 31.8g, of which sugars 7.3g; Fat 4.4g, of which saturates 0.6g; Cholesterol 0mg; Calcium 45mg; Fibre 3.5g; Sodium 26mg.
Lentil and Pasta Soup Energy 206kcal/865kJ; Protein 8.1g; Carbohydrate 23.5g, of which sugars 1.7g; Fat 9.5g, of which saturates 3g; Cholesterol 9mg; Calcium 24mg; Fibre 1.9g; Sodium 42mg.

Potage of Lentils

In this soup, red lentils and vegetables are simmered in the slow cooker until very soft, then puréed to give a rich and velvety consistency. On a hot day, serve chilled with extra lemon juice.

Serves 4
45ml/3 tbsp olive oil
1 onion, chopped
2 celery sticks, chopped
1 carrot, sliced
2 garlic cloves, chopped
1 potato, diced

250g/9oz/generous 1 cup
    red lentils
750ml/1¼ pints/3 cups
    hot vegetable stock
2 bay leaves
1 small lemon
2.5ml/½ tsp ground cumin
cayenne pepper or Tabasco sauce,
    to taste
salt and ground black pepper
lemon slices and chopped fresh
    flat leaf parsley, to serve

1 Heat the oil in a frying pan. Add the onion and cook, stirring frequently, for 5 minutes, or until beginning to soften. Stir in the celery, carrot, garlic and potato. Cook for a further 3–4 minutes.

2 Transfer the fried vegetables to the ceramic cooking pot and switch to high. Add the lentils, hot vegetable stock, bay leaves and a pared strip of lemon rind and stir to combine. Cover the slow cooker with the lid and cook on the auto or high setting for about 1 hour.

3 Leave the cooker on auto or switch to low and cook for a further 4–5 hours, or until the vegetables and lentils are soft and very tender.

4 Remove and discard the bay leaves and the lemon rind. Process the soup in a food processor or blender until smooth. Transfer the soup back to the cleaned cooking pot, stir in the cumin and cayenne pepper or Tabasco, and season.

5 Cook the soup on high for a further 45 minutes, or until piping hot. Squeeze in lemon juice to taste and check the seasoning. Ladle into warmed bowls and top each portion with lemon slices and a sprinkling of chopped fresh parsley.

Minestrone with Pesto

Pesto is stirred into this slow-cooker version of minestrone to add extra flavour and colour. This soup makes an excellent supper dish when served with bread. To save time, you can use ready-made bottled pesto.

Serves 4
30ml/2 tbsp olive oil
1 onion, finely chopped
2 celery sticks, finely chopped
1 large carrot, finely chopped
1 potato, weighing about 115g/4oz,
    cut into 1cm/½in cubes
1 litre/1¾ pints/4 cups hot
    vegetable stock
75g/3oz green beans, cut into
    5cm/2in pieces

1 courgette (zucchini), thinly sliced
2 Italian plum tomatoes, peeled
    and chopped
200g/7oz can cannellini beans,
    drained and rinsed
¼ Savoy cabbage, shredded
40g/1½oz dried 'quick-cook'
    spaghetti or vermicelli, broken
    into short lengths
salt and ground black pepper

For the pesto
about 20 fresh basil leaves
1 garlic clove
10ml/2 tsp pine nuts
15ml/1 tbsp freshly grated
    Parmesan cheese
15ml/1 tbsp freshly grated
    Pecorino cheese
30ml/2 tbsp olive oil

1 Heat the olive oil in a pan, then add the onion, celery and carrot and cook, stirring, for 7 minutes, until they begin to soften.

2 Transfer the fried vegetables to the ceramic cooking pot. Add the potato cubes and vegetable stock, cover the cooking pot with the lid and cook on high for 1¼ hours.

3 Add the green beans, courgette, tomatoes and cannellini beans to the pot. Cover and cook for 1 hour, then stir in the cabbage and pasta and cook for a further 20 minutes.

4 Meanwhile, place all the pesto ingredients in a food processor. Blend to a smooth sauce, adding 15–45ml/1–3 tbsp water through the feeder tube to loosen the mixture if necessary.

5 Stir 30ml/2 tbsp of the pesto sauce into the soup. Check the seasoning, adding more if necessary. Serve hot, in warmed bowls, with the remaining pesto spooned on top of each serving.

Potage of Lentils Energy 300kcal/1265kJ; Protein 15.8g; Carbohydrate 40.1g, of which sugars 3.6g; Fat 9.6g, of which saturates 1.3g; Cholesterol 0mg; Calcium 47mg; Fibre 3.9g; Sodium 456mg.
Minestrone Energy 263kcal/1098kJ; Protein 8.5g; Carbohydrate 25.1g, of which sugars 7g; Fat 14.9g, of which saturates 2.8g; Cholesterol 5mg; Calcium 103mg; Fibre 5.4g; Sodium 1034mg.

Italian Farmhouse Soup

Root vegetables form the base of this chunky, minestrone-style main meal soup. Cooked in one pot, it is simple to make as well as versatile – you can vary the vegetables according to what you have to hand.

Serves 4
30ml/2 tbsp olive oil
1 onion, roughly chopped
3 carrots, cut into large chunks
175–200g/6–7oz turnips, cut into large chunks
about 175g/6oz swede (rutabaga), cut into large chunks
400g/14oz can chopped Italian tomatoes
15ml/1 tbsp tomato purée (paste)
5ml/1 tsp dried mixed herbs
5ml/1 tsp dried oregano
50g/2oz dried (bell) peppers, washed and thinly sliced (optional)
1.5 litres/2½ pints/6¼ cups vegetable stock or water
50g/2oz/½ cup dried small macaroni or conchiglie
400g/14oz can red kidney beans, rinsed and drained
30ml/2 tbsp chopped fresh flat leaf parsley
salt and ground black pepper
freshly grated Parmesan cheese, to serve

1 Heat the olive oil in a large pan, add the onion and cook over a low heat for about 5 minutes until softened. Add the carrot, turnip and swede chunks, canned chopped tomatoes, tomato purée, dried mixed herbs, dried oregano and dried peppers, if using. Stir in salt and pepper to taste.

2 Pour in the vegetable stock or water and bring to the boil. Stir well, cover the pan, then lower the heat and simmer for 30–40 minutes, stirring occasionally.

3 Add the pasta to the pan and bring quickly to the boil, stirring. Lower the heat and simmer, uncovered, for about 5–7 minutes until the pasta is only just tender, or according to the instructions on the packet. Stir frequently.

4 Stir in the kidney beans. Heat through for 2–3 minutes, then remove the pan from the heat and stir in the parsley. Taste the soup for seasoning. Serve hot in warmed soup bowls, with grated Parmesan cheese handed separately.

Bean and Pistou Soup

This hearty vegetarian soup is typical of provençal-style cooking. It is cooked slowly in a bean pot in the oven and richly flavoured with a home-made garlic and fresh basil pistou sauce.

Serves 4–6
150g/5oz/scant 1 cup dried haricot (navy) beans, soaked overnight in cold water
150g/5oz/scant 1 cup dried flageolet or cannellini beans, soaked overnight in cold water
1 onion, chopped
1.2 litres/2 pints/5 cups hot vegetable stock
2 carrots, roughly chopped
225g/8oz Savoy cabbage, shredded
1 large potato, about 225g/8oz, roughly chopped
225g/8oz green beans, chopped
salt and ground black pepper
basil leaves, to garnish

For the pistou
4 garlic cloves
8 large sprigs basil leaves
90ml/6 tbsp olive oil
60ml/4 tbsp freshly grated Parmesan cheese

1 Soak a bean pot in cold water for 20 minutes then drain. Drain the soaked haricot and flageolet or cannellini beans and place in the bean pot. Add the onion and pour over sufficient cold water to come 5cm/2in above the beans. Cover and place the pot in an unheated oven. Set the oven to 200°C/400°F/Gas 6 and cook for about 1½ hours, or until the beans are tender.

2 Drain the beans and onion. Place half the beans and onion in a food processor and process to a paste. Return the drained beans and the bean paste to the pot. Add the vegetable stock.

3 Add the chopped carrots, shredded cabbage, chopped potato and green beans to the bean pot. Season with salt and pepper, cover and return the pot to the oven. Reduce the oven temperature to 180°C/350°F/Gas 4 and cook for 1 hour, or until all the vegetables are cooked right through.

4 Meanwhile, place the garlic and basil in a mortar and pound with a pestle, then gradually beat in the oil. Stir in the grated Parmesan. Stir half the pistou into the soup and then ladle into warmed soup bowls. Top each serving with a spoonful of the remaining pistou and serve garnished with basil.

Farmhouse Soup Energy 248kcal/1047kJ; Protein 10.2g; Carbohydrate 38.6g, of which sugars 14.9g; Fat 7g, of which saturates 1.1g; Cholesterol 0mg; Calcium 139mg; Fibre 10.6g; Sodium 422mg.
Bean and Pistou Soup Energy 305kcal/1281kJ; Protein 17.2g; Carbohydrate 34.6g, of which sugars 7.5g; Fat 11.8g, of which saturates 3.3g; Cholesterol 10mg; Calcium 215mg; Fibre 10.8g; Sodium 133mg.

Black-eyed Bean and Tomato Broth

This delicious soup, made with black-eyed beans and turmeric-tinted tomato broth, is flavoured with tangy lemon and speckled with chopped fresh coriander. It is ideal for serving at parties as it can be made in advance – simply multiply the quantities to the amount required.

Serves 4

175g/6oz/1 cup black-eyed
  beans (peas), soaked overnight
15ml/1 tbsp olive oil

2 onions, chopped
4 garlic cloves, chopped
1 medium-hot or 2–3 mild fresh
  chillies, chopped
5ml/1 tsp ground cumin
5ml/1 tsp ground turmeric
250g/9oz fresh or canned
  tomatoes, diced
600ml/1 pint/2½ cups
  vegetable stock
25g/1oz fresh coriander (cilantro)
  leaves, roughly chopped
juice of ½ lemon
salt and ground black pepper
pitta bread, to serve

1 Put the black-eyed beans in a pan and add enough cold water to cover. Bring to the boil, then cook on a high heat for about 5–10 minutes, skimming off any foam that rises to the top. Remove from the heat, cover the pan with a tight-fitting lid and leave to stand for 2 hours.

2 Drain the beans, return to the pan, cover with fresh cold water, then simmer for 35–40 minutes, or until the beans are tender. Drain and set aside.

3 Heat the olive oil in a pan, add the chopped onions, garlic and fresh chilli and cook for 5 minutes, or until the onion has started to soften and turn translucent.

4 Stir the cumin and turmeric into the pan and cook, stirring, for a minute until the spices release their fragrances. Add the fresh or canned tomatoes, the vegetable stock, half the chopped coriander and the drained beans, and simmer gently for 20–30 minutes.

5 Stir in the lemon juice, season with salt and pepper and add the remaining coriander. Serve immediately with pitta bread.

Old Country Mushroom, Bean and Barley Soup

This hearty and rustic soup is easy to make as all the ingredients are simply placed in one pot and then cooked together. It is perfect on a freezing cold day, when you can gather in the kitchen while it slowly cooks on the stove. Serve in warmed bowls, with plenty of rye or pumpernickel bread to mop up the delicious broth.

Serves 6–8

30–45ml/2–3 tbsp small haricot
  (navy) beans, soaked overnight

45–60ml/3–4 tbsp green split peas
45–60ml/3–4 tbsp yellow split peas
90–105ml/6–7 tbsp pearl barley
1 onion, chopped
2 carrots, sliced
3 celery sticks, diced or sliced
½ baking potato, peeled and cut
  into chunks
10g/¼oz or 45ml/3 tbsp mixed
  flavourful dried mushrooms
5 garlic cloves, sliced
2 litres/3½ pints/8 cups water
2 vegetable stock (bouillon) cubes
salt and ground black pepper
30–45ml/2–3 tbsp chopped fresh
  parsley, to garnish
rye or pumpernickel bread, to serve

1 Place the haricot beans, green and yellow split peas, pearl barley, chopped onion, carrots, celery, potato, mixed mushrooms and garlic into a large, heavy pan. Pour in the water.

2 Bring the mixture to the boil, then reduce the heat, cover with a tight-fitting lid and simmer gently for about 1½ hours, or until the beans are tender.

3 Crumble the stock cubes into the soup. Taste for seasoning, adjusting if necessary – remember the stock cubes will be quite salty. Ladle into warmed bowls, garnish with parsley and serve with rye or pumpernickel bread.

Cook's Tip
Ensure that you do not add the stock cubes until near the end of the cooking time as the salt will prevent the beans from becoming tender.

Bean Broth Energy 222kcal/934kJ; Protein 14.3g; Carbohydrate 31.8g, of which sugars 10.9g; Fat 5.1g, of which saturates 0.6g; Cholesterol 0mg; Calcium 273mg; Fibre 13.9g; Sodium 50mg.
Old Country Soup Energy 130kcal/553kJ; Protein 6.7g; Carbohydrate 26.1g, of which sugars 2.2g; Fat 0.6g, of which saturates 0.1g; Cholesterol 0mg; Calcium 24mg; Fibre 1.8g; Sodium 20mg.

Spicy Carrot Dip

When carrots are cooked over a gentle heat in a slow cooker their flavour intensifies and becomes deliciously sweet, making them the perfect partner for hot, spicy flavourings.

Serves 4
1 onion, finely chopped
3 carrots, grated, plus extra
 to garnish (optional)

grated rind and juice of 1 orange
15ml/1 tbsp hot curry paste
150ml/¼ pint/⅔ cup natural
 (plain) yogurt
handful of fresh basil leaves
15ml/1 tbsp fresh lemon juice
dash Tabasco sauce (optional)
salt and ground black pepper

1 Put the onion, carrots, orange rind and juice, and curry paste in the ceramic cooking pot and stir well to combine. Cover with the lid and cook on high for 2 hours, or until the carrots are soft and tender.

2 Uncover the pot and leave to cool for about 10 minutes, then transfer the mixture to a food processor or blender and process until smooth.

3 Transfer the carrot purée to a mixing bowl and leave, uncovered, for about 1 hour to cool completely.

4 Add the yogurt to the cooled carrot purée. Tear the basil leaves roughly into small pieces, then stir them into the mixture until thoroughly combined.

5 Stir in the lemon juice and Tabasco, if using, then season to taste with salt and pepper. Serve at room temperature, within a few hours of making.

> **Cook's Tip**
> *Serve this versatile dip as an appetizer or on its own with wheat crackers or fiery tortilla chips, or with a variety of raw vegetables for a healthy snack.*

Cheese-stuffed Pears

These pears, made in the slow cooker, make a sublime dish with their scrumptious creamy topping. If you don't have a very large slow cooker, choose short squat pears rather than long, tapering ones, so that they will fit in a single layer.

Serves 4
50g/2oz/¼ cup ricotta cheese
50g/2oz/¼ cup dolcelatte cheese

15ml/1 tbsp honey
½ celery stick, finely sliced
8 green olives, pitted and
 roughly chopped
4 dates, pitted and cut into
 thin strips
pinch of paprika
2 medium barely ripe pears
150ml/¼ pint/⅔ cup fresh
 apple juice
mixed salad leaves, to serve
 (optional)

1 Place the ricotta cheese in a bowl and crumble in the dolcelatte. Add the honey, celery, olives, dates and paprika and mix together well until creamy and thoroughly blended.

2 Halve the pears lengthways. Use a melon baller or teaspoon to remove the cores and make a hollow for the filling.

3 Divide the ricotta filling equally between the pears, packing it into the hollow, then arrange the fruit in a single layer in the ceramic cooking pot.

4 Pour the apple juice around the pears, then cover with the lid. Cook on high for 1½–2 hours, or until the fruit is tender. (The cooking time will depend on the ripeness of the pears.)

5 Remove the pears from the slow cooker and brown them under a hot grill (broiler) for a few minutes. Serve with mixed salad leaves, if you like.

> **Cook's Tip**
> *These pears go particularly well with slightly bitter and peppery leaves, such as chicory and rocket (arugula). Try them tossed in a walnut oil dressing.*

Spiced Carrot Dip Energy 58kcal/241kJ; Protein 2.5g; Carbohydrate 9.5g, of which sugars 8.4g; Fat 1.3g, of which saturates 0.4g; Cholesterol 0mg; Calcium 80mg; Fibre 1.3g; Sodium 34mg.
Cheese-stuffed Pears Energy 236kcal/992kJ; Protein 6.9g; Carbohydrate 35.6g, of which sugars 35.6g; Fat 8.2g, of which saturates 5.0g; Cholesterol 24mg; Calcium 141mg; Fibre 4.1g; Sodium 261mg.

Mini Baked Potatoes with Blue Cheese

Baked potatoes are one of the ultimate slow-cooked foods. These mini versions are perfect as finger food for a party, especially as you can prepare them in advance.

Makes 20
20 small new or salad potatoes

60ml/4 tbsp vegetable oil
coarse salt
120ml/4fl oz/½ cup sour cream
25g/1oz blue cheese, such as
 Roquefort or Stilton, crumbled
30ml/2 tbsp chopped fresh
 chives, for sprinkling

1 Preheat the oven to 180°C/350°F/Gas 4. Wash and dry the potatoes. Pour the oil into a bowl. Add the potatoes and toss to coat thoroughly.

2 Dip the potatoes in the coarse salt to coat lightly. Spread out the potatoes in one layer on a baking sheet. Bake for about 45–50 minutes until tender.

3 Put the sour cream into a small bowl and add the blue cheese. Blend together until well combined.

4 Cut a cross in the top of each cooked potato with a sharp knife. Press the sides of each potato gently with your fingers to make them open up.

5 While the potatoes are still hot, top each one with a generous dollop of the blue cheese mixture. It will melt down into the potato nicely. Sprinkle with chives on a serving dish and serve hot or at room temperature.

> **Cook's Tip**
> This dish works just as well as a light snack. If you don't want to be bothered with lots of fiddly small potatoes, simply bake one large floury potato per person. Use whatever blue cheese is available to make the creamy topping.

Wild Mushroom and Sun-dried Tomato Soufflés

These impressive little soufflés are baked in individual earthenware pots. They are packed with rich, Italian flavours and are remarkably easy to prepare and cook.

Serves 4
25g/1oz/½ cup dried
 cep mushrooms
40g/1½oz/3 tbsp butter, plus
 extra for greasing
20ml/4 tsp grated
 Parmesan cheese
40g/1½oz/⅓ cup plain
 (all-purpose) flour
250ml/8fl oz/1 cup milk
50g/2oz/½ cup grated mature
 (sharp) Cheddar cheese
4 eggs, separated
2 sun-dried tomatoes in oil,
 drained and chopped
15ml/1 tbsp chopped
 fresh chives
salt and ground black pepper

1 Place the ceps in a bowl, pour over enough warm water to cover and leave to soak for 15 minutes. Grease four individual earthenware soufflé dishes with a little butter. Sprinkle the grated Parmesan into the soufflé dishes and rotate each dish to coat the sides with cheese. Preheat the oven to 190°C/375°F/Gas 5.

2 Melt the butter in a large pan, remove from the heat and stir in the flour. Cook over low heat for 1 minute, stirring constantly. Remove the pan from the heat and gradually stir in the milk. Return to the heat and bring to the boil, stirring constantly, until the sauce has thickened.

3 Remove the sauce from the heat, then stir in the grated Cheddar cheese and plenty of seasoning. Beat in the egg yolks, one at a time, then stir in the chopped sun-dried tomatoes and the chives. Drain the soaked mushrooms, then coarsely chop them and add them to the cheese sauce.

4 Whisk the egg whites until they stand in soft peaks. Mix one spoonful into the sauce then carefully fold in the rest. Divide the mixture among the soufflé dishes and bake for 25 minutes, or until the soufflés are golden brown on top, well risen and just firm to the touch. Serve immediately – before they sink.

Mini Baked Potatoes Energy 63kcal/262kJ; Protein 1.1g; Carbohydrate 6.3g, of which sugars 0.7g; Fat 3.9g, of which saturates 1.3g; Cholesterol 5mg; Calcium 14mg; Fibre 0.4g; Sodium 22mg.
Mushroom Soufflés Energy 290kcal/1207kJ; Protein 14.7g; Carbohydrate 11.6g, of which sugars 3.9g; Fat 20.8g, of which saturates 11.2g; Cholesterol 232mg; Calcium 274mg; Fibre 0.6g; Sodium 305mg.

Mushroom and Bean Pâté

Making pâté in the slow cooker results in this light and tasty version. It is delicious served on triangles of wholemeal toast for a vegetarian appetizer, or with crusty French bread as a light lunch served with salad.

Serves 8
450g/1lb/6 cups mushrooms, sliced
1 onion, finely chopped
2 garlic cloves, crushed
1 red (bell) pepper, seeded
 and diced
30ml/2 tbsp vegetable stock
30ml/2 tbsp dry white wine
400g/14oz can red kidney beans,
 rinsed and drained
1 egg, beaten
50g/2oz/1 cup fresh wholemeal
 (whole-wheat) breadcrumbs
10ml/2 tsp chopped fresh thyme
10ml/2 tsp chopped fresh rosemary
salt and ground black pepper
salad leaves, fresh herbs and
 tomato wedges, to garnish

1 Put the mushrooms, onion, garlic, red pepper, stock and wine in the ceramic cooking pot. Cover and cook on high for 2 hours, then set aside for about 10 minutes to cool.

2 Transfer the mixture to a food processor or blender and add the kidney beans. Process to make a smooth purée, stopping the machine once or twice to scrape down the sides.

3 Lightly grease and line a 900g/2lb loaf tin (pan). Put an inverted saucer or metal pastry ring in the bottom of the ceramic cooking pot. Pour in about 2.5cm/1in of hot water, and set to high.

4 Transfer the vegetable mixture to a bowl. Add the egg, breadcrumbs and herbs, and season. Mix thoroughly, then spoon into the loaf tin and cover with cling film (plastic wrap) or foil.

5 Put the tin in the slow cooker and pour in enough boiling water to come just over halfway up the sides of the tin. Cover with the lid and cook on high for 4 hours, or until lightly set.

6 Remove the tin and place on a wire rack until cool. Chill for several hours, or overnight. Turn the pâté out of the tin, remove the lining paper and serve garnished with salad leaves, herbs and tomato wedges.

Red Lentil and Goat's Cheese Pâté

The smoky, earthy flavour of red lentils is a perfect partner for tangy goat's cheese in this pâté that is made in the slow cooker.

Serves 8
225g/8oz/1 cup red lentils
1 shallot, very finely chopped
1 bay leaf
475ml/16fl oz/2 cups near-boiling
 vegetable stock
115g/4oz/½ cup soft goat's cheese
5ml/1 tsp ground cumin
3 eggs, lightly beaten
salt and ground black pepper
Melba toast and rocket (arugula)
 leaves, to serve

1 Rinse the lentils, drain, then place in the ceramic cooking pot and add the shallot, bay leaf and hot vegetable stock. Switch the slow cooker to high, cover and cook for 2 hours, or until the liquid has been absorbed and the lentils are soft and pulpy. Stir once or twice towards the end of cooking time.

2 Turn off the slow cooker. Transfer the lentil mixture to a bowl, remove the bay leaf and leave to cool uncovered. Meanwhile, wash and dry the ceramic cooking pot.

3 Lightly grease a 900ml/1½ pint/3¾ cup loaf tin (pan) with oil and line the base with baking parchment. Put an upturned saucer or metal pastry ring in the bottom of the ceramic cooking pot and pour in about 2.5cm/1in of hot water. Set the cooker to high.

4 Put the goat's cheese in a bowl with the cumin and beat together until creamy. Gradually mix in the eggs until blended. Stir in the lentil mixture and season well with salt and pepper.

5 Place the mixture in the tin. Cover with clear film (plastic wrap) or foil. Put the tin in the slow cooker and pour in boiling water to come just over halfway up the sides. Cover with the lid and cook for 3–3½ hours, until the pâté is lightly set.

6 Remove the tin from the slow cooker and place on a wire rack to cool completely. Chill for several hours, or overnight.

7 To serve, turn the pâté out of the tin, peel off the parchment and cut into slices. Serve with Melba toast and rocket leaves.

Mushroom and Bean Pâté Energy 85kcal/358kJ; Protein 5.5g; Carbohydrate 12.3g, of which sugars 3.8g; Fat 1.6g, of which saturates 0.4g; Cholesterol 28mg; Calcium 47mg; Fibre 3.7g; Sodium 187mg.
Red Lentil Pâté Energy 136kcal/573kJ; Protein 9.8g; Carbohydrate 16g, of which sugars 0.9g; Fat 4.1g, of which saturates 2.6g; Cholesterol 13mg; Calcium 34mg; Fibre 1.4g; Sodium 97mg.

Layered Vegetable Terrine

A combination of vegetables
and herbs layered and
slowly baked in a spinach-
lined loaf tin. Delicious
served hot or warm with
a simple salad garnish.

Serves 6
3 red (bell) peppers, halved
450g/1lb main crop
  waxy potatoes

115g/4oz spinach leaves,
  trimmed
25g/1oz/2 tbsp butter
pinch grated nutmeg
115g/4oz/1 cup vegetarian
  Cheddar cheese, grated
1 courgette (zucchini), sliced
  lengthways and blanched
salt and ground black pepper
salad leaves and tomatoes,
  to serve

1 Preheat the oven to 180°C/350°F/Gas 4. Place the peppers in a roasting pan and roast, cores in place, for 30–45 minutes until charred. Remove from the oven. Place in a plastic bag to cool. Peel the skins and remove the cores. Halve the potatoes and boil in lightly salted water for 10–15 minutes.

2 Blanch the spinach for a few seconds in boiling water. Drain and pat dry on kitchen paper. Line the base and sides of a 900g/2lb loaf tin (pan) with the spinach, making sure the leaves overlap slightly.

3 Slice the potatoes thinly and lay one-third of the potatoes over the base, dot with a little of the butter and season with salt, pepper and nutmeg. Sprinkle a little cheese over.

4 Arrange three of the peeled pepper halves on top. Sprinkle a little cheese over and then a layer of courgettes. Lay another one-third of the potatoes on top with the remaining peppers and some more cheese, seasoning as you go. Lay the final layer of potato on top and scatter over any remaining cheese. Fold the spinach leaves over. Cover with foil.

5 Place the loaf tin in a roasting pan and pour boiling water around the outside, making sure the water comes to halfway up the sides of the tin. Bake for about 45 minutes to 1 hour. Remove from the oven and turn the loaf out on to a serving plate. Serve sliced with salad leaves and tomatoes.

Onion and Potato Cake

Serve this ever-popular dish with a fresh green salad accompaniment. It is also particularly good alongside a selection of roasted vegetables. The slow cooking time will vary a little depending on the potatoes and how thinly they are sliced: use a food processor or mandolin (if you have one) to make paper-thin slices. The mound of potatoes will cook down to make a thick buttery cake.

Serves 6
900g/2lb new potatoes, peeled
  and thinly sliced
2 medium onions, very
  finely chopped
salt and ground black pepper
115g/4oz/½ cup butter

1 Preheat the oven to 190°C/375°F/Gas 5. Lightly butter a 20cm/8in round cake tin (pan) and line the base with a circle of baking parchment.

2 Arrange some of the potato slices evenly in the bottom of the tin and then sprinkle some of the onions over them. Season with salt and pepper. Reserve 25g/1oz/2 tbsp of the butter and dot the mixture with tiny pieces of the remaining butter.

3 Repeat these layers, using up all the ingredients and finishing with a layer of potatoes. Melt the reserved butter and brush it over the top.

4 Cover the potatoes with foil, put in the hot oven and cook for 1–1½ hours, until tender and golden. Remove from the oven and leave to stand, still covered, for 10–15 minutes.

5 Carefully turn out the onion cake on to a warmed plate and serve with a salad or as an accompaniment to a main meal.

> **Cook's Tip**
> If using old potatoes, cook and serve in an earthenware or ovenproof glass dish. Then remove the cover for the final 10–15 minutes to lightly brown the top.

Vegetable Terrine Energy 205kcal/854kJ; Protein 8.3g; Carbohydrate 19.2g, of which sugars 7.7g; Fat 10.6g, of which saturates 6.6g; Cholesterol 27mg; Calcium 196mg; Fibre 3g; Sodium 203mg.
Onion and Potato Cake Energy 272kcal/1133kJ; Protein 3.5g; Carbohydrate 29.5g, of which sugars 5.8g; Fat 16.3g, of which saturates 10.1g; Cholesterol 41mg; Calcium 29mg; Fibre 2.4g; Sodium 135mg.

Baked Tomato Casserole

This is a beautifully fresh-tasting tomato dish. Slow baking in the oven helps to intensify the flavour of the tomatoes and the spices add a subtle piquancy.

Serves 4
40ml/2½ tbsp olive oil
45ml/3 tbsp chopped fresh flat
  leaf parsley
1kg/2¼lb firm ripe tomatoes
5ml/1 tsp caster (superfine) sugar
40g/1½oz/scant 1 cup
  day-old breadcrumbs
2.5ml/½ tsp chilli powder
  or paprika
salt
chopped parsley, to garnish
rye bread, to serve

1 Preheat the oven to 200°C/400°F/Gas 6. Brush a large baking dish with 15ml/1 tbsp of the oil.

2 Sprinkle the chopped flat leaf parsley over the base of the dish. Cut the tomatoes into even slices, discarding the two end slices of each. Arrange the slices of tomato in the dish so that they overlap slightly. Sprinkle them with a little salt and the caster sugar.

3 In a mixing bowl, stir together the breadcrumbs, the remaining oil and chilli powder or paprika. Sprinkle this mixture over the top of the tomatoes.

4 Place the dish in the preheated oven and bake for about 40–50 minutes until the tomatoes are tender and the breadcrumb topping is golden brown and crisp. If the topping is getting too brown during cooking, loosely cover the dish with foil. Serve hot or cold, garnished with chopped parsley and accompanied by rye bread.

> **Variation**
> To vary this recipe, replace half the quantity of tomatoes with 450g/1lb courgettes (zucchini). Slice the courgettes evenly and arrange alternate slices of courgette and tomato in the dish, overlapping the slices as before.

New Potato and Vegetable Casserole

Here is a simple one-pot meal that is ideal for feeding large numbers of people. It is packed with nutritious vegetables that are lightly spiced and has lots of garlic.

Serves 4
60ml/4 tbsp olive oil
1 large onion, chopped
2 small aubergines (eggplants),
  cut into small cubes
4 courgettes (zucchini), cut into
  small chunks
1 green (bell) pepper, seeded
  and chopped
1 red or yellow (bell) pepper,
  seeded and chopped
115g/4oz/1 cup fresh or
  frozen peas
115g/4oz green beans
450g/1lb new or salad
  potatoes, cubed
2.5ml/½ tsp cinnamon
2.5ml/½ tsp ground cumin
5ml/1 tsp paprika
4–5 tomatoes, skinned
400g/14oz can chopped tomatoes
30ml/2 tbsp chopped fresh parsley
3–4 garlic cloves, crushed
350ml/12fl oz/1½ cups hot
  vegetable stock
salt and ground black pepper
black olives, to garnish
fresh parsley sprigs, to garnish

1 Preheat the oven to 190°C/375°F/Gas 5. Heat 45ml/3 tbsp of the oil in a heavy frying pan, add the onion and cook until softened and golden. Add the aubergines and cook, stirring, for about 3 minutes.

2 Add the courgettes, green and red or yellow peppers, peas, beans and potatoes, together with the spices and seasoning. Continue to cook the mixture for about 3 minutes, stirring all the time. Transfer to a shallow ovenproof dish.

3 Halve, seed and chop the fresh tomatoes and mix with the canned tomatoes, chopped fresh parsley, garlic and the remaining olive oil in a bowl.

4 Pour the hot vegetable stock over the vegetable mixture and then spoon over the prepared tomato mixture.

5 Cover the dish with the lid and bake in the preheated oven for 30–45 minutes until the vegetables are tender. Serve hot, garnished with black olives and parsley.

Baked Tomato Casserole Energy 155kcal/649kJ; Protein 3.1g; Carbohydrate 15.7g, of which sugars 8.2g; Fat 9.3g, of which saturates 1.4g; Cholesterol 0mg; Calcium 46mg; Fibre 3.1g; Sodium 101mg.
Potato Casserole Energy 307kcal/1282kJ; Protein 9.4g; Carbohydrate 39.9g, of which sugars 17.8g; Fat 13.3g, of which saturates 2.1g; Cholesterol 0mg; Calcium 92mg; Fibre 8.7g; Sodium 30mg.

Harvest Vegetable and Lentil Bake

This oven-baked dish is easy to prepare and is delicious served with warm garlic bread. Try adding a few sun-dried tomatoes with the lentils, if you like.

Serves 6

15ml/1 tbsp sunflower or olive oil
2 leeks, sliced
1 garlic clove, crushed
4 celery sticks, chopped
2 carrots, sliced
2 parsnips, diced
1 sweet potato, diced
225g/8oz swede (rutabaga), diced
175g/6oz/¾ cup whole brown or green lentils
450g/1lb tomatoes, peeled, seeded and chopped
15ml/1 tbsp chopped fresh thyme
15ml/1 tbsp chopped fresh marjoram
900ml/1½ pints/3¾ cups hot vegetable stock
15ml/1 tbsp cornflour (cornstarch)
45ml/3 tbsp water
salt and ground black pepper
warm garlic bread, to serve

1 Preheat the oven to 180°C/350°F/Gas 4. Heat the oil in a large, flameproof casserole. Add the leeks, garlic and celery, and cook over low heat, stirring occasionally, for about 3 minutes, until the leeks are just beginning to soften.

2 Add the carrots, parsnips, sweet potato, swede, brown or green lentils, tomatoes, thyme, marjoram and vegetable stock and season to taste with salt and pepper. Stir the vegetables well to combine. Bring to the boil, stirring occasionally, to make sure that the vegetables do not stick to the base of the pan.

3 Cover and bake for about 50 minutes, until the vegetables and lentils are cooked through and tender, removing the casserole from the oven and gently stirring the vegetable mixture once or twice during the cooking time.

4 Remove the casserole from the oven. Mix the cornflour with 45ml/3 tbsp cold water in a small bowl to make a smooth paste. Stir the mixture into the casserole and heat on top of the stove, stirring until the mixture comes to the boil and thickens, then simmer gently for 2 minutes, stirring constantly. Taste and adjust the seasoning, if necessary, then serve in warmed bowls. Hand around garlic bread.

Tagine of Yam, Carrots and Prunes

A tagine featuring tender caramelized vegetables.

Serves 4–6

45ml/3 tbsp olive oil
25–30 button (pearl) onions, blanched and peeled
900g/2lb yam, cut into chunks
2–3 carrots, cut into chunks
150g/5oz ready-to-eat pitted prunes
5ml/1 tsp ground cinnamon
2.5ml/½ tsp ground ginger
10ml/2 tsp clear honey
450ml/¾ pint/scant 2 cups vegetable stock
small bunch of fresh coriander (cilantro), finely chopped
small bunch of mint, finely chopped
salt and ground black pepper

1 Preheat the oven to 200°C/400°F/Gas 6. Heat the oil in a flameproof casserole. Cook the onions for 5 minutes, then set aside half of them. Cook the yam and carrots until browned. Stir in the prunes, cinnamon, ginger, honey and stock. Season well.

2 Cover and bake for 45 minutes. Stir in the reserved onions and bake for 10 minutes. Stir in the coriander and mint, and serve.

Mixed Vegetable Casserole

A gloriously simple and nutritious dish.

Serves 4

1 aubergine (eggplant), diced
115g/4oz/½ cup okra, halved
225g/8oz/2 cups frozen peas
225g/8oz/1½ cups green beans
4 courgettes (zucchini), diced
2 onions, finely chopped
450g/1lb potatoes, diced
1 red (bell) pepper, sliced
400g/14oz can chopped tomatoes
150ml/¼ pint/⅔ cup vegetable stock
60ml/4 tbsp olive oil
75ml/5 tbsp chopped fresh parsley
5ml/1 tsp paprika
salt
3 tomatoes, sliced and 1 courgette (zucchini), sliced, for the topping

1 Preheat the oven to 190°C/375°F/Gas 5. Add the vegetables to a flameproof casserole. Stir in the tomatoes, stock, oil, parsley, paprika and salt. Top with slices of tomatoes and courgette.

2 Cover and cook for 1 hour, until tender. Serve hot or cold.

Harvest Bake Energy 202kcal/857kJ; Protein 9.4g; Carbohydrate 36.2g, of which sugars 10.3g; Fat 3.2g, of which saturates 0.5g; Cholesterol 0mg; Calcium 70mg; Fibre 6.4g; Sodium 60mg.
Tagine of Yam Energy 431kcal/1825kJ; Protein 5.6g; Carbohydrate 86.4g, of which sugars 23g; Fat 9.5g, of which saturates 1.5g; Cholesterol 0mg; Calcium 97mg; Fibre 7.6g; Sodium 27mg.
Casserole Energy 573kcal/2416kJ; Protein 32.5g; Carbohydrate 81.5g, of which sugars 19.5g; Fat 15.3g, of which saturates 2.5g; Cholesterol 0mg; Calcium 250mg; Fibre 25.7g; Sodium 60mg.

Tagine of Butter Beans, Cherry Tomatoes and Olives

This slow-cooked bean dish is delicious served with a leafy salad and fresh, crusty bread.

Serves 4

115g/4oz/²/₃ cup butter (lima) beans, soaked overnight
30–45ml/2–3 tbsp olive oil
1 onion, chopped
2–3 garlic cloves, crushed
25g/1oz fresh root ginger, peeled and chopped
pinch of saffron threads
16 cherry tomatoes
generous pinch of sugar
handful of fleshy black olives, pitted
5ml/1 tsp ground cinnamon
5ml/1 tsp paprika
small bunch of flat leaf parsley
salt and ground black pepper

1 Rinse the soaked beans and place them in a large pan with plenty of water. Bring to the boil and boil for about 10 minutes, skimming off any foam that rises to the surface. Reduce the heat and simmer gently for 1–1½ hours until tender. Drain the beans and refresh under cold water.

2 Heat the olive oil in a heavy pan. Add the onion and cook, stirring frequently, for about 6–7 minutes or until beginning to soften, but do not let it brown. Add the garlic and ginger, and cook for about 4 minutes. Stir in the saffron threads, followed by the cherry tomatoes and a sprinkling of sugar.

3 As the tomatoes begin to soften in the pan, stir in the butter beans. When the tomatoes have heated through, stir in the black olives, ground cinnamon and paprika. Season to taste with salt and ground black pepper and sprinkle over the parsley. Serve immediately.

Cook's Tip
If you forget to soak the dried beans the night before, you could use two 400g/14oz cans of pre-cooked butter beans instead. Make sure you rinse the beans well before adding as canned beans tend to be salty.

Mushroom and Fennel Hotpot

Hearty and richly flavoured, this tasty stew is ideal for making in the slow cooker. The dried mushrooms swell up a great deal after soaking, so a little goes a long way in terms of both flavour and quantity.

Serves 4

25g/1oz/½ cup dried shiitake mushrooms
1 small head of fennel
30ml/2 tbsp olive oil
12 shallots, peeled
225g/8oz/3 cups button (white) mushrooms, trimmed and halved
250ml/8fl oz/1 cup dry (hard) cider
25g/1oz/½ cup sun-dried tomatoes
30ml/2 tbsp/½ cup sun-dried tomato paste
1 bay leaf
salt and ground black pepper
chopped fresh parsley, to garnish

1 Place the dried shiitake mushrooms in a heatproof bowl. Pour over just enough hot water to cover them and leave to soak for about 15–20 minutes. Meanwhile, trim and slice the head of fennel.

2 Heat the oil in a heavy pan. Add the shallots and fennel, then cook for about 10 minutes over medium heat, until the vegetables are soft and just beginning to brown. Add the button mushrooms to the pan and cook for a further 2–3 minutes, stirring occasionally.

3 Transfer the vegetable mixture to the ceramic cooking pot. Drain the shiitake mushrooms, adding 30ml/2 tbsp of the soaking liquid to the pot. Chop them and add to the pot.

4 Pour the dry cider into the pot and stir in the sun-dried tomatoes and tomato paste. Add the bay leaf. Cover the cooker with the lid and cook on high for 3–4 hours, or until the vegetables are tender.

5 Remove the bay leaf and season to taste with salt and ground black pepper. Serve sprinkled with plenty of chopped fresh parsley.

Tagine Energy 138kcal/578kJ; Protein 5.5g; Carbohydrate 12.8g, of which sugars 3.5g; Fat 7.6g, of which saturates 1.1g; Cholesterol 0mg; Calcium 51mg; Fibre 5.2g; Sodium 605mg.
Mushroom Hotpot Energy 94kcal/394kJ; Protein 2.1g; Carbohydrate 4.2g, of which sugars 4g; Fat 6g, of which saturates 0.9g; Cholesterol 0mg; Calcium 28mg; Fibre 2.4g; Sodium 17mg.

Root Vegetable Casserole with Caraway Dumplings

Soft cheese gives this slow-cooker casserole a creamy richness.

Serves 3

300ml/½ pint/1¼ cups dry (hard) cider
175ml/6fl oz/¾ cup boiling vegetable stock
2 leeks
2 carrots
2 small parsnips
225g/8oz potatoes
1 sweet potato, about 175g/6oz
1 bay leaf

7.5ml/1½ tsp cornflour (cornstarch)
115g/4oz full-fat soft cheese with garlic and herbs
salt and ground black pepper

For the dumplings

115g/4oz/1 cup self-raising (self-rising) flour
5ml/1 tsp caraway seeds
50g/2oz/scant ½ cup shredded vegetable suet (US chilled, grated shortening)
1 courgette (zucchini), grated
about 75ml/5 tbsp cold water

1 Reserve 15ml/1 tbsp of the cider and pour the rest into the ceramic cooking pot with the stock. Cover and switch to high.

2 Meanwhile, prepare the vegetables. Trim the leeks and cut into 2cm/¾in slices. Peel the carrots, parsnips, potatoes and sweet potato and cut into 2cm/¾in chunks. Add to the ceramic cooking pot with the bay leaf. Cover and cook for 3 hours.

3 In a bowl, blend the cornflour with the reserved cider. Add the cheese and mix together, then blend in a few spoonfuls of the cooking liquid. Stir into the vegetables. Season with salt and pepper. Cover and cook for 1–2 hours, or until almost tender.

4 Towards the end of the cooking time, make the dumplings. Sift the flour into a bowl and stir in the caraway seeds, suet, courgettes, salt and pepper. Stir in enough water to make a soft dough. Shape the mixture into 12 walnut-size dumplings.

5 Place the dumplings on top of the casserole, cover and cook for a further hour, or until the vegetables and dumplings are cooked. Serve in warmed deep soup plates.

Spicy Root Vegetable Gratin

Subtly spiced, this rich gratin is slowly baked in the oven and is substantial enough to serve on its own for lunch or supper. It can also work well as a tasty side dish to accompany a selection of grilled vegetables.

Serves 4

2 large potatoes, total weight about 450g/1lb
2 sweet potatoes, total weight about 275g/10oz

175g/6oz celeriac
15ml/1 tbsp unsalted butter
5ml/1 tsp curry powder
5ml/1 tsp ground turmeric
2.5ml/½ tsp ground coriander
5ml/1 tsp mild chilli powder
3 shallots, chopped
150ml/¼ pint/⅔ cup single (light) cream
150ml/¼ pint/⅔ cup milk
salt and ground black pepper
chopped fresh flat leaf parsley, to garnish

1 Peel the potatoes, sweet potatoes and celeriac and cut into thin, even slices using a sharp knife or the slicing attachment on a food processor. Immediately place the vegetables in a bowl of cold water to prevent them from discolouring.

2 Preheat the oven to 180°C/350°F/Gas 4. Heat half the butter in a heavy pan, add the curry powder, ground turmeric and coriander and half the chilli powder. Cook for 2 minutes, then leave to cool slightly.

3 Drain the vegetables, then pat them dry with kitchen paper. Place in a bowl, add the spice mixture and the shallots, and mix well. Arrange the vegetables in a shallow baking dish, seasoning well with salt and pepper between the layers.

4 In a bowl, mix together the cream and milk until well blended. Pour the mixture over the vegetables in the dish, then sprinkle the remaining chilli powder on top.

5 Cover the dish with baking parchment and bake for about 45 minutes. Remove the baking parchment, dot the vegetables with the remaining butter and bake for a further 50 minutes, or until the top is golden brown. Serve the gratin garnished with chopped parsley.

Root Casserole Energy 616kcal/2584kJ; Protein 11.9g; Carbohydrate 74.9g, of which sugars 17.1g; Fat 28.9g, of which saturates 15.9g; Cholesterol 35mg; Calcium 256mg; Fibre 9.5g; Sodium 369mg.
Spicy Gratin Energy 268kcal/1129kJ; Protein 5.8g; Carbohydrate 37.7g, of which sugars 9.8g; Fat 11.6g, of which saturates 7.1g; Cholesterol 31mg; Calcium 127mg; Fibre 3.6g; Sodium 117mg.

Mixed-bean Hotpot

This impressive slow-cooker dish has a deliciously rich and tangy tomato sauce.

Serves 6

40g/1½oz/3 tbsp butter
4 shallots, peeled and finely chopped
40g/1½oz/⅓ cup plain
   (all-purpose) or wholemeal
   (whole-wheat) flour
300ml/½ pint/1¼ cups passata
   (bottled strained tomatoes)
120ml/4fl oz/½ cup unsweetened
   apple juice
60ml/4 tbsp soft light brown sugar
60ml/4 tbsp tomato ketchup
60ml/4 tbsp dry sherry
60ml/4 tbsp cider vinegar
60ml/4 tbsp light soy sauce
400g/14oz can butter (lima) beans
400g/14oz can flageolet (small
   cannellini) beans
400g/14oz can chickpeas
175g/6oz green beans, cut into
   2.5cm/1in lengths
225g/8oz/3 cups mushrooms, sliced
450g/1lb unpeeled potatoes
15ml/1 tbsp olive oil
15ml/1 tbsp chopped fresh thyme
15ml/1 tbsp fresh marjoram
salt and ground black pepper
fresh herbs, to garnish

1 Melt the butter in a pan, add the shallots and fry gently for 5–6 minutes, until softened. Add the flour and cook for 1 minute, stirring all the time, then gradually stir in the passata. Stir in the apple juice, sugar, ketchup, sherry, vinegar and soy sauce. Bring the mixture to the boil, stirring constantly until it thickens.

2 Rinse the beans and chickpeas and drain well. Place them in the ceramic cooking pot with the green beans and mushrooms and pour over the sauce. Stir well, then cover with the lid and cook on high for 3 hours.

3 Meanwhile, thinly slice the potatoes and par-boil them for about 4 minutes. Drain, then toss them in the oil to lightly coat.

4 Stir the fresh herbs into the bean mixture and season with salt and pepper. Arrange the potato slices on top of the beans, overlapping them slightly so that they completely cover the beans. Cover and cook for 2 hours, or until the potatoes are tender.

5 Place the ceramic cooking pot under a medium grill (broiler) and cook for 4–5 minutes to brown the potato topping. Serve garnished with herbs.

Spicy Bean Chilli with Cornbread

This slow-cooker chilli has a tasty cornbread topping.

Serves 4

115g/4oz/generous ½ cup dried
   red kidney beans, soaked for
   6 hours or overnight
115g/4oz/generous ½ cup dried
   black-eyed beans (peas), soaked
   for 6 hours or overnight
1 bay leaf
15ml/1 tbsp vegetable oil
1 large onion, finely chopped
1 garlic clove, crushed
5ml/1 tsp ground cumin
5ml/1 tsp chilli powder
5ml/1 tsp mild paprika
2.5ml/½ tsp dried marjoram
450g/1lb mixed vegetables such
   as potatoes, carrots, aubergines
   (eggplants), parsnips and celery
1 vegetable stock (bouillon) cube
400g/14oz can chopped tomatoes
15ml/1 tbsp tomato purée (paste)
salt and ground black pepper

For the cornbread topping

250g/9oz/2¼ cups fine cornmeal
30ml/2 tbsp wholemeal
   (whole-wheat) flour
7.5ml/1½ tsp baking powder
1 egg, plus 1 egg yolk lightly beaten
300ml/½ pint/1¼ cups milk

1 Drain the beans and rinse well. Place in a pan with 600ml/ 1 pint/2½ cups of cold water and the bay leaf. Bring to the boil and boil rapidly for 10 minutes. Turn off the heat, leave to cool slightly, then add to the ceramic cooking pot and switch to high.

2 Heat the oil in a pan, add the onion and cook for 7–8 minutes. Add the garlic, cumin, chilli powder, paprika and marjoram and cook for 1 minute. Transfer to the ceramic cooking pot and stir.

3 Peel or trim the vegetables as necessary, then cut into 2cm/¾in chunks. Add to the pot, submerging those that may discolour. Cover and cook for 3 hours, until the beans are tender.

4 Add the stock cube and tomatoes to the pot, then stir in the tomato purée and season with salt and pepper. Replace the lid and cook for 30 minutes until the mixture is at boiling point.

5 Make the topping. Combine the cornmeal, flour, baking powder and a pinch of salt in a bowl. Make a well in the centre and add the egg, egg yolk and milk. Mix, then spoon over the bean mixture. Cover and cook for 1 hour, or until the topping is firm. Serve.

Mixed-bean Hotpot Energy 483kcal/2042kJ; Protein 18.5g; Carbohydrate 73.3g, of which sugars 24.8g; Fat 13.8g, of which saturates 4.5g; Cholesterol 14mg; Calcium 134mg; Fibre 10.9g; Sodium 826mg.
Spicy Chilli Energy 613kcal/2595kJ; Protein 29.6g; Carbohydrate 97.4g, of which sugars 15.8g; Fat 14.5g, of which saturates 3.4g; Cholesterol 112mg; Calcium 257mg; Fibre 13.4g; Sodium 413mg.

Mushroom and Courgette Lasagne

This dish can be prepared in the slow cooker early in the day, then left to cook.

Serves 6
30ml/2 tbsp olive oil
50g/2oz/¼ cup butter
450g/1lb courgettes (zucchini), thinly sliced
1 onion, finely chopped
450g/1lb/6 cups chestnut mushrooms, thinly sliced
2 garlic cloves, crushed
6–8 non-pre-cook lasagne sheets
50g/2oz/½ cup freshly grated Parmesan cheese
salt and ground black pepper
fresh oregano leaves, to garnish

For the tomato sauce
15g/½oz dried porcini mushrooms
120ml/4fl oz/½ cup hot water
1 onion
1 carrot
1 celery stick
30ml/2 tbsp olive oil
2 x 400g/14oz cans chopped tomatoes
15ml/1 tbsp sun-dried tomato paste
5ml/1 tsp sugar
5ml/1 tsp dried basil or mixed herbs

For the white sauce
40g/1½oz/3 tbsp butter
40g/1½oz/⅓ cup plain (all-purpose) flour
900ml/1½ pints/3¾ cups milk
freshly grated nutmeg

1 Make the tomato sauce. Put the dried porcini mushrooms in a bowl. Pour over the hot water and leave to soak for 15 minutes. Transfer the porcini and liquid to a sieve (strainer) set over a bowl and squeeze the mushrooms with your hands to release as much liquid as possible. Chop the mushrooms finely and set aside. Strain the soaking liquid through a fine sieve and reserve.

2 Chop the onion, carrot and celery finely. Heat the olive oil in a pan and fry the vegetables until softened. Place in a food processor with the tomatoes, tomato paste, sugar, herbs, porcini and soaking liquid, and blend to a purée.

3 For the lasagne, heat the olive oil and half the butter in a large, heavy pan. Cook the courgette slices in batches, turning frequently, for 5–8 minutes, until lightly coloured on both sides. Remove from the pan with a slotted spoon and transfer to a bowl. Melt the remaining butter in the pan, and cook the onion for about 3 minutes, stirring. Add the mushrooms and garlic and cook for 5 minutes. Add to the courgettes and season with salt and pepper.

4 For the white sauce, melt the butter in a large pan, then add the flour and cook, stirring, for 1 minute. Turn off the heat and gradually whisk in the milk. Bring to the boil and cook, stirring, until the sauce is smooth and thick. Season with salt, black pepper and nutmeg.

5 Ladle half of the tomato sauce into the ceramic cooking pot and spread out to cover the base. Add half the vegetable mixture, spreading it evenly. Top with about one-third of the white sauce, then about half the lasagne sheets, breaking them to fit the cooking pot. Repeat these layers, then top with the remaining white sauce and sprinkle with grated Parmesan.

6 Cover the ceramic cooking pot with the lid and cook on low for 2–2½ hours or until the lasagne is tender. If you like, brown the top under a medium grill (broiler). Garnish with the fresh oregano leaves, and serve immediately.

Pasta with Mushrooms

The slow cooker is ideal for making this pasta sauce of mushrooms, garlic and sun-dried tomatoes, together with white wine and stock.

Serves 4
15g/½oz dried porcini mushrooms
120ml/4fl oz/½ cup hot water
2 cloves garlic, finely chopped
2 large pieces sun-dried tomato in olive oil, drained, sliced into strips
120ml/4fl oz/½ cup dry white wine
120ml/4fl oz/½ cup hot vegetable stock
225g/8oz/2 cups chestnut mushrooms, thinly sliced
1 handful fresh flat leaf parsley, roughly chopped
450g/1lb/4 cups dried short pasta shapes, such as ruote, penne, fusilli or eliche
salt and ground black pepper
rocket (arugula) and/or fresh flat leaf parsley, to garnish

1 Put the dried porcini mushrooms in a large bowl. Pour over the hot water and leave to soak for 15 minutes.

2 While the mushrooms are soaking, put the garlic, tomatoes, wine, stock and chestnut mushrooms into the ceramic cooking pot and switch the slow cooker to high.

3 Transfer the porcini mushrooms to a sieve (strainer) set over a bowl, then squeeze them with your hands to release as much liquid as possible. Reserve the soaking liquid. Chop the porcini finely. Add the liquid and the chopped porcini to the ceramic cooking pot, and cover the slow cooker with the lid. Cook on high for 1 hour, stirring halfway through the cooking time to make sure the mushrooms cook evenly.

4 Switch the slow cooker to the low setting and cook for a further 1–2 hours, until the mushrooms are tender.

5 Cook the pasta in boiling salted water for about 10 minutes, or according to the instructions on the packet. Drain the pasta and transfer it to a large warmed bowl. Stir the chopped parsley into the sauce in the cooking pot and season to taste with salt and ground black pepper. Add the sauce to the pasta in the bowl and toss well. Serve immediately, garnished with rocket and/or parsley.

Lasagne Energy 421kcal/1757kJ; Protein 15.5g; Carbohydrate 32.9g, of which sugars 15g; Fat 26.2g, of which saturates 12.4g; Cholesterol 49mg; Calcium 346mg; Fibre 3.8g; Sodium 310mg.
Pasta with Mushrooms Energy 420kcal/1787kJ; Protein 15.1g; Carbohydrate 84.9g, of which sugars 5.1g; Fat 2.6g, of which saturates 0.3g; Cholesterol 0 mg; Calcium 61mg; Fibre 4.8g; Sodium 14mg.

Courgettes with Rice

This tasty slow-cooked rice dish is first simmered on the stove and then finished in the oven.

Serves 4

1kg/2¼lb courgettes (zucchini)
60ml/4 tbsp olive oil
3 onions, finely chopped
3 garlic cloves, crushed
5ml/1 tsp chilli powder
400g/14oz can chopped tomatoes
200g/7oz/1 cup risotto or
    short grain rice
600–750ml/1–1¼ pints/
    2½–3 cups vegetable stock
30ml/2 tbsp chopped fresh parsley
30ml/2 tbsp chopped fresh dill
salt and ground white pepper
sprigs of dill and olives,
    to garnish
thick natural (plain) yogurt,
    to serve

1 Preheat the oven to 190°C/375°F/Gas 5. Top and tail the courgettes and slice into large chunks.

2 Heat half the olive oil in a large pan and gently fry the onions and garlic until just soft. Stir in the chilli powder and tomatoes and simmer for about 5–8 minutes before adding the courgettes. Add salt to taste.

3 Cook over low to medium heat for 10–15 minutes, before stirring the rice into the pan.

4 Add the stock to the pan, cover and simmer for 45 minutes, or until the rice is tender. Stir the mixture occasionally.

5 Season with pepper, and stir in the parsley and dill. Transfer to an ovenproof dish and bake in the oven for about 45 minutes.

6 Halfway through cooking, brush the remaining oil over the courgette mixture. Garnish with the dill sprigs and olives. Serve with the natural yogurt.

Cook's Tip
Add extra liquid, as necessary, while simmering the rice on the stove to prevent the mixture from sticking to the pan.

Rosemary Risotto with Borlotti Beans

The low, constant heat of the slow cooker produces a delicious risotto. Easy-cook rice means that all the liquid can be added at the same time, rather than gradually, as with a traditional risotto.

Serves 3

400g/14oz can borlotti beans
15g/½oz/1 tbsp butter
15ml/1 tbsp olive oil
1 onion, finely chopped
2 garlic cloves, crushed
120ml/4fl oz/½ cup dry white wine
225g/8oz/generous 1 cup easy-
    cook (converted) Italian rice
750ml/1¼ pints/3 cups boiling
    vegetable stock
60ml/4 tbsp mascarpone cheese
5ml/1 tsp chopped fresh rosemary
65g/2½oz/¾ cup freshly grated
    Parmesan cheese, plus extra to
    serve (optional)
salt and ground black pepper

1 Rinse the beans well and drain. Place two-thirds of the beans in a food processor or blender and process to a coarse paste. Transfer the remaining beans to a bowl and set aside.

2 Heat the butter and oil in a pan, add the onion and garlic and fry gently for 7–8 minutes until soft. Transfer the mixture to the ceramic cooking pot and stir in the wine and the bean paste. Cover with the lid and cook on high for 1 hour.

3 Add the rice to the pot, then stir in the stock. Re-cover with the lid and cook for about 45 minutes, stirring once halfway through cooking. The rice should be almost tender and most of the stock should have been absorbed.

4 Stir the reserved beans, mascarpone and rosemary into the risotto. Cover again with the lid and cook for a further 15 minutes, until the rice is tender but still has a little bite.

5 Stir the Parmesan cheese into the risotto and season to taste with salt and ground black pepper. Turn off the slow cooker, cover and leave to stand for 5 minutes, so that the risotto absorbs the flavours fully and the rice completes cooking.

6 Spoon the rice into warmed serving bowls and serve immediately, sprinkled with extra Parmesan, if you like.

Courgettes with Rice Energy 201kcal/837kJ; Protein 5.6g; Carbohydrate 30.1g, of which sugars 8g; Fat 6.6g, of which saturates 1g; Cholesterol 0mg; Calcium 72mg; Fibre 3g; Sodium 10mg.
Rosemary Risotto Energy 651kcal/2740kJ; Protein 25g; Carbohydrate 87g, of which sugars 4.6g; Fat 22.2g, of which saturates 10.5g; Cholesterol 41.9mg; Calcium 357mg; Fibre 7.1g; Sodium 1462mg.

Clay-pot Saffron Risotto with Spinach

Rice cooks to perfection in the moist environment of a clay pot. This risotto can be made without the constant checking usually needed.

Serves 4
a few saffron threads
30ml/2 tbsp boiling water
15ml/1 tbsp olive oil
50g/2oz/¼ cup butter
1 onion, finely chopped

350g/12oz/1¾ cups risotto rice
900ml/1½ pints/3¾ cups warm
    vegetable stock
150ml/¼ pint/⅔ cup dry
    white wine
225g/8oz baby spinach leaves
300ml/½ pint/1¼ cups hot
    vegetable stock
40g/1½oz/¼ cup shelled
    walnuts, chopped
75g/3oz Parmesan cheese, shaved
salt and ground black pepper

1 Soak a large clay pot in cold water for 20 minutes, then drain. Meanwhile, place the saffron in a bowl, cover with the boiling water and set aside.

2 Heat the oil and half the butter in a large, heavy pan. Add the onion and cook gently for 5 minutes, or until soft, stirring occasionally. Add the rice and stir for about 3 minutes, until the grains are thoroughly coated in oil and butter.

3 Pour the stock into the clay pot, add the saffron water, wine and the rice mixture, and stir together. Cover and place in an unheated oven. Set the oven to 190°C/375°F/Gas 5 and cook for 50 minutes, stirring after 30 minutes.

4 Stir in the spinach, add the stock, then cover and cook for 10 minutes, or until the rice is tender. Stir in the walnuts, the remaining butter and half the Parmesan cheese. Season and serve sprinkled with the remaining Parmesan shavings.

> **Cook's Tip**
> Risotto is made from Italian short grain rice, of which there are several varieties. Arborio rice is widely available, but you may also find carnaroli and vialone nano. When cooked, risotto rice has a creamy consistency but the grains retain a slight 'bite'.

Vegetable Paella

A colourful assortment of vegetables is slowly baked with rice to make this dish.

Serves 4
1 large aubergine (eggplant)
45ml/3 tbsp extra virgin olive or
    sunflower oil
2 onions, quartered and sliced
2 garlic cloves, crushed
300g/11oz/1½ cups short grain
    Spanish or risotto rice
1.2–1.5 litres/2–2½ pints/
    5–6¼ cups vegetable stock

1 red (bell) pepper, halved, seeded
    and sliced
1 yellow (bell) pepper, halved,
    seeded and sliced
200g/7oz fine green beans, halved
115g/4oz/scant 2 cups chestnut
    mushrooms, quartered, or
    brown cap (cremini) or button
    (white) mushrooms, halved
1 dried chilli, crushed
115g/4oz/1 cup frozen peas
salt and ground black pepper
fresh coriander (cilantro) leaves,
    to garnish

1 Soak a clay pot or Chinese sand pot in cold water for 20 minutes, then drain. Cut the aubergine in half lengthways, then cut it crossways into thin slices.

2 Heat 30ml/2 tbsp of the oil in a large frying pan, add the aubergine slices and cook until golden. Transfer to the clay pot. Add the remaining oil, and cook the onion, stirring occasionally, for a few minutes until golden.

3 Add the garlic and rice and cook for 1–2 minutes, stirring, until the rice becomes transparent. Pour 900ml/1½ pints/3¾ cups of the stock into the clay pot, then add the rice mixture.

4 Stir in the peppers, green beans, mushrooms, chilli and seasoning. Cover the pot and place in an unheated oven.

5 Set the oven to 200°C/400°F/Gas 6 and cook for 1 hour, or until the rice is almost tender. After 40 minutes, remove the pot from the oven and add a little more stock to moisten the paella. Stir well, re-cover and return to the oven.

6 Add the peas and a little more stock to the paella and cook for a further 10 minutes. Adjust the seasoning and sprinkle over the coriander. Lightly stir through and then serve.

Clay-pot Risotto Energy 630kcal/2618kJ; Protein 17.2g; Carbohydrate 72.6g, of which sugars 2.3g; Fat 26.9g, of which saturates 11.4g; Cholesterol 45mg; Calcium 356mg; Fibre 1.8g; Sodium 362mg.
Vegetable Paella Energy 458kcal/1911kJ; Protein 11.8g; Carbohydrate 80g, of which sugars 14.3g; Fat 10.3g, of which saturates 1.5g; Cholesterol 0mg; Calcium 80mg; Fibre 7.1g; Sodium 10mg.

Savoury Nut Loaf

Ideal as an alternative to the traditional meat roast, this slow-cooker vegetarian dish is perfect for special occasions. It is also good with a fresh tomato sauce.

Serves 4
30ml/2 tbsp olive oil, plus extra
   for greasing
1 onion, finely chopped
1 leek, finely chopped
2 celery sticks, finely chopped
225g/8oz/3 cups mushrooms,
   chopped
2 garlic cloves, crushed
425g/15oz can lentils, rinsed
   and drained
115g/4oz/1 cup mixed nuts, such
   as hazelnuts, cashew nuts and
   almonds, finely chopped
50g/2oz/½ cup plain
   (all-purpose) flour
50g/2oz/½ cup grated mature
   (sharp) Cheddar cheese
1 egg, beaten
45–60ml/3–4 tbsp chopped fresh
   mixed herbs
salt and ground black pepper
chives and sprigs of fresh flat leaf
   parsley, to garnish

1 Place an upturned saucer or metal pastry ring in the base of the ceramic cooking pot. Pour in about 2.5cm/1in hot water and switch the slow cooker to high. Lightly grease the base and sides of a 900g/2lb loaf tin (pan) or terrine that will fit in the cooker. Line the base and sides with baking parchment.

2 Heat the oil in a large pan, add the onion, leek, celery, mushrooms and garlic, then cook for 10 minutes until softened. Remove the pan from the heat, then stir in the lentils, nuts and flour, cheese, egg and herbs. Season with salt and pepper.

3 Spoon the nut mixture into the prepared loaf tin or terrine, pressing right into the corners. Level the surface, then cover the tin with a piece of foil. Place in the ceramic cooking pot and pour in enough near-boiling water to come just over halfway up the side of the dish. Cover the slow cooker with the lid and cook for 3–4 hours, or until the loaf is firm to the touch.

4 Leave the loaf to cool in the tin for about 15 minutes, then turn out on to a serving plate. Serve the loaf hot or cold, cut into thick slices and garnished with fresh chives and sprigs of flat leaf parsley.

Beetroot Casserole

This slowly simmered casserole can be served as a light meal in itself or with a simple salad. It has a wonderful sweet and sour flavour.

Serves 4
50g/2oz/4 tbsp butter
1 onion, chopped
2 garlic cloves, crushed
675g/1½lb uncooked
   beetroot, peeled
2 large carrots, peeled
½ lemon
115g/4oz/1½ cups button
   (white) mushrooms
300ml/½ pint/1¼ cups hot
   vegetable stock
2 bay leaves
15ml/1 tbsp chopped fresh mint,
   plus sprigs to garnish (optional)
salt and ground black pepper

For the hot dressing
150ml/¼ pint/⅔ cup sour cream
2.5ml/½ tsp paprika, plus extra
   to garnish

1 Melt the butter in a pan and fry the onion and garlic for 5 minutes. Meanwhile, dice the beetroot and carrot. Grate the rind and squeeze the juice of the ½ lemon. Add the beetroot, carrots and mushrooms and fry for 5 minutes.

2 Pour in the stock with the lemon rind and bay leaves. Season with salt and pepper. Bring to the boil, turn down the heat, cover and simmer for 1 hour, or until the vegetables are soft.

3 Turn off the heat and stir in the lemon juice and chopped mint, if using. Leave the pan to stand, covered, for 5 minutes, to develop the flavours.

4 Meanwhile, for the dressing, gently heat the sour cream and paprika in a pan, stirring all the time, until bubbling. Transfer the beetroot mixture to a serving bowl, then spoon over the dressing. Serve garnished with mint and extra paprika, if you like.

> **Cook's Tip**
> Wear clean rubber or plastic gloves to avoid staining your hands when preparing beetroot.

Savoury Nut Loaf Energy 484kcal/2019kJ; Protein 23.7g; Carbohydrate 34.1g, of which sugars 5.1g; Fat 29g, of which saturates 5.4g; Cholesterol 69mg; Calcium 238mg; Fibre 8.7g; Sodium 128mg.
Beetroot Energy 256kcal/1064kJ; Protein 5.3g; Carbohydrate 18.5g, of which sugars 16.1g; Fat 18.5g, of which saturates 11.3g; Cholesterol 49mg; Calcium 87mg; Fibre 4.3g; Sodium 212mg.

Mixed Bean and Aubergine Tagine

A bean pot or tagine is used for slowly cooking this dish.

Serves 4
115g/4oz/generous ½ cup dried red kidney beans, soaked overnight and drained
115g/4oz/generous ½ cup dried black-eyed beans (peas) or cannellini beans, soaked overnight and drained
600ml/1 pint/2½ cups water
2 bay leaves
2 celery sticks, cut into 8 pieces
75ml/5 tbsp olive oil
1 aubergine (eggplant), about 350g/12oz, cut into chunks
1 onion, thinly sliced
3 garlic cloves, crushed
1–2 fresh red chillies, seeded and finely chopped
30ml/2 tbsp tomato purée (paste)
5ml/1 tsp paprika
2 large tomatoes, roughly chopped
300ml/½ pint/1¼ cups hot vegetable stock
15ml/1 tbsp each chopped mint, parsley and coriander (cilantro)
salt and ground black pepper
fresh herb sprigs, to garnish

For the mint yogurt
150ml/¼ pint/⅔ cup natural (plain) yogurt
30ml/2 tbsp chopped fresh mint
2 spring onions (scallions), chopped

1 Place the kidney beans in a large pan of boiling water. Bring back to the boil and boil rapidly for 10 minutes, then drain. Place the black-eyed or cannellini beans in a separate pan of boiling water and boil rapidly for 10 minutes, then drain.

2 Place the measured water in a soaked bean pot or tagine, add the bay leaves, celery and beans. Cover and place in an unheated oven set to 190°C/375°F/Gas 5. Cook for 1–1½ hours. Drain well.

3 Heat the oil in a frying pan. Cook the aubergine until browned. Set aside. Cook the onion for 5 minutes, then add the garlic and chillies for 5 minutes. Stir the tomato purée and paprika into the pan for 1–2 minutes. Reduce the oven to 160°C/325°F/Gas 3.

4 Transfer the contents of the pan to the bean pot or tagine. Add the tomatoes, cooked aubergine, drained beans and stock. Cook in the oven for 1 hour.

5 Mix together the mint yogurt ingredients. Stir the herbs into the tagine and season. Serve garnished with the herb sprigs.

Pilaff Stuffed Apples

Tangy apples are stuffed with an aromatic pilaff, then slowly baked in the oven.

Serves 4
4 cooking apples, or any firm, sour apple of your choice
30ml/2 tbsp olive oil
juice of ½ lemon
10ml/2 tsp sugar
salt and ground black pepper

For the filling
30ml/2 tbsp olive oil
a little butter
1 onion, finely chopped
2 garlic cloves
30ml/2 tbsp pine nuts
30ml/2 tbsp currants, soaked in warm water for 5–10 minutes and drained
5–10ml/1–2 tsp ground cinnamon
5–10ml/1–2 tsp ground allspice
5ml/1 tsp sugar
175g/6oz/scant 1 cup short grain rice, thoroughly rinsed and drained
1 bunch each of fresh flat leaf parsley and dill, finely chopped

To serve
1 tomato
1 lemon
a few fresh mint or basil leaves

1 Make the filling. Heat the oil and butter in a heavy pan, stir in the onion and garlic and cook until soft. Add the pine nuts and currants and cook until the nuts turn golden. Stir in the spices, sugar and rice, and pour in water to just cover. Bring to the boil.

2 Season with salt and pepper. Lower the heat and simmer for 10–12 minutes, until almost all the water has been absorbed. Stir in the herbs and turn off the heat. Cover the pan with a dish towel and the lid, and leave the rice to steam for 5 minutes.

3 Preheat the oven to 200°C/400°F/Gas 6. Using a knife, cut the stalk ends off the apples and keep to use as lids. Core each apple, removing some of the flesh to create a cavity for stuffing. Pack spoonfuls of the filling into the apples. Replace the lids and stand the apples, tightly packed, in a small baking dish.

4 In a bowl, mix together 120ml/4fl oz/½ cup water with the oil, lemon juice and sugar. Pour over and around the apples, then bake for 30–40 minutes, until tender and the juices are caramelized. Serve immediately, with a tomato and lemon garnish and a sprinkling of mint or basil leaves.

Mixed Bean Tagine Energy 328kcal/1377kJ; Protein 14.9g; Carbohydrate 35.2g, of which sugars 9.3g; Fat 15.3g, of which saturates 2.2g; Cholesterol 0mg; Calcium 96mg; Fibre 12.8g; Sodium 28mg.
Pilaff Stuffed Apples Energy 382kcal/1595kJ; Protein 5g; Carbohydrate 54.1g, of which sugars 18.8g; Fat 16.5g, of which saturates 1.9g; Cholesterol 0mg; Calcium 26mg; Fibre 2.1g; Sodium 4mg.

Pumpkin Stuffed with Apricot Pilaff

An oven-baked pumpkin filled with a fruity pilaff makes a great centrepiece.

Serves 4–6
1 pumpkin, weighing about
 1.2kg/2¹/₂lb
225g/8oz/generous 1 cup long
 grain rice, well rinsed
30–45ml/2–3 tbsp olive oil
15ml/1 tbsp butter
a few saffron threads
5ml/1 tsp coriander seeds
2–3 strips of orange peel, pith
 removed and finely sliced
45–60ml/3–4 tbsp shelled
 pistachio nuts
30–45ml/2–3 tbsp dried
 cranberries, soaked in boiling
 water for 5 minutes and drained
175g/6oz/³/₄ cup ready-to-eat
 dried apricots, sliced or chopped
1 bunch of fresh basil, leaves torn
1 bunch each of fresh coriander
 (cilantro), mint and flat leaf
 parsley, coarsely chopped
salt and ground black pepper
lemon wedges and thick natural
 (plain) yogurt, to serve

1 Preheat the oven to 200°C/400°F/Gas 6. Wash the pumpkin and cut off the stalk end to use as a lid. Scoop all the seeds out of the middle with a spoon, and pull out the stringy bits. Replace the lid, put the pumpkin on a baking tray and bake for 1 hour.

2 Meanwhile, put the rice in a pan and pour in enough water to cover. Add a pinch of salt and bring to the boil, then partially cover the pan and simmer for 10–12 minutes, until the water has been absorbed and the rice is cooked but still has a bite.

3 Heat the oil and butter in a heavy pan. Stir in the saffron, coriander seeds, orange peel, pistachios, cranberries and apricots, then stir in the cooked rice. Season with salt and pepper. Turn off the heat, cover the pan with a dish towel and the lid and leave the pilaff to steam for 10 minutes, then toss in the herbs.

4 Spoon the pilaff into the cavity in the pumpkin. Put the lid back on and bake in the oven for a further 20 minutes.

5 To serve, remove the lid and slice a round off the top of the pumpkin. Place the ring on a plate and spoon some pilaff in the middle. Prepare the rest in the same way. Serve with lemon wedges and a bowl of yogurt.

Onions Stuffed with Goat's Cheese and Sun-dried Tomatoes

Long, gentle cooking is the best way to get maximum flavour from onions, so the slow cooker is the natural choice for this delicious stuffed-onion dish.

Serves 4
2 large onions, unpeeled
30ml/2 tbsp olive oil (or use oil
 from the sun-dried tomatoes)
150g/5oz/²/₃ cup firm goat's
 cheese, crumbled or cubed
50g/2oz/1 cup fresh white
 breadcrumbs
8 sun-dried tomatoes in olive oil,
 drained and chopped
1 garlic clove, finely chopped
2.5ml/¹/₂ tsp fresh thyme
30ml/2 tbsp chopped fresh parsley
1 small egg, beaten
45ml/3 tbsp pine nuts
150ml/¹/₄ pint/²/₃ cup near-boiling
 vegetable stock
salt and ground black pepper
chopped fresh parsley, to garnish

1 Bring a large pan of water to the boil. Add the whole onions in their skins and boil for 10 minutes.

2 Drain the onions and leave until cool enough to handle, then cut each onion in half horizontally and peel. Using a teaspoon, remove the centre of each onion, leaving a thick shell.

3 Very finely chop the flesh from one of the scooped-out onion halves and place in a bowl. Stir in 5ml/1 tsp of the olive oil or oil from the sun-dried tomatoes, then add the goat's cheese, breadcrumbs, sun-dried tomatoes, garlic, thyme, parsley, egg and pine nuts. Season with salt and pepper and mix well.

4 Divide the stuffing among the onions and cover each one with a piece of oiled foil. Brush the base of the ceramic cooking pot with 15ml/1 tbsp of oil, then pour in the stock. Put the onions in the base of the cooking pot, cover and cook on high for 4 hours, or until the onions are tender but still hold their shape.

5 Remove the onions from the slow cooker and transfer them to a grill (broiler) pan. Remove the foil and drizzle with the remaining oil. Brown under the grill for 3–4 minutes, taking care not to burn the nuts. Serve immediately, garnished with parsley.

Onions with Cheese Energy 330kcal/1370kJ; Protein 13.8g; Carbohydrate 14.3g, of which sugars 11.3g; Fat 24.7g, of which saturates 8.4g; Cholesterol 83.7mg; Calcium 98mg; Fibre 1.9g; Sodium 349mg.
Pumpkin Energy 345kcal/1443kJ; Protein 9.9g; Carbohydrate 50.1g, of which sugars 18.6g; Fat 12g, of which saturates 2.6g; Cholesterol 5mg; Calcium 299mg; Fibre 9.6g; Sodium 93mg.

Couscous-stuffed Sweet Peppers

This slow-cooker recipe for stuffed peppers couldn't be easier. The peppers are softened in boiling water before filling to ensure really tender results. Choose red, yellow or orange peppers for this dish, but avoid green ones because they tend to discolour after a couple of hours of cooking.

Serves 4

4 (bell) peppers
75g/3oz/½ cup instant couscous
75ml/2½fl oz/⅓ cup boiling vegetable stock
15ml/1 tbsp olive oil
10ml/2 tsp white wine vinegar
50g/2oz ready-to-eat dried apricots, finely chopped
75g/3oz feta cheese, cut into tiny cubes
3 ripe tomatoes, skinned, seeded and chopped
45ml/3 tbsp toasted pine nuts
30ml/2 tbsp finely chopped fresh parsley
salt and ground black pepper
flat leaf parsley, to garnish

1 Halve the peppers lengthways, then remove the cores and seeds. Place the peppers in a large heatproof bowl and pour over boiling water to cover. Leave to stand for about 3 minutes, then drain thoroughly and set aside.

2 Meanwhile, put the couscous in a small bowl and pour over the stock. Leave to stand for about 5 minutes, until all the water has been absorbed.

3 Using a fork, fluff up the couscous, then stir in the oil, vinegar, apricots, feta cheese, tomatoes, pine nuts and parsley, and season to taste with salt and ground black pepper.

4 Place spoonfuls of the couscous mixture into the pepper halves, gently packing it down using the back of the spoon.

5 Place the peppers, filling side up, in the ceramic cooking pot, then pour 150ml/¼ pint/⅔ cup near-boiling water around them.

6 Cover the cooker with the lid, switch to the high setting and cook for 2–3 hours, or until the peppers are tender. Brown them under a hot grill (broiler) for 2 minutes, if you like, and serve garnished with fresh parsley.

Stuffed Onions, Potatoes and Courgettes

The vegetarian filling of these oven-roasted vegetables is mildly spiced and has the sharp tang of lemon juice. They are also excellent cold and are good served as an appetizer, as well as a main course.

Serves 4

4 potatoes, peeled
4 onions, skinned
4 courgettes (zucchini), halved widthways
2–4 garlic cloves, chopped
45–60ml/3–4 tbsp olive oil
45–60ml/3–4 tbsp tomato purée (paste)
1.5ml/¼ tsp ras curry powder
large pinch of ground allspice
seeds of 2–3 cardamom pods
juice of ½ lemon
30–45ml/2–3 tbsp chopped fresh parsley
90–120ml/6–8 tbsp hot vegetable stock
salt and ground black pepper
salad, to serve (optional)

1 Bring a large pan of salted water to the boil. Starting with the potatoes, then the onions and finally the courgettes, add to the boiling water and cook until they become almost tender but not cooked through. Allow about 10 minutes for the potatoes, 8 minutes for the onions and 4–6 minutes for the courgettes. Remove the vegetables from the pan and leave to cool.

2 When the vegetables are cool enough to handle, hollow them out using a knife and spoon. Preheat the oven to 190°C/375°F/Gas 5.

3 Finely chop the cut-out vegetable flesh and put it in a bowl. Add the garlic, half the olive oil, the tomato purée, curry powder, allspice, cardamom seeds, lemon juice, parsley, salt and pepper and mix well together. Use the stuffing mixture to fill the hollowed vegetables.

4 Arrange the stuffed vegetables in a roasting pan and drizzle with the vegetable stock and the remaining oil. Roast for about 35–40 minutes, or until they are golden brown. Serve warm or cold, with a salad, if you like.

Sweet Peppers Energy 303kcal/1266kJ; Protein 33.7g; Carbohydrate 33.6g, of which sugars 17g; Fat 15.8g, of which saturates 3.9g; Cholesterol 13mg; Calcium 105mg; Fibre 4.3g; Sodium 285mg.
Stuffed Onions Energy 347kcal/1452kJ; Protein 10.2g; Carbohydrate 56.7g, of which sugars 22.1g; Fat 10.3g, of which saturates 1.6g; Cholesterol 0mg; Calcium 135mg; Fibre 8.2g; Sodium 62mg.

Spicy Parsnip and Chickpea Stew

Sweet parsnips go very well with the spices in this Indian-style vegetable stew, made in the slow cooker.

Serves 4

5 garlic cloves, finely chopped
1 small onion, chopped
5cm/2in piece fresh root ginger, finely chopped
2 green chillies, seeded and chopped
75ml/5 tbsp cold water
60ml/4 tbsp groundnut (peanut) oil
5ml/1 tsp cumin seeds
10ml/2 tsp coriander seeds
5ml/1 tsp ground turmeric
2.5ml/1/2 tsp chilli powder or mild paprika
50g/2oz/1/2 cup cashew nuts, toasted and ground
225g/8oz tomatoes, peeled and chopped
400g/14oz can chickpeas, drained and rinsed
900g/2lb parsnips, cut into chunks
350ml/12fl oz/11/2 cups boiling vegetable stock
juice of 1 lime, to taste
salt and ground black pepper
chopped fresh coriander (cilantro) leaves, toasted cashew nuts and natural (plain) yogurt, to serve

1 Reserve 10ml/2 tsp of the garlic, then place the remainder in a food processor or blender with the onion, ginger and half the chilli. Add the water and process to a smooth paste.

2 Heat the oil in a large frying pan, add the cumin seeds and cook for 30 seconds. Stir in the coriander seeds, turmeric, chilli powder or paprika and the ground cashew nuts. Add the ginger and chilli paste and cook, stirring frequently, until the paste bubbles and the water starts to evaporate.

3 Add the tomatoes to the pan and cook for 1 minute. Transfer the mixture to the ceramic cooking pot and switch the slow cooker to high. Add the chickpeas and parsnips to the pot and stir to coat in the spicy tomato mixture, then stir in the stock and season with salt and pepper. Cover with the lid and cook on high for 4 hours, or until the parsnips are tender.

4 Stir half the lime juice, the reserved garlic and green chilli into the stew. Re-cover and cook for 30 minutes more, then taste and add more lime juice if needed. Spoon on to plates and sprinkle with fresh coriander leaves and toasted cashew nuts. Serve immediately, with a generous spoonful of natural yogurt.

Spiced Clay-pot Chickpeas

This sweet and spicy dish has a well-developed flavour after long, slow cooking in a clay pot. Serve it hot as a main course with rice or couscous, or serve cold as a salad, drizzled with olive oil and lemon juice.

Serves 4

250g/9oz/11/2 cups dried chickpeas, soaked overnight in cold water
30ml/2 tbsp olive oil
2 onions, cut into wedges
10ml/2 tsp ground cumin
1.5ml/1/4 tsp ground turmeric
1.5ml/1/4 tsp cayenne pepper
15ml/1 tbsp ground coriander
5ml/1 tsp ground cinnamon
300ml/1/2 pint/11/4 cups hot vegetable stock
2 carrots, sliced
115g/4oz/1/2 cup ready-to-eat dried apricots, halved
50g/2oz/scant 1/2 cup raisins
25g/1oz/1/4 cup flaked (sliced) almonds
30ml/2 tbsp chopped fresh coriander (cilantro)
30ml/2 tbsp chopped fresh flat leaf parsley
salt and ground black pepper

1 Soak a bean clay pot in cold water for 20 minutes, then drain. Place the chickpeas in a pan with plenty of cold water. Bring to the boil and boil rapidly for 10 minutes, then place the chickpeas in the bean pot, pour in lukewarm water and cover.

2 Place in an unheated oven and set the temperature to 200°C/400°F/Gas 6. Cook for 1 hour, then reduce the oven temperature to 160°C/325°/Gas 3. Cook for another hour, or until the chickpeas are tender.

3 Meanwhile, place the olive oil and onions in a frying pan and cook for 6–8 minutes, or until softened. Add the cumin, turmeric, cayenne, coriander and cinnamon and cook for 2–3 minutes. Stir in the stock, carrots, apricots, raisins and almonds and bring the mixture to the boil.

4 Drain the chickpeas, add the spicy vegetable mixture to the clay pot and stir. Cover and return to the oven for 30 minutes.

5 Season with salt and pepper, stir in half the fresh coriander and parsley, and serve sprinkled with the remainder.

Spicy Parsnip Stew Energy 453kcal/1899kJ; Protein 14.8g; Carbohydrate 50.1g, of which sugars 16.6g; Fat 23g, of which saturates 4.3g; Cholesterol 0mg; Calcium 148mg; Fibre 15.8g; Sodium 394mg.
Spiced Chickpeas Energy 403kcal/1696kJ; Protein 17.1g; Carbohydrate 58.5g, of which sugars 27.1g; Fat 12.8g, of which saturates 1.4g; Cholesterol 0mg; Calcium 167mg; Fibre 10.9g; Sodium 45mg.

Spicy Chickpea and Aubergine Stew

Aubergines and chickpeas go particularly well with the warm spices in this substantial stew. Serve with boiled rice, or on its own with some Indian breads, if you prefer.

Serves 4

3 garlic cloves
2 large onions
3 large aubergines (eggplants)
200g/7oz/1 cup chickpeas,
   soaked overnight
60ml/4 tbsp olive oil
2.5ml/½ tsp ground cumin
2.5ml/½ tsp ground cinnamon
2.5ml/½ tsp ground coriander
3 x 400g/14oz cans
   chopped tomatoes
salt and ground black pepper
boiled rice (optional), to serve

For the garnish
30ml/2 tbsp olive oil
1 onion, sliced
1 garlic clove, sliced
sprigs of fresh coriander (cilantro)

1 Chop the garlic and onions and set aside. Cut the aubergines into bitesize cubes. Place the aubergine cubes in a colander and sprinkle them with salt. Sit the colander in a bowl and leave for 30 minutes, to allow the bitter juices to escape. Rinse the aubergine with cold water and dry on kitchen paper. Set aside.

2 Drain the chickpeas and put in a pan with enough water to cover. Bring to the boil and boil vigorously for 10 minutes, skimming off any foam that rises to the surface. Reduce the heat and simmer for 1–1½ hours, or until tender. Drain.

3 Heat the oil in a large pan. Add the garlic and onion, and cook until soft. Add the spices and cook, stirring, for a few seconds. Add the aubergine and stir. Cook for 5 minutes.

4 Add the tomatoes and chickpeas and season with salt and pepper. Cover and simmer for 20 minutes.

5 To make the garnish, heat the olive oil in a frying pan and, when very hot, add the sliced onion and garlic. Fry, stirring constantly, until golden and crisp.

6 Serve the stew with boiled rice, if using, topped with onion and garlic and garnished with fresh coriander.

Saffron and Pickled Walnut Pilaff

Fragrant saffron gives this lovely slow-cooker dish a warm, spiced flavour and a glorious colour.

Serves 4

5ml/1 tsp saffron threads
50g/2oz/½ cup pine nuts
45ml/3 tbsp olive oil
1 large onion, finely chopped
3 garlic cloves, crushed
1.5ml/¼ tsp ground allspice
4cm/1½in piece fresh root
   ginger, grated
750ml/1¼ pints/3 cups boiling
   vegetable stock
300g/10oz/generous 1½ cups
   easy-cook (converted) rice
50g/2oz/½ cup pickled walnuts,
   drained and roughly chopped
40g/1½2oz/¼ cup raisins
45ml/3 tbsp roughly
   chopped fresh parsley or
   coriander (cilantro)
salt and ground black pepper
parsley or coriander (cilantro)
   leaves, to garnish
natural (plain) yogurt, to serve

1 Put the saffron threads in a heatproof bowl with 15ml/1 tbsp boiling water and leave to stand. Meanwhile, heat a large frying pan and dry-fry the pine nuts until golden. Set them aside.

2 Heat the oil in a pan, add the onion and fry for 8 minutes. Stir in the garlic, allspice and ginger and cook for 2 minutes, stirring constantly. Transfer to the ceramic cooking pot. Pour the stock into the cooking pot and stir to combine, then cover with the lid and switch to high. Cook for 1 hour.

3 Sprinkle the rice into the cooking pot, then stir to mix thoroughly. Re-cover with the lid and cook for 1 hour, or until the rice is almost tender and most of the stock has been absorbed. Add a little extra stock or water to the pot if the mixture is already becoming dry.

4 Stir the saffron and soaking liquid into the rice, then add the pine nuts, walnuts, raisins and parsley or coriander, and stir well to combine. Season to taste with salt and ground black pepper.

5 Re-cover the pot with the lid and cook for 15 minutes, until the rice is very tender and all the ingredients are completely warmed through. Garnish with fresh parsley or coriander leaves and serve with a bowl of natural yogurt.

Chickpea Stew Energy 201kcal/843kJ; Protein 7.1g; Carbohydrate 22.3g, of which sugars 10.4g; Fat 10g, of which saturates 1.4g; Cholesterol 0mg; Calcium 57mg; Fibre 5.9g; Sodium 175mg.
Pilaff Energy 585kcal/2456kJ; Protein 10.2g; Carbohydrate 77.1g, of which sugars 11.1g; Fat 28.5g, of which saturates 3.1g; Cholesterol 0mg; Calcium 72mg; Fibre 2g; Sodium 222mg.

Spiced Indian Rice with Spinach, Tomatoes and Cashew Nuts

This all-in-one rice dish is simple to prepare in the slow cooker and makes a delicious, nutritious meal for all the family. It can also be served as a tasty accompaniment to a spicy vegetable curry.

Serves 4
30ml/2 tbsp sunflower oil
15ml/1 tbsp ghee or
    unsalted butter
1 onion, finely chopped
2 garlic cloves, crushed
3 tomatoes, peeled, seeded
    and chopped
275g/10oz/1½ cups easy-cook
    (converted) brown rice
5ml/1 tsp each ground coriander
    and ground cumin, or 10ml/2 tsp
    dhana jeera powder
2 carrots, coarsely grated
750ml/1¼ pints/3 cups boiling
    vegetable stock
175g/6oz baby spinach
    leaves, washed
50g/2oz/½ cup unsalted cashew
    nuts, toasted
salt and ground black pepper

1 Heat the oil and ghee or butter in a heavy pan, add the onion and fry gently for 6–7 minutes, until soft. Add the garlic and chopped tomatoes and cook for a further 2 minutes.

2 Rinse the rice in a sieve (strainer) under cold running water, drain well and transfer to the pan. Add the coriander and cumin or dhana jeera powder and stir for a few seconds. Turn off the heat and transfer the mixture from the pan to the ceramic cooking pot.

3 Stir the carrots into the cooking pot, then pour in the stock, season with salt and pepper, and stir to mix. Switch the slow cooker on to high. Cover and cook for 1 hour.

4 Lay the spinach on the surface of the rice, replace the lid and cook for a further 30–40 minutes, or until the spinach has wilted and the rice is cooked and tender.

5 Stir the spinach into the rice in the pot and check the seasoning, adding a little more salt and pepper, if necessary. Sprinkle the cashew nuts over the rice and serve immediately.

Vegetable Kashmiri

Tender vegetables simmered in the slow cooker in a spicy and aromatic yogurt sauce make a lovely vegetarian main meal.

Serves 4
10ml/2 tsp cumin seeds
8 black peppercorns
2 green cardamom pods, seeds only
5cm/2in cinnamon stick
2.5ml/½ tsp grated nutmeg
45ml/3 tbsp vegetable oil
1 fresh green chilli, seeded
    and chopped
2.5cm/1in piece fresh root
    ginger, grated
5ml/1 tsp chilli powder
2.5ml/½ tsp salt
2 large potatoes, cut into
    2.5cm/1in chunks
225g/8oz cauliflower florets
400ml/14fl oz/1⅔ cups boiling
    vegetable stock
150ml/¼ pint/⅔ cup Greek
    (US strained plain) yogurt
225g/8oz okra, thickly sliced
toasted flaked (sliced) almonds
    and sprigs of fresh coriander
    (cilantro), to garnish

1 Put the cumin seeds, peppercorns, cardamom seeds, cinnamon stick and nutmeg in a mortar or spice grinder, and grind to a fine powder.

2 Heat the oil in a frying pan, add the chilli and ginger and fry for 2 minutes, stirring all the time. Add the chilli powder, salt and ground spice mixture to the pan, and fry gently for 2–3 minutes, stirring constantly to prevent the spices from sticking to the pan.

3 Transfer the mixture to the ceramic cooking pot and stir in the potatoes and cauliflower. Pour in all but a few spoonfuls of the stock, cover with the lid, and cook on high for 2 hours.

4 In a bowl, stir the remaining hot stock into the yogurt, then pour over the vegetable mixture in the cooking pot, and stir until thoroughly combined.

5 Add the okra to the pot, stir, cover and cook for a further 1½–2 hours, or until all the vegetables are very tender. Serve the curry straight from the ceramic cooking pot, or spoon into a warmed serving dish. Sprinkle with toasted almonds and fresh coriander sprigs, to garnish.

Spiced Indian Rice Energy 473kcal/1989kJ; Protein 10.1g; Carbohydrate 72.1g, of which sugars 9.2g; Fat 18g, of which saturates 4.5g; Cholesterol 8mg; Calcium 111mg; Fibre 4.8g; Sodium 349mg.
Vegetable Kashmiri Energy 294kcal/1231kJ; Protein 9g; Carbohydrate 35.5g, of which sugars 7g; Fat 13.8g, of which saturates 4g; Cholesterol 6mg; Calcium 161mg; Fibre 5.1g; Sodium 427mg.

Vegetable and Cashew Nut Biriani

This hearty slow-cooker dish is full of Indian flavours.

Serves 4
1 small aubergine (eggplant), sliced
3 onions, 1 chopped, 2 finely sliced
2 garlic cloves
2.5cm/1in piece fresh root
    ginger, peeled
about 60ml/4 tbsp sunflower oil
3 parsnips, cut into 2cm/¾in pieces
5ml/1 tsp ground cumin
5ml/1 tsp ground coriander
2.5ml/½ tsp chilli powder
750ml/1¼ pints/3 cups boiling
    vegetable stock
1 red (bell) pepper, sliced
275g/10oz/generous 1½ cups
    easy-cook (converted) basmati
    or white rice
175g/6oz/1½ cup unsalted
    cashew nuts
40g/1½oz/¼ cup sultanas
    (golden raisins)
salt and ground black pepper
2 hard-boiled eggs, quartered, and
    sprigs of fresh coriander
    (cilantro), to garnish

1 Sprinkle the aubergine slices with salt in a colander. Leave for 30 minutes, then rinse thoroughly, pat dry and cut into bitesize pieces. Add the chopped onion to a food processor with the garlic and ginger. Add enough cold water to process to a paste.

2 Heat 30ml/2 tbsp of the oil in a frying pan, and cook the sliced onions for 10 minutes. Add the aubergine and parsnips and cook for 4 minutes. Transfer to the ceramic cooking pot and set to high.

3 Add 15ml/1 tbsp oil to the pan, and fry the onion paste with the cumin, coriander and chilli powder for 3–4 minutes. Stir in one-third of the stock, then transfer the mixture to the pot. Add the remaining stock and the pepper to the pot, then season and cover. Cook for 2–3 hours. Spoon the rice over the vegetables, then re-cover and cook for 45–55 minutes, until the rice is tender.

4 Meanwhile, heat the remaining oil in a clean frying pan, add the nuts and stir-fry for 2 minutes. Add the sultanas and fry for a few seconds. Drain the nuts and sultanas on kitchen paper.

5 Stir half the cashew nuts and sultanas into the vegetable rice. Turn off the slow cooker, cover and leave to stand for 5 minutes. Spoon the biriani on to a serving dish. Top with the remaining nuts and sultanas. Serve garnished with eggs and coriander.

Rice with Lime and Lemon Grass

The nutty flavour of brown rice is enhanced by the fragrance of limes and lemon grass in this tasty slow-cooker dish.

Serves 4
2 limes
1 lemon grass stalk
15ml/1 tbsp sunflower oil
1 onion, chopped
2.5cm/1in piece fresh root ginger,
    peeled and very finely chopped
7.5ml/1½ tsp coriander seeds
7.5ml/1½ tsp cumin seeds
750ml/1¼ pints/3 cups boiling
    vegetable stock
275g/10oz/1½ cups easy-cook
    (converted) brown rice
60ml/4 tbsp chopped fresh
    coriander (cilantro)
salt and ground black pepper
spring onions (scallions), toasted
    coconut strips and lime wedges,
    to garnish

1 Using a cannelle knife (zester) or fine grater, pare the rind from the limes, taking care not to remove any of the bitter white pith. Set the rind aside.

2 Cut off the lower portion of the lemon grass stalk, discarding the papery top end of the stalk. Finely chop the lemon grass and set aside.

3 Heat the oil in a large pan. Add the onion and cook over low heat for 5 minutes. Stir in the ginger, coriander and cumin seeds, lemon grass and lime rind, and cook for 2–3 minutes. Transfer the mixture to the ceramic cooking pot.

4 Pour the vegetable stock into the cooking pot, briefly stir to combine, then cover with the lid and switch the slow cooker to high. Cook for 1 hour.

5 Rinse the rice in cold running water until the water runs clear, then drain and add to the ceramic cooking pot. Cook for 45 minutes to 1½ hours, or until the rice is tender and has absorbed all the stock.

6 Stir the fresh coriander into the rice and season with salt and pepper. Fluff up the grains with a fork and serve garnished with strips of spring onion, toasted coconut and lime wedges.

Vegetable Biriani Energy 801kcal/3360kJ; Protein 18.7g; Carbohydrate 103.4g, of which sugars 25.7g; Fat 37.6g, of which saturates 6.7g; Cholesterol 0mg; Calcium 129mg; Fibre 9.2g; Sodium 230mg.
Rice with Lime Energy 308kcal/1304kJ; Protein 5.6g; Carbohydrate 64g, of which sugars 5.1g; Fat 5.1g, of which saturates 0.9g; Cholesterol 0mg; Calcium 17mg; Fibre 2g; Sodium 129mg.

Baked Mushrooms with Hazelnuts

Large mushrooms, full of texture and flavour, are topped with crunchy hazelnut pieces, fresh parsley, and garlic-flavoured oil, before being slowly baked in the oven.

90ml/6 tbsp olive oil
8 large field (portabello) mushrooms
50g/2oz/½ cup hazelnuts, coarsely chopped
30ml/2 tbsp chopped fresh parsley
salt and ground black pepper

Serves 4
2 garlic cloves
grated rind of 1 lemon

1 Crush the garlic cloves with a little salt, using a mortar and pestle or on a chopping board. Place the crushed garlic in a small bowl and stir in the grated lemon rind and the olive oil. Leave the mixture to stand for at least 30 minutes to allow all the flavours to develop.

2 Preheat the oven to 200°C/400°F/Gas 6. Arrange the mushrooms, stalk side up, in a single layer in a large, ovenproof earthenware dish. Drizzle about 60ml/4 tbsp of the garlic and lemon oil over them and bake in the preheated oven for about 10 minutes.

3 Remove the mushrooms from the oven, and baste them with the remaining garlic and lemon oil, then sprinkle the chopped hazelnuts evenly over the top. Bake in the oven for about 10–15 minutes more, until the mushrooms are tender. Season with salt and pepper and sprinkle with the chopped parsley. Serve immediately.

> **Cook's Tips**
> • Almost any unsalted nuts can be used in this recipe in place of the hazelnuts. Try pine nuts, cashew nuts, almonds or walnuts.
> • Nuts can go rancid quickly, so for the freshest flavour buy in small quantities, or buy them in shells and remove the shells just before using.

Baked Aubergines with Cheese

This wonderful slow-baked dish of aubergines is cloaked in a thick cheese sauce, which, when cooked, has a topping like a soufflé. It is delicious hot but even better cold and, although it takes a while to prepare, is the perfect dish to make ahead of time for barbecues or a picnic lunch.

about 60ml/4 tbsp olive oil
25g/1oz/2 tbsp butter
30ml/2 tbsp plain (all-purpose) flour
500ml/17fl oz/2¼ cups hot milk
about ⅛ of a whole nutmeg, freshly grated
cayenne pepper
4 large (US extra large) eggs, lightly beaten
400g/14oz/3½ cups grated cheese, such as Gruyère, or a mixture of Parmesan and Cheddar
salt and ground black pepper

Serves 4–6
2 large aubergines (eggplants), cut into 5mm/¼in thick slices

1 Layer the aubergine slices in a bowl or colander, sprinkling each layer with salt, and leave to drain for at least 30 minutes. Rinse well, then pat dry with kitchen paper.

2 Heat the oil in a large frying pan, then fry the aubergine slices until golden brown on both sides. Remove from the pan and set aside.

3 Melt the butter in a heavy pan, then add the flour and cook for 1 minute, stirring. Remove from the heat and gradually stir in the hot milk. Return to the heat and slowly bring to the boil, stirring constantly, until the sauce thickens and becomes smooth. Season with nutmeg, cayenne pepper, salt and black pepper and leave to cool.

4 When the sauce is cool, beat in the eggs, then mix in the grated cheese, reserving a little to sprinkle on top of the dish. Preheat the oven to 180°C/350°F/Gas 4.

5 In an ovenproof dish, arrange a layer of the aubergine, then pour over some sauce. Repeat, ending with sauce. Sprinkle with the cheese. Bake for about 35–40 minutes, until golden and firm. Serve hot or leave to cool before eating.

Baked Mushrooms Energy 255kcal/1052kJ; Protein 5.2g; Carbohydrate 1.7g, of which sugars 1g; Fat 25.4g, of which saturates 3.1g; Cholesterol 0mg; Calcium 43mg; Fibre 3.1g; Sodium 12mg.
Aubergines Energy 296kcal/1228kJ; Protein 14.7g; Carbohydrate 6.6g, of which sugars 5.1g; Fat 23.6g, of which saturates 10.6g; Cholesterol 39mg; Calcium 297mg; Fibre 3.4g; Sodium 297mg.

Three Vegetable Kugel

Grated seasonal vegetables are baked until crisp on top and creamy and tender inside. This version of the classic Jewish casserole combines the traditional flavours and method but uses a more contemporary combination of vegetables.

Serves 4

2 courgettes (zucchini), coarsely grated
2 carrots, coarsely grated
2 potatoes, peeled and coarsely grated
1 onion, grated
3 eggs, lightly beaten
3 garlic cloves, chopped
pinch of sugar
15ml/1 tbsp finely chopped fresh parsley
2–3 pinches of dried basil
30–45ml/2–3 tbsp matzo meal
105ml/7 tbsp olive oil or vegetable oil
salt and ground black pepper

1 Preheat the oven to 180°C/350°F/Gas 4. Put the courgettes, carrots, potatoes, onion, eggs, garlic, sugar, parsley, basil, salt and pepper in a bowl and combine.

2 Add the matzo meal to the bowl and stir together until the mixture forms a thick batter.

3 Pour half the olive or vegetable oil into an ovenproof dish. Spoon in the vegetable mixture, then evenly pour over the remaining oil.

4 Bake in the preheated oven for 40–60 minutes, or until the vegetables are tender and the kugel top is golden brown. Serve immediately.

> **Cook's Tip**
> Matzo is a thin, brittle unleavened bread, rather like a cracker. It is usually made with only plain (all-purpose) flour and water, although some have additional flavourings, like onion. Matzo is traditionally eaten during the Jewish Passover festival in place of the forbidden bread. Matzo meal is made by grinding matzos, and comes in fine or medium texture.

Mediterranean Baked Vegetables

This colourful selection of vegetables is baked in the oven in a shallow clay pot. It makes an excellent vegetarian meal.

Serves 4–6

75ml/5 tbsp olive oil
2 onions, halved and sliced
1 garlic clove, crushed
15ml/1 tbsp finely chopped fresh sage
4 large, well-flavoured tomatoes, quartered
3 courgettes (zucchini), thickly sliced
2 small yellow (bell) peppers, quartered and seeded
2 small red (bell) peppers, quartered and seeded
60ml/4 tbsp fresh white or wholemeal (whole-wheat) breadcrumbs
60ml/4 tbsp freshly grated Parmesan cheese
8–10 pitted black olives
salt and ground black pepper
sage leaves, to garnish

1 Heat 30ml/2 tbsp of the olive oil in a heavy frying pan, add the onions and cook, stirring occasionally, for 6–8 minutes until softened and beginning to colour.

2 Add the garlic to the pan and continue cooking until the onions are really soft and golden. Stir in the sage and season well with salt and pepper.

3 Transfer the onions to a large earthenware baking dish. Spread them out evenly in the base, then arrange the tomatoes, courgettes and peppers on top.

4 Preheat the oven to 200°F/400°C/Gas 6. Drizzle the remaining oil over the mixed vegetables and season well. Bake in the oven for 30 minutes.

5 Sprinkle the fresh white or wholemeal breadcrumbs and Parmesan cheese over the vegetables and arrange the black olives on top.

6 Return to the oven for a further 10–15 minutes, or until the vegetables are tender. Serve garnished with sage leaves.

Vegetable Kugel Energy 358kcal/1488kJ; Protein 9.2g; Carbohydrate 26.6g, of which sugars 5.7g; Fat 24.5g, of which saturates 4.2g; Cholesterol 143mg; Calcium 63mg; Fibre 2.9g; Sodium 71mg.
Baked Vegetables Energy 260kcal/1083kJ; Protein 9.5g; Carbohydrate 24.9g, of which sugars 15.4g; Fat 14.2g, of which saturates 3.7g; Cholesterol 10mg; Calcium 192mg; Fibre 4.9g; Sodium 275mg.

Cheese-topped Roast Baby Vegetables

A simple way of serving baby vegetables. Slow roasting really helps to bring out their flavour, and the cheese topping turns it into a dish that can be enjoyed on its own for supper.

Serves 4
1kg/2¼lb mixed baby vegetables, such as aubergines (eggplants), onions or shallots, courgettes (zucchini), corn on the cob and mushrooms

1 red (bell) pepper, seeded and cut into large pieces
1–2 garlic cloves, finely chopped
15–30ml/1–2 tbsp olive oil
30ml/2 tbsp chopped fresh mixed herbs
225g/8oz cherry tomatoes
115g/4oz/1 cup coarsely grated mozzarella cheese
salt and ground black pepper
black olives, to serve (optional)

1 Preheat the oven to 220°C/425°F/Gas 7. Cut all the vegetables in half lengthways.

2 Place the halved baby vegetables and pepper pieces in an ovenproof dish with the finely chopped garlic and plenty of salt and ground black pepper. Drizzle the oil over and toss the vegetables to coat them. Bake the vegetables for 20 minutes, or until they are tinged brown at the edges, stirring once during the cooking time.

3 Remove the ovenproof dish from the oven and stir in the chopped fresh mixed herbs. Sprinkle the cherry tomatoes over the surface and top with the coarsely grated mozzarella cheese.

4 Return to the oven and bake for a further 5–10 minutes until the cheese has melted and is bubbling. Serve immediately, with black olives, if you like.

> **Variation**
> This dish can also be made with a mixture of regular-sized vegetables. Simply chop them all into bitesize pieces and continue from Step 2.

Tomato and Potato Bake

This recipe is a great way for livening up potatoes to serve as a meal on their own or to accompany other vegetable dishes. The ingredients are first fried together on the stove before being slowly baked in the oven.

Serves 4
4 large ripe tomatoes
120ml/4fl oz/½ cup olive oil
1 large onion, finely chopped
3 garlic cloves, crushed
1kg/2¼lb maincrop waxy potatoes
coarse sea salt and ground black pepper
15ml/1 tbsp fresh flat leaf parsley, to garnish

1 Prepare the tomatoes. Place them in a large heatproof bowl and cover with near-boiling water. Leave submerged for about 2–3 minutes, then remove and leave to cool slightly.

2 The skin of the tomatoes should have loosened enough to peel off easily. Cut into wedges and remove the seeds and discard. Chop the flesh.

3 Preheat the oven to 180°C/350°F/Gas 4. Heat the oil in a flameproof casserole. Fry the onion, stirring frequently, for about 5 minutes until softened and just starting to brown. Add the garlic to the pan and cook for 2–3 minutes.

4 Add the tomatoes to the pan, season with salt and pepper and cook, stirring, for 1 minute. Cut the potatoes into wedges and add to the pan. Cook for 10 minutes.

5 Season the mixture again and cover the casserole with a tight-fitting lid. Place on the middle shelf of the oven and cook for 45 minutes to 1 hour. Garnish with fresh parsley and serve.

> **Cook's Tip**
> Make sure that the potatoes are completely and evenly coated in the oil for even cooking.

Cheese-topped Vegetables Energy 212kcal/883kJ; Protein 9.2g; Carbohydrate 24.3g, of which sugars 18.4g; Fat 9.4g, of which saturates 4.5g; Cholesterol 17mg; Calcium 174mg; Fibre 4.8g; Sodium 128mg.
Tomato Bake Energy 399kcal/1670kJ; Protein 5.9g; Carbohydrate 49.3g, of which sugars 10.6g; Fat 21.2g, of which saturates 3.2g; Cholesterol 0mg; Calcium 41mg; Fibre 4.6g; Sodium 39mg.

Drachena

A cross between an omelette and a pancake, this is a savoury dish which is slowly baked in the oven. It is popular in Russia and other European countries.

Serves 2–3
4 tomatoes
15ml/1 tbsp olive oil
1 bunch spring onions (scallions), finely sliced
1 garlic clove, crushed
45ml/3 tbsp wholemeal (whole-wheat) rye flour
60ml/4 tbsp milk
150ml/¼ pint/⅔ cup sour cream
4 eggs, beaten
30ml/2 tbsp chopped fresh parsley
25g/1oz/2 tbsp butter, melted
salt and ground black pepper
green salad, to serve

1 Place the tomatoes in a large heatproof bowl and cover with near-boiling water. Leave them submerged for 2–3 minutes, then remove and leave to cool slightly. The skin should have loosened enough to peel off easily. Cut into wedges, discard the seeds and chop the flesh.

2 Preheat the oven to 180°C/350°F/Gas 4. Heat the oil in a frying pan and gently cook the spring onions for 3–5 minutes. Add the garlic and cook for 1 minute more, or until the spring onions are soft.

3 Sprinkle the spring onions and garlic into the base of a lightly greased shallow 20cm/8in ovenproof dish, and sprinkle over the chopped tomatoes.

4 Mix the flour to a smooth paste in a bowl with the milk. Gradually add the sour cream, then mix with the beaten eggs. Stir in the fresh parsley and melted butter. Season with salt and black pepper.

5 Pour the egg mixture over the vegetables. Bake in the oven for 40–45 minutes, or until hardly any liquid seeps out when a knife is pushed into the middle.

6 Run a knife around the edge of the dish to loosen, then cut into wedges and serve immediately, with a fresh green salad.

Baked Potatoes with a Creamy Cheese Filling

In this simple recipe, potatoes are cooked in the oven, then filled with a rich cream and cheese filling before being browned under the grill. They make a very tasty hot meal.

Serves 6
3 baking potatoes
115g/4oz/1 cup mature (sharp) Cheddar cheese, grated
90ml/6 tbsp single (light) cream
sea salt and ground black pepper

1 Preheat the oven to 200°C/400°F/Gas 6. Scrub the potatoes and pat dry. Prick each one with a fork and cook directly on the middle shelf of the oven for 1¼–1½ hours until cooked through and tender.

2 Remove the potatoes from the oven and cut each one in half. Place the halves on a baking sheet and make shallow dips in the centre of each half, raising the potato up at the edges.

3 In a bowl, mix together the grated cheese and cream until well combined. Divide the mixture between the potato halves, packing it into the dips. Preheat the grill (broiler).

4 Grill (broil) the potatoes for 5 minutes until the cheese has melted and bubbles. Serve hot, sprinkled with salt and pepper.

Cook's Tip
You can speed up this recipe by starting the potatoes off in the microwave. Prick the scrubbed potatoes well and place in a covered microwave dish. Cook on high until starting to soften – test after 2 minutes, then every minute. Place in the oven to crisp the skins and finish cooking for about 45 minutes.

Drachena Energy 384kcal/1598kJ; Protein 13.4g; Carbohydrate 19.4g, of which sugars 7.9g; Fat 28.9g, of which saturates 13.5g; Cholesterol 302mg; Calcium 155mg; Fibre 2.4g; Sodium 187mg.
Baked Potatoes Energy 179kcal/748kJ; Protein 7.1g; Carbohydrate 16.5g, of which sugars 1.7g; Fat 9.4g, of which saturates 6.1g; Cholesterol 27mg; Calcium 161mg; Fibre 1g; Sodium 154mg.

Truffade

Baked until meltingly soft, this warming cheese and potato supper is the perfect slow bake to come home to. In France, where it originated, it would be made with a Tomme or Cantal cheese – look for them in good cheese stores.

Serves 4–6
1 large onion, thinly sliced
675g/1½lb baking potatoes, very thinly sliced
150g/5oz/1¼ cups grated hard cheese, such as Tomme, Cantal or mature (sharp) Cheddar
freshly grated nutmeg
coarse sea salt and ground black pepper
mixed salad leaves, to serve

1 Preheat the oven to 180°C/350°F/Gas 4. Lightly grease the base of a shallow baking dish or roasting pan with the oil or melted butter.

2 Arrange a layer of sliced onion over the base of the dish, then add a layer of sliced potatoes and about half of the grated cheese. Finish with the remaining onions and top with a layer of sliced potatoes.

3 Brush the top layer of potatoes with oil or melted butter and season with nutmeg, salt and pepper.

4 Sprinkle the remaining grated cheese over the top and bake for about 1 hour, or until the vegetables are tender and the top is golden brown.

5 Leave the dish to stand for about 5 minutes, then cut into wedges and serve with a salad.

> **Variation**
> *In France, they also make other versions of this dish, with the cheese chopped rather than grated. The ingredients are mixed and cooked slowly in white cooking fat in a heavy frying pan on top of the stove.*

Baked Scalloped Potatoes with Feta Cheese and Olives

Thinly sliced potatoes are slowly baked with Greek feta cheese, black and green olives and olive oil. This dish is excellent served with toasted pitta bread.

Serves 4
4–6 large, unpeeled potatoes, total weight about 900g/2lb
150ml/¼ pint/⅔ cup extra virgin olive oil
leaves from a sprig of rosemary
275g/10oz/2½ cups feta cheese, coarsely crumbled
115g/4oz/1 cup pitted, mixed black and green olives
300ml/½ pint/1¼ cups hot vegetable stock
salt and ground black pepper
toasted pitta bread, to serve

1 Preheat the oven to 200°C/400°F/Gas 6. Bring a large pan of salted water to the boil and cook the potatoes for 15 minutes until only just tender.

2 Drain the potatoes and set them aside until they are cool enough to handle. Carefully remove the peel from the potatoes using a small sharp knife, and cut them into thin slices.

3 Brush the base and sides of a 1.5 litre/2½ pint/6¼ cup rectangular ovenproof dish with some of the olive oil.

4 Arrange half the potatoes in the dish in an even layer. Top with half of the rosemary, cheese and olives, and season with salt and pepper. Arrange the rest of the potatoes in an even layer on top.

5 Add the remaining rosemary leaves, crumbled cheese and olives, and drizzle with the remaining olive oil. Pour the hot vegetable stock over the top and season the top layer with salt and plenty of ground black pepper.

6 Bake for 35 minutes, covering the dish loosely with foil after about 20 minutes to prevent the top from getting too brown. Serve hot, straight from the dish, with the toasted pitta bread.

Truffade Energy 117kcal/494kJ; Protein 3.2g; Carbohydrate 20.8g, of which sugars 3.4g; Fat 2.9g, of which saturates 1.7g; Cholesterol 7mg; Calcium 40mg; Fibre 1.6g; Sodium 48mg.
Scalloped Potatoes Energy 584kcal/2429kJ; Protein 14.8g; Carbohydrate 37.3g, of which sugars 4g; Fat 42.7g, of which saturates 13.7g; Cholesterol 48mg; Calcium 279mg; Fibre 3.1g; Sodium 1662mg.

Pan Haggerty

This Northumberland dish of potatoes, onions and cheese is slowly simmered on the stove. Use a firm-fleshed potato, such as Romano or Maris Piper, which will hold its shape.

Serves 2
1 large onion
450g/1lb potatoes
30ml/2 tbsp olive oil

25g/1oz/2 tbsp butter
2 garlic cloves, crushed
115g/4oz/1 cup grated mature
   (sharp) Cheddar cheese
45ml/3 tbsp chopped fresh
   chives, plus extra to garnish
coarse sea salt and ground
   black pepper

1 Halve and thinly slice the onion, using a sharp knife or a mandolin. Peel and thinly slice the potatoes.

2 Heat the oil and butter in a large heavy frying pan. Remove from the heat and cover the base with a layer of potatoes, followed by layers of onion slices, garlic, cheese and chives, and plenty of salt and ground black pepper.

3 Continue layering the vegetables and cheese, ending with grated cheese. Cover the pan with a tight-fitting lid or foil, and cook the pan haggerty over low heat on the stove for about 30–40 minutes, or until the potatoes and onion are tender when tested with a knife.

4 Preheat the grill (broiler) to hot. Uncover the pan, cover the pan handle with foil to protect it, if necessary, and brown the top under the grill. Serve the pan haggerty straight from the pan, sprinkled with extra chives to garnish.

> **Variations**
> • Other hard cheeses such as Red Leicester or Monterey Jack work well in this recipe.
> • For a slightly sweeter flavour and extra colour, use 1 sliced red onion in place of the brown-skinned variety.

Cheesy Potato Cake

This unusual dish is made from a layered ring of potatoes, cheese and fresh herbs. Slow baking gives the ingredients a rich flavour.

Serves 4
3 large potatoes
1 small onion, finely sliced
   into rings

200g/7oz/1¾ cups red Leicester
   or mature (sharp) Cheddar
   cheese, grated
fresh thyme sprigs
150ml/¼ pint/⅔ cup single
   (light) cream
salt and ground black pepper
salad leaves, to serve

1 Preheat the oven to 200°C/400°F/Gas 6. Peel the potatoes and cook in boiling water for 10 minutes, until they are just starting to soften. Remove from the water and pat dry.

2 Finely slice the potatoes, using the straight edge of a grater or a mandolin. Grease the base and sides of an 18cm/7in cake tin (pan) with butter and lay some of the potatoes on the base to cover it completely. Season with salt and pepper.

3 Sprinkle some of the sliced onion rings over the potato slices and top with a little of the cheese. Sprinkle over some fresh thyme and then continue to layer the ingredients, finishing with cheese and a little more seasoning.

4 Press the potato layers right down with your hand into the cake tin. (The mixture may seem quite high at this point but it will cook down.)

5 Pour the cream over and give the tin a shake to distribute it evenly. Cook in the oven for 50–55 minutes, until the potatoes are tender. Remove from the oven and cool. Invert on to a plate and cut into wedges. Serve with a few salad leaves.

> **Variation**
> You can make this main dish even more substantial by topping the wedges with slices of roasted red (bell) peppers.

Potato Cake Energy 408kcal/1706kJ; Protein 17.1g; Carbohydrate 30.2g, of which sugars 4g; Fat 24.1g, of which saturates 15.6g; Cholesterol 69mg; Calcium 417mg; Fibre 2g; Sodium 392mg.
Pan Haggerty Energy 542kcal/2257kJ; Protein 19.6g; Carbohydrate 42.2g, of which sugars 7.2g; Fat 33.9g, of which saturates 15g; Cholesterol 60mg; Calcium 429mg; Fibre 3.3g; Sodium 413mg.

Slow-cooked Spiced Onions

Onions marinated and then slowly baked in a spicy sauce are fabulous with grilled or roasted vegetables.

Serves 4
675g/1½lb Spanish (Bermuda)
  or red onions

90ml/6 tbsp olive or sunflower oil
  or a mixture of both
pinch of saffron threads
2.5ml/½ tsp ground ginger
5ml/1 tsp ground black pepper
5ml/1 tsp ground cinnamon
15ml/1 tbsp sugar

1 Slice the onions very thinly and place them in a shallow dish. In a bowl, blend together the olive and/or sunflower oil, saffron, ground ginger, black pepper, cinnamon and sugar, and pour over the onions. Stir gently to mix, then set the onions aside for about 2 hours.

2 Preheat the oven to 160°C/325°F/Gas 3 and pour the onions and the marinade into a casserole or ovenproof dish.

3 Fold a large piece of foil into three and place over the top of the casserole or ovenproof dish, securing it with a lid.

4 Cook in the oven for about 45 minutes, or until the onions are very soft, then increase the oven temperature to 200°C/400°F/ Gas 6. Remove the lid and foil and cook for a further 5–10 minutes, or until the onions are lightly glazed. Serve immediately.

Cook's Tips
• Onions that are grown in warmer climates are milder than those from cooler regions. Consequently, Spanish onions, also known as Bermuda onions, have a mild, sweet flavour. Their skins are a rich golden colour and they are one of the largest varieties available.
• When slicing onions, chop off the neck and just a little of the base to help the onion stay together. Score a line with a knife down the side of the onion and peel away the outer skin and the first layer of flesh.

Oven-roasted Red Onions

The wonderful taste of these slow-cooked red onions is enhanced still further with the powerful flavours of fresh rosemary and juniper berries, and the added tangy sweetness of balsamic vinegar.

Serves 4
4 large or 8 small red onions
45ml/3 tbsp olive oil
6 juniper berries, crushed
8 small rosemary sprigs
30ml/2 tbsp balsamic vinegar
salt and ground black pepper

1 Soak a clay onion baker in cold water for 15 minutes, then drain. If the base of the baker is glazed, only the lid will need to be soaked.

2 Trim the roots from the onions and remove the skins, if you like. Cut the onions from the tip to the root, cutting the large onions into quarters and the small onions in half.

3 Rub the onions with olive oil, salt and black pepper and the juniper berries. Place the onions in the baker, inserting the rosemary in among the onions. Pour the remaining olive oil and vinegar over.

4 Cover and place in an unheated oven. Set the oven to 200°C/400°F/Gas 6 and cook for 40 minutes. Remove the lid and cook for a further 10 minutes. Serve immediately.

Variation
Add a similar quantity of long, thin potato wedges to the onion. Use a larger dish so that the vegetables are still in one layer.

Cook's Tip
To help hold back the tears during preparation, chill the onions first for about 30 minutes and then remove the root end last. The root contains the largest concentration of the sulphuric compounds that make the eyes water.

Slow-cooked Onions Energy 224kcal/926kJ; Protein 2.1g; Carbohydrate 17.3g, of which sugars 13.4g; Fat 16.9g, of which saturates 2.4g; Cholesterol 0mg; Calcium 60mg; Fibre 2.4g; Sodium 6mg.
Oven-roasted Red Onions Energy 128kcal/530kJ; Protein 1.8g; Carbohydrate 11.9g, of which sugars 8.4g; Fat 8.6g, of which saturates 1.2g; Cholesterol 0mg; Calcium 38mg; Fibre 2.1g; Sodium 5mg.

Baked Onions

Onions deserve to be used more as a vegetable in their own right. They become deliciously sweet and mildly flavoured when boiled or slowly baked, and can be cooked very conveniently in the oven when baking potatoes or parsnips.

Serves 4
4 large onions

1 Preheat the oven to 180°C/350°F/Gas 4. Put a little cold water into a roasting pan in which the onions will fit in a single layer. Arrange the unpeeled onions in the pan.

2 Bake the onions in the preheated oven for about 1 hour. The onions are ready when they feel soft and tender when squeezed at the sides. Peel the skins and serve immediately.

Sweet and Sour Onion Salad

This recipe features whole baby onions that are slowly simmered in a tasty, tangy stock until tender. It makes a great side dish for a summer salad or at a barbecue.

Serves 6
450g/1lb baby (pearl)
 onions, peeled
50ml/2fl oz/¼ cup wine vinegar

45ml/3 tbsp olive oil
40g/1½oz/3 tbsp caster
 (superfine) sugar
45ml/3 tbsp tomato purée (paste)
1 bay leaf
2 parsley sprigs
65g/2½oz/½ cup raisins
salt and ground black pepper

1 Put all the ingredients into a large, heavy pan with about 300ml/½ pint/1¼ cups water and stir well. Bring to the boil and simmer gently, uncovered, for 45 minutes, or until the onions are tender and most of the liquid has evaporated.

2 Remove the bay leaf and parsley from the pan. Check the seasoning, adding salt and pepper if necessary. Transfer the onions to a serving dish. Serve at room temperature.

Baked Fennel with a Crumb Crust

The aniseed flavour of baked fennel makes it a good accompaniment to all kinds of dishes – it goes very well with pasta.

Serves 4
3 fennel bulbs, cut lengthways
 into quarters

30ml/2 tbsp olive oil
1 garlic clove, chopped
50g/2oz/1 cup day-old wholemeal
 (whole-wheat) breadcrumbs
30ml/2 tbsp chopped fresh flat
 leaf parsley
salt and ground black pepper
a few fronds of fennel leaves,
 to garnish (optional)

1 Cook the fennel in a pan of boiling salted water for about 10 minutes. Preheat the oven to 190°C/375°F/Gas 5.

2 Drain the fennel and place in a large earthenware baking dish or baking tray, then brush with half the olive oil.

3 In a bowl, mix together the garlic, breadcrumbs and chopped parsley, then stir in the rest of the oil. Sprinkle the mixture evenly over the fennel, then season well with salt and pepper.

4 Bake the fennel for 30 minutes or until it is tender and the breadcrumb topping is crisp and golden. Serve hot, garnished with a few fronds of fennel leaves, if you like.

> **Variation**
> *For a cheese-topped version, add 60ml/4 tbsp finely grated strong-flavoured cheese, such as mature (sharp) Cheddar, Red Leicester or Parmesan, to the breadcrumb mixture in step 3.*

> **Cook's Tips**
> • *Fennel has a distinctive liquorice flavour. All parts of the plant are edible.*
> • *When buying fennel, look for compact, unblemished white-green bulbs. The leaves should look fresh and green. Tougher specimens will have bulbs that spread at the top.*

Baked Onions Energy 90kcal/375kJ; Protein 3g; Carbohydrate 19.8g, of which sugars 14g; Fat 0.5g, of which saturates 0g; Cholesterol 0mg; Calcium 63mg; Fibre 3.5g; Sodium 8mg.
Onion Salad Energy 138kcal/578kJ; Protein 1.5g; Carbohydrate 21.5g, of which sugars 19.7g; Fat 5.7g, of which saturates 0.8g; Cholesterol 0mg; Calcium 30mg; Fibre 1.5g; Sodium 27mg.
Baked Fennel Energy 114kcal/477kJ; Protein 3g; Carbohydrate 12.6g, of which sugars 3.1g; Fat 6.1g, of which saturates 0.8g; Cholesterol 0mg; Calcium 67mg; Fibre 4.3g; Sodium 114mg.

Roasted Tomatoes and Garlic

This recipe is so simple to prepare, yet tastes absolutely wonderful. Use a large, shallow earthenware dish that will allow the tomatoes to sear and char in a very hot oven.

Serves 4
8 well-flavoured tomatoes
  (see Cook's Tips), halved
12 garlic cloves, unpeeled
60ml/4 tbsp extra virgin
  olive oil
3–4 bay leaves
salt and ground black pepper
45ml/3 tbsp fresh oregano leaves,
  to garnish

1 Preheat the oven to 230°C/450°F/Gas 8. Select a large, shallow ovenproof dish that will hold all the tomato halves snugly in a single layer.

2 Arrange the halved tomatoes in the dish and tuck the whole, unpeeled garlic cloves evenly in among the tomatoes.

3 Brush the tomatoes all over with the extra virgin olive oil, and tuck in the bay leaves. Sprinkle plenty of ground black pepper over the top.

4 Bake in the preheated oven for about 30–40 minutes, or until the tomatoes have softened and are sizzling in the dish with the edges tinged a golden brown colour.

5 Season with a little salt and more black pepper, if needed. Garnish with oregano leaves and serve immediately.

Braised Potatoes and Onions

Layers of thinly sliced potato and onions are gently braised in the oven in butter and stock. This savoury potato dish makes a tasty accompaniment to any vegetarian meal.

Serves 6
450g/1lb maincrop potatoes
2 onions

2 garlic cloves, crushed
50g/2oz/4 tbsp butter, softened
  and diced
300ml/½ pint/1¼ cups hot
  vegetable stock
coarse sea salt and ground
  black pepper
15ml/1 tbsp finely chopped
  fresh parsley, to garnish

1 Preheat the oven to 180°C/350°F/Gas 4. Grease the base and sides of a 1.5 litre/2½ pint/6¼ cup ovenproof dish.

2 Scrub the potatoes and slice them as thinly as possible. Slice the onions to about the same thickness.

3 Line the dish with some of the sliced potatoes. Sprinkle some onions and garlic on top. Layer up the remaining potatoes and onions, seasoning between each layer.

4 Push the vegetables down into the dish and dot the top with the butter. Pour the stock over and bake in the oven for about 1½ hours, covering with foil if the top starts to over brown. Serve with parsley and plenty of salt and pepper.

Variation
If you want to make this dish more substantial, sprinkle some grated cheese over the top for the last 30 minutes of cooking.

Cook's Tip
A mandolin is a handy kitchen utensil that would be useful for preparing the potatoes and onions in this recipe. The vegetables are sliced by rubbing them across an adjustable blade.

Cook's Tips
• If possible, try to find ripe plum tomatoes to use for this recipe as they not only keep their shape better than other varieties, but they have a more intense flavour. In addition, they do not tend to fall apart when roasted in the oven at such a high temperature.
• Leave the stalks on the tomatoes, if you like, for a more interesting-looking dish.

Braised Potatoes Energy 118kcal/494kJ; Protein 1.5g; Carbohydrate 12.9g, of which sugars 1.6g; Fat 7.1g, of which saturates 4.4g; Cholesterol 18mg; Calcium 9mg; Fibre 0.9g; Sodium 59mg.
Roasted Tomatoes Energy 138kcal/571kJ; Protein 2g; Carbohydrate 6.6g, of which sugars 5.6g; Fat 11.7g, of which saturates 1.8g; Cholesterol 0mg; Calcium 36mg; Fibre 2.5g; Sodium 19mg.

Braised Red Cabbage with Beetroot

The moist, gentle cooking of the clay pot finishes this vegetable side dish to perfection. Serve with casseroles and mixed roasted vegetables.

Serves 6–8
675g/1½lb red cabbage
30ml/2 tbsp olive oil
1 Spanish (Bermuda) onion, sliced
30ml/2 tbsp light muscovado (brown) sugar
2 tart eating apples, peeled, cored and sliced
300ml/½ pint/1¼ cups hot vegetable stock
60ml/4 tbsp red wine vinegar
375g/13oz raw beetroot (beet), peeled and coarsely grated
salt and ground black pepper

1 Soak a large clay pot or bean pot in cold water for 20 minutes, then drain. Finely shred the red cabbage and place in the clay pot.

2 Heat the olive oil in a frying pan and cook the onion for about 6–8 minutes, stirring frequently, until soft and transparent. Stir in the sugar and fry the onion gently until it is caramelized and golden. Take care not to overcook.

3 Stir in the apple slices, vegetable stock and red wine vinegar, then transfer the mixture to the clay pot. Season with salt and ground black pepper.

4 Cover and place in an unheated oven. Set the oven temperature to 190°C/375°F/Gas 5 and cook for 1 hour.

5 Stir in the beetroot, re-cover the pot and cook for a further 20–30 minutes, or until the cabbage and beetroot are tender. Serve immediately.

Cook's Tip
When buying cabbage, choose one that is firm and heavy for its size. The leaves should look healthy – avoid any with curling leaves or blemishes. These guidelines apply to any type of cabbage – red, green or white.

New Potatoes with Thyme and Lemon

These tasty potatoes are oven-roasted in a clay pot. They are the perfect accompaniment to grilled or roasted vegetables, and are ideal for serving as an alternative to traditional roast potatoes.

Serves 4
675g/1½lb small new potatoes
4 garlic cloves, sliced
8 thyme sprigs
4 strips finely pared lemon rind
75ml/5 tbsp olive oil
coarsely ground black pepper
coarse sea salt

1 Soak a clay pot in cold water for 20 minutes, then drain. Scrub the new potatoes and rinse thoroughly in cold water. Place the potatoes in the pot.

2 Add the sliced garlic cloves, fresh thyme sprigs and pared lemon rind to the pot, tucking them in among the potatoes. Sprinkle over plenty of coarsely ground black pepper and coarse sea salt.

3 Drizzle the olive oil all over the potatoes. Cover the pot with the lid and place in an unheated oven. Set the oven to 200°C/400°F/Gas 6 and cook for 1 hour, or until just tender.

4 If you wish, remove the lid and bake in the oven for a further 15–20 minutes, until slightly golden. If you prefer to keep the skins soft, remove the potatoes from the oven and leave to stand for 10 minutes before serving.

Cook's Tips
• Thyme is an aromatic, woody herb that goes particularly well with lemon. It has a strong aroma and pungent flavour and grows wild in most warm climates. Thyme is often associated with dishes from the Mediterranean.
• You could easily make this dish with older potatoes – simply peel them, if you like, then cut into even chunks or wedges before adding to the pot.

Braised Cabbage Energy 99kcal/415kJ; Protein 2.5g; Carbohydrate 16.2g, of which sugars 15g; Fat 3.1g, of which saturates 0.4g; Cholesterol 0mg; Calcium 63mg; Fibre 3.5g; Sodium 39mg.
New Potatoes Energy 242kcal/1011kJ; Protein 2.9g; Carbohydrate 27.2g, of which sugars 2.2g; Fat 14.3g, of which saturates 2.1g; Cholesterol 0mg; Calcium 10mg; Fibre 1.7g; Sodium 19mg.

Potato Wedges with Tomato and Chilli Salsa

This is a healthier version of traditionally baked potato skins; the clay pot keeps the potato flesh wonderfully moist and fluffy.

Serves 4
6 potatoes, about 115g/4oz each
45ml/3 tbsp olive oil
salt and ground black pepper

For the tomato and chilli salsa
4 juicy ripe tomatoes
1 sun-dried tomato in olive oil, drained
3 spring onions (scallions)
1–2 red or green chillies, halved and seeded
15ml/1 tbsp extra virgin olive oil
10ml/2 tsp lemon juice

1 Soak a clay pot or a potato pot in cold water for 20 minutes, then drain. Scrub the potatoes and dry with kitchen paper. Cut each potato lengthways into four wedges. Brush with a little of the oil and sprinkle with salt and pepper.

2 Place the potatoes in the clay pot and cover with the lid. Place the pot in an unheated oven, set the temperature to 200°C/400°F/Gas 6 and cook for 55–60 minutes, or until the potatoes are tender.

3 Meanwhile, finely chop the tomatoes, sun-dried tomato, spring onions and chilli and mix together with the olive oil and lemon juice. Cover and leave to stand for about 30 minutes to allow the flavours to mingle.

4 Uncover the potatoes, brush with the remaining olive oil and bake, uncovered, for a further 15 minutes until slightly golden. Divide the potato wedges and salsa among four serving bowls and plates, and serve immediately.

> **Cook's Tip**
> *Varieties of floury potatoes that produce a fluffy texture when baked are best for these wedges. Good types to use include Maris Piper, Désirée, King Edward and Pentland Squire.*

Potatoes with Roasted Garlic

Potatoes slowly roasted in their skins retain a deep, earthy taste, and, as a bonus, they absorb less fat too. The whole garlic cloves will mellow during the cooking to give a deliciously pungent and sweet but not overly-strong taste. They can be served alongside the potatoes, or squeeze the soft flesh out of the skins and use as a garnish.

Serves 4
1kg/2¼lb small floury potatoes
60–75ml/4–5 tbsp sunflower oil
10ml/2 tsp walnut oil
2 whole garlic bulbs, unpeeled
salt and ground black pepper

1 Preheat the oven to 240°C/475°F/Gas 9. Gently scrub the potatoes, place in a large pan of cold water and bring to the boil. Boil vigorously for a couple of minutes, then drain and leave to dry.

2 Combine the sunflower and walnut oils in a roasting pan and place in the oven to get really hot. Add the potatoes and garlic to the pan and coat evenly in the oil.

3 Sprinkle the potatoes and garlic with plenty of salt and ground black pepper. Place the pan in the oven and cook for about 10 minutes.

4 Reduce the oven temperature to 200°C/400°F/Gas 6. Continue cooking, basting occasionally with the oil, for a further 30–40 minutes.

5 Serve immediately. Accompany each portion of the potatoes with several cloves of the roasted garlic for eating whole or squeezing over the potatoes.

> **Cook's Tip**
> *Some people are fearful of whole roasted garlic cloves, but they do lose much of their strength and become soft and sweet during cooking. If anyone really does not want the garlic paste, you can save the cloves for your next soup or mashed potato.*

Potato Wedges Energy 238kcal/1001kJ; Protein 4g; Carbohydrate 30.8g, of which sugars 4.9g; Fat 11.9g, of which saturates 1.8g; Cholesterol 0mg; Calcium 23mg; Fibre 2.6g; Sodium 28mg.
Potatoes with Garlic Energy 312kcal/1310kJ; Protein 6.2g; Carbohydrate 44.3g, of which sugars 3.7g; Fat 13.4g, of which saturates 1.7g; Cholesterol 0mg; Calcium 20mg; Fibre 3.5g; Sodium 29mg.

Potatoes Baked with Fennel, Onions, Garlic and Saffron

Vegetables are gently braised in a delicious stock in the oven. This slow-cooked dish makes a very sophisticated and attractive accompaniment, especially to egg-based vegetarian meals.

Serves 4–6

500g/1¼lb small waxy potatoes, cut into chunks or wedges
good pinch of saffron threads (12–15 threads)
1 garlic bulb, separated into cloves
12 small red or yellow onions, peeled but left whole
3 fennel bulbs, cut into wedges, feathery tops reserved for garnish (optional)
4–6 fresh bay leaves
6–9 fresh thyme sprigs
175ml/6fl oz/¾ cup vegetable stock
30ml/2 tbsp sherry or balsamic vinegar
2.5ml/½ tsp sugar
5ml/1 tsp fennel seeds, crushed
2.5ml/½ tsp paprika
45ml/3 tbsp olive oil
salt and ground black pepper

1 Boil the potato chunks or wedges in a large pan of boiling salted water for 8–10 minutes. Drain. Preheat the oven to 190°C/375°F/Gas 5. Soak the saffron threads in 30ml/2 tbsp warm water for 10 minutes.

2 Peel and finely chop two of the garlic cloves and set aside. Place the potatoes, whole red or yellow onions, remaining unpeeled garlic cloves, fennel wedges, fresh bay leaves and thyme sprigs in a large roasting pan or dish. Mix together the stock and the saffron and its soaking liquid in a jug (pitcher) or measuring cup.

3 Add the vinegar and sugar to the stock mixture, then pour the liquid over the vegetables. Stir in the fennel seeds, paprika, chopped garlic and oil, and season with salt and pepper.

4 Cook the vegetables in the oven for 1–1¼ hours, stirring occasionally, until they are just tender. Chop the reserved fennel tops, if using, and sprinkle them over the vegetables to garnish. Season with more salt and pepper and serve immediately.

Potatoes, Peppers and Shallots Roasted with Rosemary

These luscious roasted potatoes soak up both the taste and wonderful aromas of the shallots and rosemary.

Serves 4

500g/1¼lb waxy potatoes
12 shallots
2 yellow (bell) peppers
45–60ml/3–4 tbsp olive oil
2 rosemary sprigs
salt and ground black pepper
crushed peppercorns, to garnish

1 Preheat the oven to 200°C/400°F/Gas 6. Par-boil the potatoes in their skins in a pan of boiling salted water for about 5 minutes. Drain and, when they are cool enough to handle, peel and halve each one lengthways.

2 Peel the shallots, allowing them to fall into their natural segments. Cut each sweet pepper lengthways into eight strips, discarding the seeds and pith.

3 Oil a shallow ovenproof dish thoroughly with 15ml/1 tbsp olive oil. Arrange the potatoes and peppers in alternating rows and stud with the shallots.

4 Cut the rosemary sprigs into 5cm/2in lengths and tuck them in among the vegetables. Season with salt and pepper, and pour over the remaining oil, tossing the vegetables to coat evenly.

5 Place in the oven, uncovered, for 30–40 minutes until all the vegetables are tender. Turn the vegetables occasionally to cook and brown evenly. Serve hot or at room temperature, garnished with crushed peppercorns.

Cook's Tip
This dish is excellent served with a simple dish of roast or grilled vegetables. It also makes a delicious light meal in itself and is the perfect comfort food.

Potatoes with Fennel Energy 162kcal/676kJ; Protein 4.4g; Carbohydrate 23.6g, of which sugars 7.1g; Fat 6.2g, of which saturates 0.9g; Cholesterol 0mg; Calcium 49mg; Fibre 4.9g; Sodium 23mg.
Potatoes with Rosemary Energy 176kcal/742kJ; Protein 4.2g; Carbohydrate 33.6g, of which sugars 12.6g; Fat 3.7g, of which saturates 0.6g; Cholesterol 0mg; Calcium 40mg; Fibre 4.1g; Sodium 20mg.

Berrichonne Potatoes

This is a traditional slow-cooked French potato dish with a difference. The potatoes on top will be crispy and golden brown, while underneath they will be tender and moist.

350ml/12fl oz/1½ cups hot
   vegetable stock
coarse sea salt and ground
   black pepper
15ml/1 tbsp chopped fresh
   parsley, to garnish

Serves 4
900g/2lb maincrop potatoes
25g/1oz/2 tbsp butter
1 onion, finely chopped

1 Preheat the oven to 200°C/400°F/Gas 6. Peel the potatoes and trim them into barrel shapes. Leave the potatoes to stand in a bowl of cold water.

2 Melt the butter in a heavy frying pan. Add the onions, stir and cover with a lid. Cook for 5–6 minutes, until they are soft but not browned.

3 Spoon the onions into the base of a 1.5 litre/2½ pint/6¼ cup rectangular shallow ovenproof dish. Lay the potatoes over the onion mixture and pour the stock over, making sure it comes halfway up the sides of the dish.

4 Season with a little salt and plenty of ground black pepper. Place in the preheated oven and cook for 1 hour, until the potatoes are tender.

5 Garnish with chopped fresh parsley and serve.

Cook's Tip
Use the best stock you can find for this dish. If you do not have any home-made stock, then try to find tubs of fresh stock available in supermarkets. If you use a stock (bouillon) cube, you may not need to add any more salt.

Orange Candied Sweet Potatoes

This dish is the classic accompaniment to a traditional Thanksgiving dinner. Long simmering in orange juice and maple syrup in the slow cooker results in deliciously sweet and tender potatoes. For a really fresh, festive look, serve this dish with extra orange segments.

Serves 8
900g/2lb sweet potatoes
150ml/¼ pint/⅔ cup orange juice
30ml/2 tbsp maple syrup
5ml/1 tsp freshly grated ginger
2.5ml/½ tsp ground cinnamon
2.5ml/½ tsp ground cardamom
5ml/1 tsp salt
ground black pepper
orange segments, to serve (optional)

1 Peel the sweet potatoes and cut them into 2cm/¾in cubes. Put the cubes into a large heatproof bowl and pour over just enough near-boiling water to cover. Leave them to stand for about 5 minutes.

2 Meanwhile, put the orange juice, maple syrup, ginger, cinnamon and cardamom in the ceramic cooking pot. Season with the salt and stir the mixture until well combined. Switch the slow cooker to high.

3 Drain the sweet potato cubes and add them to the ceramic cooking pot. Gently stir to coat the pieces in the spicy orange mixture. Cover and cook for 4–5 hours, until tender, stirring twice during cooking.

4 Stir the orange segments, if using, into the sweet potatoes, and season to taste with plenty of ground black pepper. Serve immediately.

Variation
You can serve this rich vegetable dish as a purée, if you prefer (but omit the orange segments). Transfer the cooked candied sweet potatoes to a food processor, adding a little of the sauce, and blend until smooth. You may need to add a little more of the sauce to make a soft, creamy, spoonable purée.

Berrichonne Energy 289kcal/1213kJ; Protein 8.6g; Carbohydrate 37.5g, of which sugars 3.8g; Fat 12.6g, of which saturates 5.9g; Cholesterol 32mg; Calcium 20mg; Fibre 2.5g; Sodium 425mg.
Orange Candied Potatoes Energy 53kcal/226kJ; Protein 2.9g; Carbohydrate 13.7g, of which sugars 11.8g; Fat 0g, of which saturates 0g; Cholesterol 0mg; Calcium 5mg; Fibre 0.2g; Sodium 158mg.

Roasted Sweet Potatoes, Onions and Beetroot in Coconut Paste

Sweet potatoes and beetroot become wonderfully sweet when slowly roasted. They work well with savoury onions and an aromatic coconut, ginger and garlic paste.

Serves 4

30ml/2 tbsp groundnut (peanut) or mild olive oil
450g/1lb sweet potatoes, peeled and cut into strips or chunks
4 beetroot (beets), cooked, peeled and cut into wedges
450g/1lb small onions, halved
5ml/1 tsp coriander seeds, crushed
3–4 small whole fresh red chillies
salt and ground black pepper
chopped fresh coriander (cilantro), to garnish

For the paste

2 large garlic cloves, chopped
1–2 green chillies, seeded and chopped
15ml/1 tbsp chopped fresh root ginger
45ml/3 tbsp chopped fresh coriander (cilantro)
75ml/5 tbsp coconut milk
30ml/2 tbsp groundnut (peanut) or mild olive oil
grated rind of 1/2 lime
2.5ml/1/2 tsp soft light brown sugar

1 To make the paste, process the garlic, chillies, ginger, coriander and coconut milk in a food processor or blender. Transfer the paste into a small bowl and beat in the oil, grated lime rind and light brown sugar. Preheat the oven to 200°C/400°F/Gas 6.

2 Heat the oil in a large roasting pan in the oven for 5 minutes. Add the sweet potatoes, beetroot, onions and coriander seeds, tossing them in the hot oil. Roast the vegetables for 10 minutes.

3 Stir in the paste and the whole red chillies. Season well with salt and pepper, and shake the pan to toss the vegetables and coat them thoroughly with the paste.

4 Return the vegetables to the oven and cook for a further 25–35 minutes, or until the vegetables are tender. During cooking, stir the mixture two or three times to prevent the coconut and ginger paste from sticking to the roasting pan. Serve the vegetables immediately, garnished with a little chopped fresh coriander.

Spinach Braised with Sweet Potatoes

Sweet potatoes make an interesting alternative to the ordinary variety. Here, the garlic and ginger subtly complement the slow-cooked potatoes and spinach.

Serves 4

30ml/2 tbsp sunflower oil
1 onion, chopped
1 garlic clove, finely chopped
2.5cm/1in piece fresh root ginger, peeled and grated
2.5ml/1/2 tsp cayenne pepper
675g/11/2lb sweet potatoes
150ml/1/4 pint/2/3 cup vegetable stock
225g/8oz spinach
45ml/3 tbsp pine nuts, toasted
salt and ground black pepper

1 Soak a clay potato pot in cold water for 20 minutes, then drain. Heat the oil in a large frying pan, add the onion, garlic, ginger and cayenne pepper and fry gently, stirring occasionally, for about 8 minutes or until the onion is softened.

2 Peel the sweet potatoes and cut them into 2.5cm/1in chunks. Add the chunks to the frying pan and stir to coat them in the oil and spices.

3 Transfer the potato mixture to the clay pot and add the vegetable stock. Cover the pot and place in an unheated oven. Set the oven to 220°C/425°F/Gas 7 and cook for 50–60 minutes, or until the potatoes are just tender, stirring halfway through cooking.

4 Wash the spinach and shred roughly. Stir into the potatoes with the toasted pine nuts, re-cover the clay pot and cook for a further 5 minutes in the oven until the spinach is wilted. Remove from the oven and leave to stand for 5 minutes. Adjust the seasoning and serve immediately.

Cook's Tip
To toast pine nuts, heat a heavy frying pan and add the nuts. Cook them for 3–4 minutes or until they turn a golden brown colour, stirring occasionally. Watch the nuts carefully – they will scorch and burn quickly if toasted for too long.

Sweet Potatoes Energy 272kcal/1143kJ; Protein 4.4g; Carbohydrate 39.8g, of which sugars 19.2g; Fat 11.8g, of which saturates 1.7g; Cholesterol 0mg; Calcium 98mg; Fibre 6.3g; Sodium 122mg.
Spinach Energy 293kcal/1231kJ; Protein 5.4g; Carbohydrate 38.5g, of which sugars 11.8g; Fat 14.2g, of which saturates 1.4g; Cholesterol 0mg; Calcium 141mg; Fibre 5.7g; Sodium 147mg.

Potato, Onion and Garlic Gratin

This tasty slow-cooker dish makes the perfect accompaniment to roasted vegetables, stews and grilled vegetables. Slowly cooking the potatoes in stock with onions and garlic gives them a deep, rich flavour.

2–4 garlic cloves, finely chopped
2.5ml/½ tsp dried thyme
900g/2lb waxy potatoes, very finely sliced
450ml/¾ pint/scant 2 cups boiling vegetable stock
coarse sea salt and ground black pepper

Serves 4
40g/1½oz/3 tbsp butter
1 large onion, finely sliced into rings

1 Lightly grease the inside of the ceramic cooking pot with 15g/½oz/1 tbsp of the butter. Spoon a layer of onions into the pot, then sprinkle over a little garlic, thyme, salt and pepper.

2 Carefully arrange an overlapping layer of potato slices on top of the onion mixture. Continue to layer the ingredients in the pot, finishing with a layer of sliced potatoes.

3 Pour just enough of the stock into the pot to cover the potatoes. Cover with the lid and cook on low for 8–10 hours, or on high for 4–5 hours, until the potatoes are tender.

4 If you like, brown the potatoes under a hot grill (broiler) for 3–4 minutes. Serve sprinkled with a little salt and pepper.

> **Variations**
> • To make this dish more substantial, sprinkle 115g/4oz/1 cup of grated Gruyère cheese over the top of the cooked potatoes and brown under a preheated grill (broiler) for 3–4 minutes until golden-brown and bubbling.
> • Alternatively, crumble 165g/5½oz/scant 1 cup soft goat's cheese on to the gratin 30 minutes before the end of cooking.
> • To vary the flavour, try using chopped rosemary or sage in place of the thyme, or use crushed juniper berries instead.

Herby Potato Bake

Wonderfully creamy potatoes, well flavoured with lots of fresh herbs, are gently baked in the oven until beautifully tender. The dish is topped with a sprinkling of cheese to make a golden, crunchy topping.

Serves 4
675g/1½lb waxy potatoes
25g/1oz/2 tbsp butter

1 onion, finely chopped
1 garlic clove, crushed
2 eggs
300ml/½ pint/1¼ cups crème fraîche or double (heavy) cream
115g/4oz/1 cup Gruyère, grated
60ml/4 tbsp chopped mixed fresh herbs, such as chervil, thyme, chives and parsley
freshly grated nutmeg
salt and ground black pepper

1 Preheat the oven to 190°C/375°F/Gas 5 and place a baking sheet in the oven to heat up. Lightly butter an ovenproof dish.

2 Peel the potatoes and cut them into matchsticks. Set aside while you make up the sauce mixture.

3 Melt the butter in a heavy frying pan and cook the onions, stirring frequently, for 4–5 minutes until beginning to soften.

4 Add the garlic to the pan and cook for a further 2–3 minutes. Remove the pan from the heat to cool slightly.

5 In a large mixing bowl, add the eggs, crème fraîche or double cream and about half of the grated Gruyère cheese. Whisk together until well combined.

6 Stir the onion mixture, chopped fresh herbs and sliced potatoes into the mixing bowl. Season with salt, ground black pepper and grated nutmeg. Mix until well combined. Spoon the mixture into the prepared dish and sprinkle over the remaining Gruyère cheese.

7 Place the dish on the hot baking sheet and cook in the oven for 50 minutes to 1 hour, until the top is golden brown and the potatoes are tender. Serve immediately, straight from the dish, as this will ensure that the potatoes stay really hot.

Potato Gratin Energy 260kcal/1092kJ; Protein 5.1g; Carbohydrate 41.9g, of which sugars 6.4g; Fat 9.1g, of which saturates 5.4g; Cholesterol 21mg; Calcium 31mg; Fibre 3.3g; Sodium 171mg.
Potato Bake Energy 614kcal/2550kJ; Protein 15.6g; Carbohydrate 30.6g, of which sugars 5g; Fat 48g, of which saturates 30.8g; Cholesterol 221mg; Calcium 310mg; Fibre 2.5g; Sodium 321mg.

Potatoes and Parsnips Baked with Garlic and Cream

As the potatoes and parsnips cook, they gradually absorb the garlic-flavoured cream, while the cheese on top browns to a crispy finish.

Serves 4–6

3 large potatoes, total weight about 675g/1½lb
350g/12oz parsnips
200ml/7fl oz/scant 1 cup single (light) cream
105ml/7 tbsp milk
2 garlic cloves, crushed
5ml/1 tsp freshly grated nutmeg
75g/3oz/¾ cup coarsely grated Gruyère cheese
salt and ground black pepper

1 Peel the potatoes and parsnips and cut them into thin slices, using a sharp knife. Place them in a pan of salted boiling water and cook for 5 minutes. Drain and leave to cool slightly.

2 Meanwhile, pour the cream and milk into a heavy pan, add the garlic and bring to the boil. Remove the pan from the heat and leave to stand for about 10 minutes.

3 Lightly grease a 25cm/10in rectangular earthenware baking dish. Preheat the oven to 180°C/350°F/Gas 4.

4 Layer the potatoes and parsnips in the prepared dish, seasoning each layer with salt, pepper and a little grated nutmeg.

5 Pour the garlic-flavoured cream and milk mixture into the dish and press the sliced potatoes and parsnips down into the liquid. The liquid should come to just underneath the top layer. Cover with lightly buttered foil and bake for 45 minutes.

6 Remove the dish from the oven and remove the foil from the dish. Sprinkle the grated Gruyère cheese over the vegetables in an even layer.

7 Return the dish to the oven and bake, uncovered, for a further 20–30 minutes, or until the potatoes and parsnips are tender and the topping is golden brown. Serve immediately.

Potato Gratin

Potatoes, layered with mustard butter and slowly baked until golden, are perfect to serve with a green salad, or as an accompaniment to a vegetable or nut roast.

Serves 4

4 large potatoes, total weight about 900g/2lb
30ml/2 tbsp butter
15ml/1 tbsp olive oil
2 large garlic cloves, crushed
30ml/2 tbsp Dijon mustard
15ml/1 tbsp lemon juice
15ml/1 tbsp fresh thyme leaves, plus extra to garnish
50ml/2fl oz/¼ cup hot vegetable stock
salt and ground black pepper

1 Thinly slice the potatoes using a knife, mandolin or the slicing attachment on a food processor. Place the potato slices in a bowl of cold water to prevent them from discolouring.

2 Preheat the oven to 200°C/400°F/Gas 6. Heat the butter and oil in a deep frying pan. Add the garlic and cook gently for 2–3 minutes until light golden, stirring constantly. Stir in the mustard, lemon juice and thyme. Remove from the heat and pour the mixture into a jug (pitcher).

3 Drain the potatoes and pat dry with kitchen paper. Place a layer of potatoes in the frying pan, season and pour over one-third of the butter mixture. Arrange another layer of potatoes on top, pour over half of the remaining butter mixture and season. Arrange a final layer of potatoes on top, pour over the remainder of the butter mixture and the stock. Season and sprinkle with the reserved thyme.

4 Cover the potatoes with baking parchment and bake for 1 hour, then remove the paper, return to the oven and cook for 15 minutes or until golden.

> **Variation**
> *Any root vegetables can be used for this recipe: try using sweet potatoes, parsnips, swede (rutabaga) or turnips.*

Potatoes and Parsnips Energy 241kcal/1009kJ; Protein 7.8g; Carbohydrate 27g, of which sugars 6.4g; Fat 11.7g, of which saturates 7.2g; Cholesterol 31mg; Calcium 174mg; Fibre 3.8g; Sodium 126mg.
Potato Gratin Energy 238kcal/1002kJ; Protein 3.9g; Carbohydrate 36.3g, of which sugars 3g; Fat 9.6g, of which saturates 4.5g; Cholesterol 16mg; Calcium 15mg; Fibre 2.3g; Sodium 70mg.

Stuffed Peaches with Mascarpone Cream

These peaches are packed with an amaretti and almond filling and then slowly baked in the oven.

Serves 4
4 large peaches, halved and
   stoned (pitted)
40g/1½oz amaretti, crumbled
30ml/2 tbsp ground almonds
45ml/3 tbsp sugar
15ml/1 tbsp unsweetened
   cocoa powder

150ml/¼ pint/⅔ cup sweet wine
25g/1oz/2 tbsp butter

For the mascarpone cream
30ml/2 tbsp caster
   (superfine) sugar
3 egg yolks
15ml/1 tbsp sweet wine
225g/8oz/1 cup
   mascarpone cheese
150ml/¼ pint/⅔ cup double
   (heavy) cream

1 Preheat the oven to 200°C/ 400°F/Gas 6. Using a teaspoon, scoop some of the flesh from the cavities in the peaches, to make a space for stuffing. Chop the scooped-out flesh.

2 Mix together the amaretti, almonds, sugar, cocoa and peach flesh. Add enough wine to make the mixture into a thick paste.

3 Place the peaches in a buttered ovenproof dish and fill them with the stuffing. Dot with the butter, then pour the remaining wine into the dish. Bake for 35 minutes.

4 To make the mascarpone cream, beat the sugar and egg yolks until thick and pale. Stir in the wine, then fold in the mascarpone. Whip the double cream until it forms soft peaks and fold into the mixture. Remove the peaches from the oven and leave to cool. Serve at room temperature, with the mascarpone cream passed round separately.

> **Cook's Tip**
> Mascarpone is a thick, velvety Italian cream cheese, made from cow's milk. It is often used in desserts, or eaten with fresh fruit.

Poached Pears in Red Wine

In this recipe, the pears take on a red blush from the wine and make a very pretty dessert. For best results, use a small slow cooker, which ensures that the pears stay submerged during cooking.

Serves 4
1 bottle fruity red wine
150g/5oz/¾ cup caster
   (superfine) sugar

45ml/3 tbsp clear honey
1 cinnamon stick
1 vanilla pod (bean), split
   lengthways
large strip of lemon or orange rind
2 whole cloves
2 black peppercorns
4 firm ripe pears
juice of ½ lemon
mint leaves, to decorate
whipped cream or sour cream,
   to serve

1 Pour the red wine into the ceramic cooking pot. Add the sugar, honey, cinnamon stick, vanilla pod, lemon or orange rind, cloves and peppercorns. Cover with the lid and cook on high for 30 minutes, stirring occasionally.

2 Meanwhile, peel the pears using a vegetable peeler, leaving the stem intact. Take a very thin slice off the base of each pear so it will stand square and upright. As each pear is peeled, toss it in the lemon juice to prevent the flesh browning when exposed to the air.

3 Place the pears in the spiced wine mixture in the cooking pot. Cover with the lid and cook for 2–4 hours, turning the pears occasionally, until they are just tender; be careful not to overcook them.

4 Transfer the pears to a bowl, using a slotted spoon. Continue to cook the wine mixture, uncovered, for a further hour, until reduced and thickened a little, then turn off the slow cooker and leave to cool. Alternatively, to save time, pour the cooking liquor into a pan and boil briskly for 10–15 minutes.

5 Strain the cooled liquid over the pears and chill for at least 3 hours. Divide the pears between four individual serving dishes and spoon a little of the wine syrup over each one. Garnish with fresh mint and serve with whipped or sour cream.

Coconut Custard

This slow-cooker dessert, made with rich, creamy coconut milk, is delicious served with a selection of fresh fruit.

Serves 4
4 eggs
75g/3oz/generous ⅓ cup soft light brown sugar
250ml/8fl oz/1 cup coconut milk
5ml/1 tsp vanilla, rose or jasmine extract
icing (confectioners') sugar, to decorate
sliced fresh fruit, to serve

1 Pour about 2.5cm/1in of hot water into the base of the ceramic cooking pot and switch the slow cooker on to the low setting. Whisk the eggs and sugar in a bowl until smooth. Gradually add the coconut milk and flavoured extract, and whisk well.

2 Strain the mixture into a jug (pitcher), then pour into four individual heatproof glasses, ramekins or one single ovenproof dish. Cover the containers with clear film (plastic wrap).

3 Place the dishes in the slow cooker and, if necessary, pour a little more boiling water around them to reach just over halfway up their sides.

4 Cover the ceramic cooking pot with the lid, then cook for 3 hours, or until the custards are lightly set. Test with a fine skewer or cocktail stick (toothpick); it should come out clean.

5 Carefully lift the dishes out of the slow cooker and leave to cool. Once cool, chill in the refrigerator until ready to serve. Decorate the custards with a light dusting of icing sugar, and serve with sliced fruit.

Cook's Tip
Line the bases of individual ramekins with rounds of baking parchment, then lightly oil the sides. After cooking and chilling, run a knife around the insides of the custards and turn out on to individual dessert plates.

Coconut Crème Caramel

This is a version of the classic French dessert made with coconut milk.

600ml/1 pint/2½ cups coconut milk
toasted slivers of coconut, to decorate

Serves 4–6
4 large (US extra large) eggs
4 egg yolks
50g/2oz/¼ cup caster (superfine) sugar

For the caramel
150g/5oz/¾ cup caster (superfine) sugar

1 Preheat the oven to 160°C/325°F/Gas 3. To make the caramel, heat the sugar and 75ml/5 tbsp water in a heavy pan, stirring until the sugar dissolves. Bring to the boil and, without stirring, let the mixture bubble until dark golden and almost like treacle.

2 Pour the caramel into an ovenproof dish, tilting the dish to swirl it around so that it covers the bottom and sides – you will need to do this quickly. Set aside and leave the caramel to set.

3 In a bowl, beat the eggs and egg yolks with the caster sugar. Heat the coconut milk in a small pan, but don't allow it to boil. Then gradually pour it on to the egg mixture, while beating constantly. Pour the mixture through a sieve (strainer) over the caramel in the dish.

4 Set the dish in a bain-marie. You can use a roasting pan or wide oven dish half-filled with water. Place it in the oven for 50 minutes, or until the custard has just set, but still feels soft when touched. Leave the dish to cool, then chill in the refrigerator for at least 6 hours, or overnight.

5 To serve, loosen the custard around the sides using a thin knife. Place a flat serving plate over the top and invert the custard, holding on to the dish and plate at the same time. Shake it a little before removing the inverted dish, then carefully lift it off as the caramel drizzles down the sides.

6 Decorate the custard with freshly grated coconut and serve immediately.

Coconut Custard Energy 175kcal/738kJ; Protein 7.5g; Carbohydrate 22.7g, of which sugars 22.7g; Fat 6.7g, of which saturates 2g; Cholesterol 227mg; Calcium 57mg; Fibre 0g; Sodium 151mg.
Coconut Caramel Energy 256kcal/1078kJ; Protein 9g; Carbohydrate 31g, of which sugars 31g; Fat 11g, of which saturates 4g; Cholesterol 338mg; Calcium 79mg; Fibre 0.4g; Sodium 200mg.

Citrus and Caramel Custards

These baked custards, made rich with cream and egg yolks, are delicately scented with tangy citrus flavours and aromatic cinnamon.

Serves 4
450ml/³/₄ pint/scant 2 cups milk
150ml/¹/₄ pint/²/₃ cup single (light) cream
1 cinnamon stick, broken in half
thinly pared rind of ¹/₂ lemon
thinly pared rind of ¹/₂ orange
4 egg yolks
5ml/1 tsp cornflour (cornstarch)
40g/1¹/₂oz/3 tbsp caster (superfine) sugar
grated rind of ¹/₂ lemon
grated rind of ¹/₂ orange
a little icing (confectioner's) sugar, to decorate

1 Place the milk and cream in a pan. Add the cinnamon stick and the strips of pared citrus rind. Bring to the boil, then simmer for 10 minutes.

2 Preheat the oven to 160°C/325°F/Gas 3. Whisk the egg yolks, cornflour and caster sugar together. Remove the rinds and cinnamon from the hot milk and cream and discard. Whisk the hot milk and cream into the egg yolk mixture.

3 Stir the grated citrus rind into the custard mixture. Pour into four individual cazuelas, or earthenware oven dishes, each about 13cm/5in in diameter. Place in a roasting pan and pour warm water into the pan to reach three-quarters of the way up their sides. Bake for 25–30 minutes, or until the custards are just set. Remove the dishes from the water; leave to cool, then chill.

4 Preheat the grill (broiler) to high. Sprinkle the custards liberally with icing sugar and place under the grill until the tops turn golden brown and caramelize. Serve immediately.

> **Cook's Tips**
> • Prepare the grated rind first, then cut strips of rind from the ungrated side of the citrus fruits using a vegetable peeler.
> • You can use a special cook's gas-gun or salamander to caramelize the tops instead of grilling (broiling) them.

Petits Pots de Crème au Mocha

The name of these lovely slow-cooker custards comes from the baking cups they are traditionally made in, called pots de crème. The addition of coffee gives the dessert an even richer, more luxurious flavour.

Serves 4
5ml/1 tsp instant coffee powder
15ml/1 tbsp soft light brown sugar
300ml/¹/₂ pint/1¹/₄ cups milk
150ml/¹/₄ pint/²/₃ cup double (heavy) cream
115g/4oz plain (semisweet) chocolate
15ml/1 tbsp coffee liqueur (optional)
4 egg yolks
whipped cream and candied cake decorations, to decorate (optional)

1 Put the instant coffee and brown sugar in a pan and stir in the milk and cream. Bring the mixture to the boil over medium heat, stirring constantly, until the coffee and sugar have dissolved completely.

2 Remove the pan from the heat and add the plain chocolate. Stir until the chocolate has melted, then stir in the coffee liqueur, if using.

3 In a bowl, whisk the egg yolks, then slowly whisk in the chocolate mixture until well blended. Strain the custard mixture into a large jug (pitcher) and divide equally among pots de crème or ramekins – first checking that they will all fit inside the ceramic cooking pot.

4 Cover each pot de crème or ramekin with a piece of foil, then transfer to the ceramic cooking pot. Pour enough hot water around the dishes to come just over halfway up their sides. Cover the slow cooker with the lid and cook on high for 2¹/₂–3 hours, or until the custards are just set and a knife inserted into the middle comes out clean.

5 Carefully remove the pots or ramekins from the cooker and leave to cool. Cover and chill in the refrigerator until ready to serve, then decorate with whipped cream and candied cake decorations, if you like.

Citrus Custards Energy 225kcal/939kJ; Protein 8g; Carbohydrate 16.6g, of which sugars 16.6g; Fat 14.6g, of which saturates 7.3g; Cholesterol 229mg; Calcium 197mg; Fibre 0g; Sodium 69mg.
Petits Pots Energy 443kcal/1840kJ; Protein 8.3g; Carbohydrate 23.7g, of which sugars 23.7g; Fat 35.7g, of which saturates 20.2g; Cholesterol 264mg; Calcium 196mg; Fibre 0.2g; Sodium 74mg.

Maple Custards

Maple syrup has a really distinctive flavour and gives these little slow-cooker desserts a wonderfully rich and indulgent taste. Try to find pure maple syrup – it will make all the difference to these custards.

Serves 6

3 eggs
120ml/4fl oz/½ cup maple syrup
250ml/8fl oz/1 cup warm milk
150ml/¼ pint/⅔ cup warm
   single (light) cream
5ml/1 tsp vanilla extract
whole nutmeg, to grate

1 Beat the eggs in a large mixing bowl, then whisk in the maple syrup, followed by the warm milk, warm cream and the vanilla extract. Grate in a little fresh nutmeg.

2 Strain the custard mixture into six individual ramekins – first checking that the dishes will all fit inside the ceramic cooking pot of the slow cooker in a single layer. Carefully cover each ramekin with a piece of kitchen foil, then place them in the ceramic cooking pot.

3 Pour very hot water around the dishes to come about three-quarters of the way up their sides. Cover with the lid and cook on low for 2½–3 hours, or until set. To test, insert a skewer in the middle; it should come out clean.

4 Transfer the custards to a wire rack. Leave for 5 minutes and serve warm, or leave to cool completely, then chill. Remove from the refrigerator about 30 minutes before serving.

Cook's Tip
Warming the milk and cream until tepid will help the custard cook and set more quickly. You can do this in a pan on the stove, or more simply, pour the milk and cream into a heatproof bowl or jug (pitcher) and place in the slow cooker filled with near-boiling water to a depth of about 5cm/2in. Switch the slow cooker to high and leave for 30 minutes. Remove the milk, then turn the slow cooker to low and use the hot water in the ceramic cooking pot to cook the custards.

Baked Coffee Custards

These delightfully rich custards are flavoured with coffee. They are ideal for a dinner party as you can bake them in the oven before the guests arrive and then chill until needed.

Serves 4
25g/1oz/6 tbsp finely ground
   fresh coffee
300ml/½ pint/1¼ cups milk
150ml/¼ pint/⅔ cup single
   (light) cream
2 eggs, beaten
30ml/2 tbsp caster
   (superfine) sugar
whipped cream and unsweetened
   cocoa powder, to decorate

1 Preheat the oven to 190°C/375°F/Gas 5. Put the ground coffee in a heatproof jug (pitcher). Heat the milk in a pan until it is nearly boiling. Pour the milk over the coffee and leave to stand for 5 minutes.

2 Strain the coffee-flavoured milk back into the pan through a fine sieve (strainer). Add the single cream and heat again until nearly boiling.

3 Beat the eggs and sugar in a large bowl. Pour the heated coffee-flavoured cream into the bowl, whisking all the time. Strain into the rinsed jug.

4 Carefully pour the egg and cream mixture into four 150ml/¼ pint/⅔ cup ramekins. Cover each with a piece of foil or baking parchment.

5 Stand the ramekins in a roasting pan and pour enough hot water into the roasting pan to come halfway up the sides of the ramekins. Bake in the preheated oven for 40 minutes, or until lightly set.

6 Remove the ramekins from the roasting pan and allow to cool. When cold, chill the custards in the refrigerator for about 2 hours. Decorate each custard with a swirl of whipped cream and a sprinkling of unsweetened cocoa powder, if you like, before serving.

Maple Custard Energy 174kcal/735kJ; Protein 8.6g; Carbohydrate 24.5g, of which sugars 18.7g; Fat 5.3g, of which saturates 1.6g; Cholesterol 116mg; Calcium 97mg; Fibre 9.1g; Sodium 120mg.
Coffee Custards Energy 207kcal/860kJ; Protein 8.4g; Carbohydrate 12.1g, of which sugars 12.1g; Fat 14.3g, of which saturates 7.6g; Cholesterol 174mg; Calcium 147mg; Fibre 0g; Sodium 96mg.

Caramel Custard with Fresh Fruit

A creamy caramel dessert
is a wonderful way to
end a meal. It is light and
delicious, and easy to make.

Serves 6
6 eggs
4 drops vanilla extract
115g/4oz/generous ½ cup sugar

750ml/1¼ pints/3 cups
    semi-skimmed (low-fat) milk
fresh fruit, such as strawberries,
    blueberries, orange and banana
    slices, and raspberries, to serve

For the caramel
30ml/2 tbsp sugar
30ml/2 tbsp water

1 To make the caramel, place the sugar and water in a heavy pan and heat until the sugar has completely dissolved and the mixture is bubbling and pale gold in colour. Watch the sugar carefully, as it can quickly burn once it begins to caramelize. Pour carefully into a 1.2 litre/2 pint/5 cup soufflé dish. Leave the caramel to cool.

2 Preheat the oven to 180°C/350°F/Gas 4. To make the custard, break the eggs one at a time into a mixing bowl and whisk until frothy.

3 Stir the vanilla extract into the whisked eggs and gradually add the sugar. Add the milk in a steady stream, whisking constantly as you pour.

4 Carefully pour the custard over the top of the caramel in the base of the soufflé dish.

5 Cook the custard in the oven for 35–40 minutes. Remove from the oven and leave to cool for 30 minutes or until the mixture is set.

6 Loosen the custard from the sides of the dish with a knife. Place a serving dish upside-down on top of the soufflé dish and invert, giving a gentle shake if necessary to turn out the custard on to the serving dish.

7 Arrange fresh fruit of your choice around the custard on the serving dish and serve immediately.

Rice Condé Sundae

Slowly cooking rice pudding on top of the hob instead of in the oven gives it a light, creamy texture, especially if you remember to stir it frequently. It is particularly good served cold with a topping of fruit and toasted nuts or a trickle of hot chocolate sauce.

Serves 4
50g/2oz/generous ¼ cup short
    grain pudding rice

5ml/1 tsp vanilla extract
2.5ml/½ tsp ground cinnamon
45ml/3 tbsp sugar
600ml/1 pint/2½ cups milk

For the toppings
soft berry fruits, such as
    strawberries, raspberries
    and cherries
chocolate sauce and
    flaked (sliced) toasted
    almonds (optional)

1 Mix the rice, vanilla extract, ground cinnamon and sugar in a pan. Pour in the milk and slowly bring the mixture to the boil, stirring constantly. Reduce the heat to low so that the mixture is barely simmering.

2 Cook the rice over low heat for about 30–40 minutes, stirring frequently to release the starch from the grains. Add extra milk to the rice if it begins to dry out a little during the cooking process.

3 When the rice grains are soft, remove the pan from the heat. Allow the rice to cool completely, stirring it occasionally, then chill in the refrigerator.

4 Before serving, stir the rice pudding and spoon it into four sundae dishes. Top with soft berry fruits, and with chocolate sauce and toasted almonds, if using.

> **Variation**
> *For a special occasion, use single cream instead of milk, and glaze the fruit with a little melted redcurrant jelly. (Add a splash of port to the jelly, if you like.)*

Custard Energy 197kcal/830kJ; Protein 10.6g; Carbohydrate 23.3g, of which sugars 23.3g; Fat 7.7g, of which saturates 2.9g; Cholesterol 198mg; Calcium 187mg; Fibre 0g; Sodium 125mg.
Rice Condé Energy 185kcal/782kJ; Protein 6.9g; Carbohydrate 34.8g, of which sugars 24.8g; Fat 2.7g, of which saturates 1.6g; Cholesterol 9mg; Calcium 204mg; Fibre 1.1g; Sodium 71mg.

Winter Fruit Poached in Mulled Wine

Poaching fresh apples and pears with dried apricots and figs in a spicy wine syrup in the slow cooker makes a seasonal winter dessert. Serve on its own or with a generous spoonful of thick cream.

Serves 4
300ml/½ pint/1¼ cups fruity
   red wine
300ml/½ pint/1¼ cups fresh
   apple or orange juice

thinly pared strip of orange or
   lemon peel
45ml/3 tbsp clear honey
1 small cinnamon stick
4 whole cloves
4 cardamom pods, split
2 pears, such as Comice or William
8 ready-to-eat figs
12 ready-to-eat dried apricots
2 eating apples, peeled, cored and
   thickly sliced

1 Pour the wine and apple or orange juice into the ceramic cooking pot. Add the citrus peel, honey, cinnamon stick, cloves and cardamom pods. Cover with the lid and cook on high for 1 hour.

2 Peel, core and halve the pears, keeping the stalk intact if possible. Place in the slow cooker with the figs and apricots. Cook for 1 hour. Gently turn the pears, then add the sliced apples and cook for a further 1½–2 hours, or until all the fruit is tender.

3 Using a slotted spoon, remove the fruit from the cooking pot and place in a serving dish. Set aside while you finish the syrup.

4 Strain the syrup into a pan, discarding the spices, then bring to the boil. Boil vigorously for about 10 minutes, until reduced by about one-third. Pour over the fruit and serve hot or cold.

> **Cook's Tip**
> *Choose tart, well-tasting apples such as Cox's Orange Pippin, Braeburn or Granny Smith. They stand up particularly well against the sweet dried fruits and spicy, robust red wine syrup.*

Baked Stuffed Apples

Using Italian amaretti to stuff the apples in this slow-cooker dessert gives a lovely almondy flavour. Dried cranberries and glacé fruit add sweetness and colour. Choose apples that will stay firm during cooking.

Serves 4
75g/3oz/6 tbsp butter, softened
45ml/3 tbsp orange or apple juice
75g/3oz/scant ½ cup light
   muscovado (brown) sugar

grated rind and juice of ½ orange
1.5ml/¼ tsp ground cinnamon
30ml/2 tbsp crushed amaretti
25g/1oz/¼ cup pecan nuts,
   chopped
25g/1oz/¼ cup dried cranberries
   or sour cherries
25g/1oz/¼ cup luxury mixed
   glacé (candied) fruit, chopped
4 large cooking apples, such
   as Bramleys
cream, crème fraîche or vanilla
   ice cream, to serve

1 Grease the ceramic cooking pot with 15g/½oz/1 tbsp of the butter, then pour in the fruit juice and switch the slow cooker to the high setting.

2 Put the remaining butter, the sugar, orange rind and juice, cinnamon and amaretti crumbs in a bowl and mix well.

3 Add the nuts and dried cranberries or sour cherries and glacé fruit to the bowl and mix well, then set aside the filling while you prepare the apples.

4 Wash and dry the apples. Remove the cores using an apple corer, then carefully enlarge each core cavity to twice its size, using the corer to shave out more flesh. Using a sharp knife, score each apple around its equator.

5 Divide the filling among the apples, packing it into the hole, then piling it on top. Stand the apples in the cooking pot and cover with the lid. Reduce the temperature to low and cook for 4 hours, or until tender.

6 Transfer the apples to warmed serving plates and spoon the sauce over the top. Serve immediately, with cream, crème fraîche or vanilla ice cream.

Winter Fruit Energy 347kcal/1476kJ; Protein 5g; Carbohydrate 78.1g, of which sugars 78.1g; Fat 1.9g, of which saturates 0g; Cholesterol 0mg; Calcium 284mg; Fibre 11.4g; Sodium 72mg.
Baked Stuffed Apples Energy 347kcal/1457kJ; Protein 1.6g; Carbohydrate 42.4g, of which sugars 41.3g; Fat 20.3g, of which saturates 10.3g; Cholesterol 40mg; Calcium 27mg; Fibre 3g; Sodium 131mg.

Papaya Cooked with Ginger

Spicy ginger enhances the delicate flavour of papaya perfectly. This slow-cooker recipe is excellent for busy people because it takes no more than 10 minutes to prepare and can then be left to cook gently. Be careful not to overcook the papaya or the flesh will become watery.

Serves 4
150ml/¼ pint/⅔ cup hot water
45ml/3 tbsp raisins
shredded finely pared rind and juice of 1 lime
2 ripe papayas
2 pieces stem ginger in syrup, drained, plus 15ml/1 tbsp syrup from the jar
8 amaretti or other dessert biscuits (cookies), coarsely crushed
25g/1oz/¼ cup pistachio nuts, chopped
15ml/1 tbsp light muscovado (brown) sugar
60ml/4 tbsp crème fraîche, plus extra to serve

1 Pour the water into the base of the ceramic cooking pot and switch the slow cooker to high. Put the raisins in a small bowl and pour over the lime juice. Stir until well combined, then leave to soak for at least 5 minutes, while preparing the remaining ingredients.

2 Cut the papayas in half and scoop out and discard their seeds using a teaspoon.

3 Finely chop the stem ginger and combine with the biscuits, raisins and lime juice, lime rind, two-thirds of the nuts, the sugar and crème fraîche.

4 Fill the papayas with the mixture and place in the cooking pot. Cover and cook for 1–1½ hours. Drizzle with the ginger syrup, sprinkle with the remaining nuts and serve immediately, with crème fraîche.

> **Variation**
> Try using chopped almonds and Greek (US strained plain) yogurt in place of the pistachio nuts and crème fraîche.

Hot Bananas with Rum and Raisins

These sticky bananas are made in the slow cooker and are utterly moreish. The rich sauce becomes almost toffee-like during the long cooking.

Serves 4
30ml/2 tbsp seedless raisins
45ml/3 tbsp dark rum
40g/1½oz/3 tbsp unsalted butter
50g/2oz/¼ cup soft light brown sugar
4 slightly under-ripe bananas, peeled and halved lengthways
1.5ml/¼ tsp grated nutmeg
1.5ml/¼ tsp ground cinnamon
25g/1oz/¼ cup flaked (sliced) almonds, toasted (optional)
whipped cream or vanilla ice cream, to serve

1 Put the raisins in a bowl and spoon over 30ml/2 tbsp of the rum. Set aside and leave to soak.

2 Cut the butter into small cubes and place in the ceramic cooking pot with the sugar and remaining 15ml/1 tbsp rum. Switch the slow cooker to high and leave uncovered for 15 minutes, until the butter and sugar have melted.

3 Add the bananas to the butter and sugar mixture, cover with the lid and cook for 30 minutes, or until the fruit is almost tender, turning over the bananas halfway through cooking time.

4 Sprinkle the nutmeg and cinnamon over the bananas, then stir in the rum and raisins. Re-cover and cook for 10 minutes.

5 Carefully lift the bananas out of the ceramic cooking pot and arrange on a serving dish or individual plates. Spoon over the sauce, then sprinkle with almonds, if using. Serve hot with whipped cream or vanilla ice cream.

> **Variation**
> If you don't like the taste of rum, try using an orange liqueur, such as Cointreau, instead. It makes a very good alternative and is a little less overpowering.

Papaya Energy 302kcal/1272kJ; Protein 4.1g; Carbohydrate 45.6g, of which sugars 36.6g; Fat 12.8g, of which saturates 5.7g; Cholesterol 17mg; Calcium 70mg; Fibre 5.7g; Sodium 136mg.
Hot Bananas Energy 323kcal/1355kJ; Protein 3g; Carbohydrate 47.1g, of which sugars 44.7g; Fat 12.1g, of which saturates 5.6g; Cholesterol 21mg; Calcium 33mg; Fibre 1.9g; Sodium 72mg.

Cassava Sweet

This sweet and sticky baked dessert is made with cassava root and coconut milk with a hint of aniseed. It is perfect with jasmine tea.

115g/4oz/generous ½ cup palm sugar (jaggery)
2.5ml/½ tsp ground aniseed
salt
675g/1½lb cassava root, peeled and coarsely grated

Serves 6–8
350ml/12fl oz/1½ cups coconut milk

1 Preheat the oven to 190°C/375°F/Gas 5. Grease a baking dish with butter.

2 In a mixing bowl, whisk the coconut milk with the palm sugar, ground aniseed and a pinch of salt, until the palm sugar has completely dissolved.

3 Beat the grated cassava root into the coconut mixture until well combined. Pour into the greased baking dish.

4 Place the dish in the oven and bake for about 1 hour, or until cooked through and golden brown on top.

5 Leave the sweet to cool a little in the dish before serving warm or at room temperature.

> **Variation**
> This dessert can also be made using sweet potatoes or yams in place of the cassava root.

> **Cook's Tip**
> To prepare the cassava root for grating, use a sharp knife to split the whole length of the root and then carefully peel off the skin using a vegetable peeler or knife. Simply grate the peeled root using a coarse grater.

Baked Peaches

This recipe uses fresh ripe peaches with a hint of cloves to give them a lovely aromatic, spicy flavour. The fruits are slowly baked in the oven until deliciously tender. This is a great dish to make the most of peaches when they are in season.

12 whole cloves
90g/3½oz/½ cup vanilla sugar
45ml/3 tbsp brandy or dry white wine (optional)
fresh mint leaves and a little sifted icing (confectioners') sugar, to decorate
shelled pistachio nuts and whipped cream or crème fraîche, to serve

Serves 6
40g/1½oz/3 tbsp unsalted butter
6 firm ripe peaches, washed

1 Preheat the oven to 180°C/350°F/Gas 4. Spread half the unsalted butter around an ovenproof dish, making sure both the sides and base are well coated.

2 Halve the peaches and remove the stones (pits) using a sharp knife. Place the peach halves, skin side down, in the prepared dish. Push a whole clove into the centre of each peach half.

3 Sprinkle the vanilla sugar over the peaches and dot the remaining butter into each peach half. Drizzle over the brandy or dry white wine, if using. Bake for 30–40 minutes, or until the peaches are tender.

4 Decorate with sprigs of fresh mint, and sprinkle over a little of the icing sugar. Serve the baked peaches hot or cold, with freshly whipped cream or crème fraîche and a few shelled pistachio nuts.

> **Cook's Tip**
> The cooking time will depend on the size and ripeness of the peaches. Small, ripe peaches will cook quicker than larger, less ripe peaches. Check them with a skewer after 30 minutes.

Baked Peaches Energy 70kcal/299kJ; Protein 1.1g; Carbohydrate 17.3g, of which sugars 17.3g; Fat 0.1g, of which saturates 0g; Cholesterol 0mg; Calcium 8mg; Fibre 1.5g; Sodium 3mg.
Cassava Sweet Energy 254kcal/1086kJ; Protein 1g; Carbohydrate 64g, of which sugars 25g; Fat 1g, of which saturates 1g; Cholesterol 2mg; Calcium 39mg; Fibre 1.8g; Sodium 0.2g.

Tapioca Pudding

This slow-cooker version of the classic tapioca pudding is made from large pearl tapioca and coconut milk and is served warm. It is very good served with fresh tropical fruits such as lychees.

Serves 4
115g/4oz/⅔ cup large pearl tapioca

475ml/16fl oz/2 cups very hot water
115g/4oz/generous ½ cup caster (superfine) sugar
pinch of salt
250ml/8fl oz/1 cup coconut milk
250g/9oz prepared tropical fruits
shredded lime rind and shaved fresh coconut, to decorate (optional)

1 Put the tapioca in a bowl and pour over enough warm water to cover generously. Leave the tapioca to soak for 1 hour until the grains swell, then drain well and set aside.

2 Pour the measured hot water into the ceramic cooking pot and switch the slow cooker to the high setting. Add the sugar and salt and stir until dissolved.

3 Cover the slow cooker with the lid and cook for about 30 minutes, until the water inside the cooking pot reaches boiling point.

4 Add the tapioca and coconut milk to the ceramic cooking pot and stir until well combined. Cover again with the lid and cook for a further 1–1½ hours, or until the tapioca grains have all turned transparent.

5 Spoon into one large dish or four individual bowls and serve warm with tropical fruits, decorated with the lime rind and coconut shavings, if using.

> **Cook's Tip**
> *This dish includes a considerable amount of sugar but you may prefer to reduce the quantity according to taste.*

Souffléed Rice Pudding

Using skimmed milk to make this baked pudding is a healthy option, but you could use whole milk if you prefer a creamier taste.

Serves 4
65g/2½oz/⅓ cup short grain pudding rice

4.5ml/3 tbsp clear honey
750ml/1¼ pints/3 cups skimmed milk
1 vanilla pod (bean) or 2.5ml/½ tsp vanilla extract
2 egg whites
5ml/1 tsp freshly grated nutmeg
wafer biscuits, to serve (optional)

1 Place the rice, honey and milk in a heavy or non-stick pan, and bring the milk to just below boiling point, watching it closely to prevent it from boiling over. Add the vanilla pod (but do not add vanilla extract at this stage, if using).

2 Reduce the heat to the lowest setting and cover the pan with a tight-fitting lid. Leave to cook for about 1–1¼ hours, stirring occasionally to prevent sticking, until most of the liquid has been absorbed.

3 Remove the vanilla pod or, if using vanilla extract, add this to the rice mixture now. Preheat the oven to 220°C/425°F/Gas 7. Grease a 1 litre/1¾ pint/4 cup baking dish with butter.

4 Place the egg whites in a large grease-free bowl and whisk them until they hold soft peaks. Using either a large metal spoon or a spatula, carefully fold the egg whites evenly into the rice and milk mixture. Transfer to the baking dish.

5 Sprinkle with grated nutmeg and bake in the oven for about 15–20 minutes, until the rice pudding has risen well and the surface is golden brown. Serve the pudding hot, with wafer biscuits, if you like.

> **Cook's Tip**
> *This pudding is also delicious if served with a topping of stewed dried fruit, such as apricots, prunes or dates.*

Tapioca Pudding Energy 273kcal/1164kJ; Protein 2.7g; Carbohydrate 66.7g, of which sugars 41.9g; Fat 1.3g, of which saturates 0.4g; Cholesterol 0mg; Calcium 43mg; Fibre 1.7g; Sodium 73mg.
Rice Pudding Energy 183kcal/773kJ; Protein 9.1g; Carbohydrate 30.4g, of which sugars 17.4g; Fat 3.3g, of which saturates 2g; Cholesterol 11mg; Calcium 230mg; Fibre 0g; Sodium 112mg.

Traditional Rice Pudding

This classic, slow-baked dessert is delectably smooth and creamy with just a hint of fragrant spices, thanks to the vanilla pod and a little fresh nutmeg.

Serves 4
600ml/1 pint/2¹/₂ cups
  creamy milk
1 vanilla pod (bean)
50g/2oz/generous ¹/₄ cup short
  grain pudding rice
45ml/3 tbsp caster
  (superfine) sugar
25g/1oz/2 tbsp butter
freshly grated nutmeg

1 Pour the creamy milk into a pan and add the vanilla pod. Bring to simmering point, then remove from the heat, cover and leave the flavour of the vanilla to mingle with the milk for about 1 hour.

2 Preheat the oven to 150°C/300°F/Gas 2. Put the rice and sugar in an ovenproof dish. Strain the vanilla-flavoured milk over the rice, discarding the vanilla pod. Stir to mix, then dot the surface with the butter.

3 Bake, uncovered, in the preheated oven for about 2 hours. After about 40 minutes, stir the pudding, gently folding the surface skin into the rice.

4 Stir the rice pudding again after a further 40 minutes. At this stage, sprinkle the surface of the pudding with the freshly grated nutmeg. Allow the pudding to finish cooking in the oven without any further stirring. Spoon into a warmed bowl and serve immediately.

> **Cook's Tips**
> • *Always use a non-stick pan when heating milk, if you have one. Otherwise the milk is likely to stick to the bottom of the pan and will easily burn.*
> • *Serve the rice pudding with a spoonful of thick cherry or raspberry jam, if you like.*

Rice Pudding with Lemon and Cinnamon

There are many versions of rice pudding to choose from, but the presence here of pistachios, lemon, cinnamon and rose petals, makes this version a distinctly unusual one.

45ml/3 tbsp sugar
900ml/1¹/₂ pints/3³/₄ cups full-fat
  (whole) milk
25g/1oz/2 tbsp unsalted butter
1 cinnamon stick
strip of lemon rind
halved pistachios and rose petals,
  to decorate (optional)

Serves 4–6
75g/3oz/scant ¹/₂ cup short grain
  pudding rice

1 Put the rice, sugar, full-fat milk, unsalted butter, cinnamon stick and lemon rind into a large heavy pan. Gently stir until all the ingredients are well combined.

2 Cover the pan with a tight-fitting lid and cook the rice over very low heat, stirring occasionally, for about 1¹/₂ hours. Add a little extra milk or water if the mixture looks like it is becoming a little dry.

3 When the rice has absorbed the liquid and become thick and creamy, remove and discard the cinnamon stick and the lemon rind.

4 Spoon the rice pudding into warmed, individual serving bowls. Sprinkle each serving with halved pistachios and rose petals, to decorate, if you like.

> **Variations**
> • *For an extra creamy version of this rice pudding, fold in 150ml/¹/₄ pint/²/₃ cup lightly whipped double (heavy) cream, just before serving.*
> • *Instead of rose petals, try decorating with some other edible flowers or leaves.*

Rice Pudding Energy 433kcal/1829kJ; Protein 5.8g; Carbohydrate 85.6g, of which sugars 65.7g; Fat 6.9g, of which saturates 3.3g; Cholesterol 112mg; Calcium 113mg; Fibre 0.5g; Sodium 68mg.
Pudding with Lemon Energy 205kcal/852kJ; Protein 5.9g; Carbohydrate 24.6g, of which sugars 14.6g; Fat 9.3g, of which saturates 5.9g; Cholesterol 30mg; Calcium 184mg; Fibre 0g; Sodium 90mg.

Caramel Rice Pudding with Fresh Fruits

This slowly baked rice pudding is finished with a crunchy caramelized topping. It is a family favourite served with plenty of fresh fruit.

Serves 4

15g/½oz/1 tbsp butter
50g/2oz/generous ¼ cup short grain pudding rice
75ml/5 tbsp demerara (raw) sugar
400g/14oz can evaporated milk made up to about 600ml/1 pint/2½ cups with water
2 fresh baby pineapples
2 figs
1 crisp eating apple
10ml/2 tsp lemon juice
salt

1 Preheat the oven to 150°C/300°F/Gas 2. Grease a soufflé dish lightly with a little of the butter.

2 Put the rice in a sieve (strainer) and wash it thoroughly under cold running water. Drain well and place it into the prepared soufflé dish.

3 Add 30ml/2 tbsp of the demerara sugar to the soufflé dish, with a pinch of salt. Pour on the diluted evaporated milk and stir gently to combine.

4 Dot the surface of the rice with the remaining butter. Bake in the preheated oven for about 2 hours, then leave to cool for 30 minutes.

5 Meanwhile, quarter the baby pineapples and the figs. Cut the apple into segments and toss the pieces in a bowl with the lemon juice. Preheat the grill (broiler).

6 Sprinkle the remaining sugar evenly over the rice. Cook under the grill for 5 minutes or until the sugar has caramelized.

7 Leave the rice to stand for 5 minutes to allow the caramel to harden, then serve with the fresh fruit.

Coconut Rice Pudding

A delicious adaptation of the classic creamy rice pudding. This dessert is baked in a clay pot and flavoured with coconut milk, finished off with a crispy coconut crust.

Serves 4

75g/3oz/scant ½ cup short grain pudding rice
40g/1½oz/3 tbsp caster (superfine) sugar
2.5ml/½ tsp vanilla extract
300ml/½ pint/1¼ cups milk
400ml/14fl oz/1⅔ cups coconut milk
105ml/7 tbsp single (light) cream
30ml/2 tbsp desiccated (dry unsweetened shredded) coconut or slivers of fresh coconut, to decorate

1 Soak a small clay pot in cold water for 15 minutes, then drain well. Add the rice, sugar, vanilla extract, milk, coconut milk and cream to the pot and mix thoroughly until all the ingredients are well combined.

2 Cover the clay pot with the lid and place in a cold oven. Set the oven temperature to 180°C/350°F/Gas 4 and cook the rice for about 1 hour.

3 Remove the lid from the clay pot, stir the pudding gently, then re-cover and cook for a further 30–45 minutes, or until the rice is tender.

4 Remove the lid, stir the pudding again, then sprinkle with desiccated coconut or slivers of fresh coconut.

5 Return the pot to the oven and bake, uncovered, for about 10–15 minutes, until the topping is just brown and crisp.

> **Variation**
> If you prefer, this rice pudding can be made with extra milk instead of the single cream to reduce the fat content of the dessert. However, use full-cream (whole) milk, for a richer, creamier flavour.

Caramel Pudding Energy 313kcal/1321kJ; Protein 9.6g; Carbohydrate 54.3g, of which sugars 44.3g; Fat 7.6g, of which saturates 4.5g; Cholesterol 25mg; Calcium 312mg; Fibre 1.9g; Sodium 147mg.
Coconut Pudding Energy 259kcal/1087kJ; Protein 5.8g; Carbohydrate 34g, of which sugars 19.9g; Fat 11.6g, of which saturates 8.2g; Cholesterol 19mg; Calcium 153mg; Fibre 1g; Sodium 153mg.

Baked Coconut Rice Pudding with Pineapple and Ginger

This rice pudding needs long, slow cooking in a low oven but it is well worth the wait.

Serves 4–6

90g/3$\frac{1}{2}$oz/$\frac{1}{2}$ cup short grain pudding rice

600ml/1 pint/2$\frac{1}{2}$ cups coconut milk

300ml/$\frac{1}{2}$ pint/1$\frac{1}{4}$ cups full-fat (whole) milk

75g/2$\frac{3}{4}$oz/scant $\frac{1}{2}$ cup caster (superfine) sugar

25g/1oz/2 tbsp butter, plus extra for greasing

45ml/3 tbsp grated fresh or desiccated (dry unsweetened shredded) coconut, toasted

1 small, ripe pineapple

30ml/2 tbsp sesame oil

5cm/2in piece fresh root ginger, peeled and grated

shavings of toasted coconut, to decorate

1 Preheat the oven to 150°C/300°F/Gas 2. Grease an ovenproof dish. In a bowl, mix the rice with the coconut milk, milk and 50g/2oz/$\frac{1}{4}$ cup of the sugar and pour it into the ovenproof dish. Dot pieces of butter over the top and place the dish in the oven.

2 After 30 minutes, take the dish out and gently stir in the toasted coconut. Return it to the oven for a further 1$\frac{1}{2}$ hours, or until almost all the milk is absorbed and a golden skin has formed on top of the pudding.

3 Meanwhile, using a sharp knife, peel the pineapple and remove the core, then cut the flesh into bitesize cubes.

4 Towards the end of the cooking time, heat the oil in a large wok or heavy pan. Stir in the ginger, stir-fry until the aroma is released, then add the pineapple cubes, turning them over to sear on both sides. Sprinkle with the remaining sugar and continue to cook until the pineapple is slightly caramelized.

5 Serve the pudding spooned into bowls and topped with the hot, caramelized pineapple and toasted coconut.

Chocolate Chip and Banana Pudding

Rich, dense and sticky, this pudding is steamed in the slow cooker, which helps the sponge to keep moist.

Serves 4

200g/7oz/1$\frac{3}{4}$ cups self-raising (self-rising) flour

75g/3oz/6 tbsp unsalted butter

2 ripe bananas, mashed

75g/3oz/6 tbsp caster (superfine) sugar

50ml/2fl oz/1$\frac{1}{4}$ cups milk

1 egg, lightly beaten

75g/3oz/$\frac{2}{3}$ cup chocolate chips or chopped unsweetened chocolate

For the chocolate sauce

90g/3$\frac{1}{2}$oz/$\frac{1}{2}$ cup caster (superfine) sugar

50ml/2fl oz/$\frac{1}{4}$ cup water

175g/6oz/1$\frac{1}{4}$ cups plain (semisweet) chocolate chips or chopped unsweetened chocolate

25g/1oz/2 tbsp unsalted butter

30ml/2 tbsp brandy or orange juice

1 Grease and line the base of a 1 litre/1$\frac{3}{4}$ pint/4 cup heatproof bowl with baking parchment. Put an inverted saucer in the base of the ceramic cooking pot and pour in 2.5cm/1in of hot water.

2 Turn the slow cooker to high. Sift the flour into a large bowl and rub in the butter until it resembles coarse breadcrumbs. Stir in the mashed bananas and the sugar and mix well.

3 In a clean bowl, whisk together the milk and egg, then beat into the banana mixture. Stir in the chocolate chips or chopped chocolate and spoon into the lined bowl. Cover with a double thickness of buttered foil and place in the cooking pot. Pour in boiling water to come just over halfway up the side of the bowl.

4 Cover and cook on high for 3–4 hours, or until well risen and a skewer comes out clean. Turn off the slow cooker and leave the pudding in the water while you make the sauce.

5 Heat the sugar and water in a pan, stirring, until the sugar has dissolved. Take off the heat and stir in the chocolate. Add the butter in the same way. Stir in the brandy or orange juice.

6 Run a knife around the inside of the bowl to loosen the pudding. Turn it out and serve hot, with the sauce poured over.

Baked Coconut Pudding Energy 414kcal/1735kJ; Protein 6g; Carbohydrate 56g, of which sugars 39g; Fat 19g, of which saturates 9g; Cholesterol 24mg; Calcium 156mg; Fibre 1.6g; Sodium 200mg.
Chocolate Pudding Energy 926kcal/3890kJ; Protein 11.1g; Carbohydrate 131.9g, of which sugars 93.2g; Fat 41.1g, of which saturates 24.6g; Cholesterol 118mg; Calcium 266mg; Fibre 3.3g; Sodium 378mg.

Sticky Coffee and Pear Pudding

This dark and moist fruity pudding is simple to make in the slow cooker.

Serves 6
115g/4oz/¹/₂ cup butter, softened, plus extra for greasing
30ml/2 tbsp ground coffee
15ml/1 tbsp near-boiling water
4 ripe pears, peeled, cored, halved and thinly sliced across each half part of the way through
juice of ¹/₂ orange
115g/4oz/generous ¹/₂ cup golden caster (superfine) sugar, plus 15ml/1 tbsp for baking

2 eggs, beaten
50g/2oz/¹/₂ cup self-raising (self-rising) flour, sifted
50g/2oz/¹/₂ cup toasted skinned hazelnuts, finely ground
45ml/3 tbsp maple syrup
fine strips of orange rind, to decorate

For the orange cream
300ml/¹/₂ pint/1¹/₄ cups whipping cream
15ml/1 tbsp icing (confectioners') sugar, sifted
finely grated rind of ¹/₂ orange

1 Pour 2.5cm/1in of hot water into the ceramic cooking pot. Place an upturned saucer in the base, then turn on to high. Grease and line the base of a deep 18cm/7in cake tin (pan). Put the coffee in a bowl and pour the water over. Stir until dissolved. Brush the pears with the orange juice.

2 Beat the butter and the 115g/4oz sugar together in a bowl until light and fluffy, then beat in the eggs. Fold in the flour, then add the hazelnuts and coffee. Spoon into the tin, and level the surface. Pat the pears dry on kitchen paper and arrange in a circle in the sponge mixture. Brush them with some maple syrup, then sprinkle with the 15ml/1 tbsp caster sugar.

3 Cover the top of the tin with foil and place in the ceramic cooking pot. Pour in boiling water to come just over halfway up the sides of the tin. Cover and cook for 3–3¹/₂ hours, until firm.

4 Make the orange cream. Whip the cream, sugar and orange rind until soft peaks form. Spoon into a bowl and chill until needed. Leave the sponge to cool in the tin for 10 minutes, then turn over on to a serving plate. Brush with the remaining maple syrup and decorate with orange rind. Serve with the orange cream.

Steamed Chocolate Puddings

Drenched in a thick chocolate syrup and packed with fruit, this slow-cooker pudding is pure indulgence.

Serves 4
1 apple, peeled and cored, diced
25g/1oz/¹/₄ cup cranberries, thawed if frozen
175g/6oz/³/₄ cup soft dark brown sugar
115g/4oz/¹/₂ cup soft margarine
2 eggs, lightly beaten

50g/2oz/¹/₂ cup self-raising (self-rising) flour, sifted
45ml/3 tbsp unsweetened cocoa powder

For the syrup
115g/4oz plain (semisweet) chocolate, chopped
30ml/2 tbsp clear honey
15g/¹/₂oz/1 tbsp unsalted butter
2.5ml/¹/₂ tsp vanilla extract

1 Pour 2.5cm/1in of hot water into the cooking pot and switch the slow cooker to high. Grease four individual heatproof bowls with oil, then line with baking parchment.

2 Place the diced apple in a bowl, then add the cranberries and 15ml/1 tbsp of the sugar. Mix well, then divide among the four bowls, gently patting it down into the base of each one.

3 Place the remaining sugar in a clean mixing bowl and add the margarine, eggs, flour and cocoa. Beat together until smooth. Spoon into the bowls and cover each with a double thickness of greased foil. Place the bowls in the cooking pot and pour in hot water to come two-thirds of the way up the sides of the bowls.

4 Cover with the lid and cook on high for 1¹/₂–2 hours, or until the puddings are well-risen and firm. Carefully remove from the slow cooker and leave to stand for 10 minutes.

5 Meanwhile, make the chocolate syrup. Put the chocolate, honey, butter and vanilla extract in a heatproof bowl and place in the hot water in the slow cooker. Leave for 10 minutes, until the butter has melted, then stir until smooth.

6 Run a knife around the edge of the puddings to loosen, then turn over on to plates. Serve immediately, with the syrup.

Coffee Pudding Energy 852kcal/3571kJ; Protein 12.5g; Carbohydrate 107g, of which sugars 45g; Fat 44.5g, of which saturates 23.8g; Cholesterol 169mg; Calcium 362mg; Fibre 5.3g; Sodium 493mg.
Steamed Puddings Energy 739kcal/3094kJ; Protein 9.1g; Carbohydrate 88.3g, of which sugars 77.2g; Fat 41.3g, of which saturates 14.4g; Cholesterol 124mg; Calcium 103mg; Fibre 3.1g; Sodium 438mg.

Date Puddings with Toffee Sauce

Fresh dates make this slow-cooker dessert an utterly irresistible treat.

Serves 6
50g/2oz/¼ cup butter, softened, plus extra for greasing
175g/6oz/generous 1 cup fresh dates, peeled, stoned (pitted) and chopped
75ml/5 tbsp boiling water
75g/3oz/½ cup light muscovado (brown) sugar
2 eggs, beaten

115g/4oz/1 cup self-raising (self-rising) flour
2.5ml/½ tsp bicarbonate of soda (baking soda)

For the sauce
50g/2oz/¼ cup butter, at room temperature
75g/3oz/½ cup light muscovado (brown) sugar
60ml/4 tbsp double (heavy) cream
30ml/2 tbsp brandy

1 Grease six individual pudding moulds or tins (pans) that will fit in the slow cooker. Pour very hot water into the ceramic cooking pot to a depth of 2cm/¾in. Switch the cooker to high.

2 Put the dates in a heatproof bowl with the boiling water and mash well with a potato masher to make a fairly smooth paste.

3 Put the butter and sugar in a mixing bowl and beat until pale and fluffy. Gradually beat in the eggs. Fold in the flour and bicarbonate of soda. Add the date paste and gently fold in.

4 Spoon the mixture into the greased moulds or tins. Cover each with a piece of foil. Place in the ceramic cooking pot and pour enough boiling water around the puddings to come just over halfway up the sides. Cover with the lid and cook on high for 1½–2 hours, or until well risen and firm. Remove the puddings from the slow cooker.

5 Meanwhile, make the sauce. Put the butter, sugar, cream and brandy in a pan and heat very gently, stirring occasionally, until the mixture is smooth. Increase the heat and boil for 1 minute.

6 Turn the warm puddings out on to individual dessert plates. Spoon the sauce over each one and serve immediately.

Blueberry Muffin Pudding

You can't cook traditional muffins in a slow cooker but this delicious alternative will satisfy your cravings.

Serves 4
75g/3oz/6 tbsp butter, plus extra for greasing
75g/3oz/6 tbsp soft light brown sugar
105ml/7 tbsp buttermilk, at room temperature

2 eggs, lightly beaten, at room temperature
225g/8oz/2 cups self-raising (self-rising) flour
pinch of salt
5ml/1 tsp ground cinnamon
150g/5oz/1¼ cup fresh blueberries
10ml/2 tsp demerara (raw) sugar, for sprinkling
custard or crème fraîche, to serve

1 Place an upturned saucer or metal pastry ring in the base of the slow cooker. Pour in about 5cm/2in of very hot water, then switch the slow cooker to high. Lightly grease a 1.5 litre/2½ pint/6¼ cup heatproof dish with butter – first making sure that it will fit the inside of your slow cooker.

2 Put the butter and sugar in a heatproof jug (pitcher) and place in the ceramic cooking pot. Leave uncovered for 20 minutes, stirring, until melted.

3 Remove the jug from the slow cooker and leave to cool until tepid, then stir in the buttermilk and mix in the beaten egg.

4 Sift the flour, salt and cinnamon into a mixing bowl. Stir in the blueberries, then make a hollow in the middle. Pour in the buttermilk mixture and stir until just combined. Do not overmix.

5 Spoon the mixture into the prepared dish, then sprinkle the top with the demerara sugar. Cover with a piece of buttered foil and place in the ceramic cooking pot. Pour in more boiling water around the dish, if necessary, to come halfway up the sides.

6 Cover the slow cooker with the lid and cook for 3–4 hours, until a skewer inserted in the middle comes out clean. Remove from the slow cooker and let the pudding cool slightly before serving with custard or crème fraîche.

Date Puddings Energy 462kcal/1932kJ; Protein 5.1g; Carbohydrate 50.3g, of which sugars 35.9g; Fat 26.9g, of which saturates 16g; Cholesterol 138mg; Calcium 109mg; Fibre 1.1g; Sodium 244mg.
Blueberry Pudding Energy 499kcal/2101kJ; Protein 10.1g; Carbohydrate 76.2g, of which sugars 34.4g; Fat 19.2g, of which saturates 10.7g; Cholesterol 153mg; Calcium 262mg; Fibre 2.2g; Sodium 367mg.

Bread Pudding

This baked dessert is spicy, rich and filling – and is an ideal winter food. Serve the pudding warm with custard or cream or, if you prefer, it is just as nice left until cold.

Makes 9 squares

225g/8oz/4 cups stale bread, weighed after removing crusts
300ml/½ pint/1¼ cups milk
50g/1¾oz/4 tbsp dark muscovado (molasses) sugar
85g/3oz/½ cup shredded vegetable suet or grated chilled butter
225g/8oz/1⅓ cups mixed dried fruit, including currants, sultanas (golden raisins), finely chopped citrus peel
15ml/1 tbsp mixed (apple pie) spice
2.5ml/½ tsp freshly grated nutmeg
finely grated rind of 1 small orange and 1 small lemon, plus a little orange or lemon juice
1 egg, lightly beaten
caster (superfine) sugar, for sprinkling

1 Break the bread into small pieces. Place in a large mixing bowl, pour the milk over and leave for about 30 minutes.

2 Preheat the oven to 180°C/350°F/Gas 4. Butter an 18cm/7in square and 5cm/2in deep ovenproof dish.

3 Break up the bread before stirring in the sugar, suet or butter, dried fruit, spices and citrus rinds. Beat in the egg, adding some orange or lemon juice to make a soft mixture.

4 Spread the mixture into the dish and level the surface. Bake for 1¼ hours, or until the top is brown and firm to the touch.

5 Sprinkle caster sugar over the surface and cool before cutting into squares.

> **Cook's Tip**
> Although the shredded suet is traditional in this recipe, you may prefer to use grated chilled butter.

Fresh Currant Bread and Butter Pudding

Fresh mixed red- and blackcurrants add a tart touch to this scrumptious baked pudding in which layers of custard-soaked bread are cooked to a crisp golden crust.

Serves 6

8 slices day-old white bread, crusts removed
50g/2oz/¼ cup butter, softened
115g/4oz/1 cup redcurrants
115g/4oz/1 cup blackcurrants
4 eggs, beaten
75g/3oz/6 tbsp caster (superfine) sugar
475ml/16fl oz/2 cups creamy milk
5ml/1 tsp vanilla extract
freshly grated nutmeg
30ml/2 tbsp demerara (raw) sugar
single (light) cream, to serve

1 Preheat the oven to 160°C/325°F/Gas 3. Generously butter a 1.2 litre/2 pint/5 cup ovenproof earthenware dish.

2 Spread the slices of bread generously with the butter, then cut them in half diagonally. Layer the slices in the dish, buttered side up, sprinkling the currants between the layers.

3 Beat the eggs and caster sugar lightly together in a large mixing bowl, then gradually whisk in the creamy milk and vanilla extract, along with a large pinch of freshly grated nutmeg.

4 Pour the milk mixture over the bread, pushing the slices down into the liquid. Sprinkle the demerara sugar and a little more nutmeg over the top. Place the dish in a roasting pan and fill with hot water to come halfway up the sides of the dish.

5 Bake for 40 minutes, then increase the oven temperature to 180°C/350°F/Gas 4 and bake for about 20 minutes more, or until the top is golden. Serve warm, with single cream.

> **Variation**
> A mixture of blueberries and raspberries would work just as well as the currants in this recipe.

Bread Pudding Energy 254kcal/1072kJ; Protein 4.3g; Carbohydrate 39.7g, of which sugars 27g; Fat 10.2g, of which saturates 5.3g; Cholesterol 31mg; Calcium 103mg; Fibre 1.4g; Sodium 147mg.
Currant Pudding Energy 328kcal/1377kJ; Protein 10.3g; Carbohydrate 42.2g, of which sugars 25.4g; Fat 14.3g, of which saturates 7.4g; Cholesterol 156mg; Calcium 186mg; Fibre 1.9g; Sodium 321mg.

Fruity Bread and Butter Pudding

Fresh currants add a tart touch to this scrumptious slow-cooker pudding.

Serves 4

40g/1½oz/3 tbsp butter, softened, plus extra for greasing
6 slices of day-old bread, crusts removed
115g/4oz/1 cup prepared redcurrants and raspberries
3 eggs, beaten
50g/2oz/¼ cup golden caster (superfine) sugar
300ml/½ pint/1¼ cups creamy milk
5ml/1 tsp vanilla extract
freshly grated nutmeg
30ml/2 tbsp demerara (raw) sugar
single (light) cream, to serve

1 Butter a 1 litre/1¾ pints/4 cup round or oval baking dish – first checking that it fits in the slow cooker. Pour 2.5cm/1in of very hot water into the ceramic cooking pot. Place an upturned saucer in the base and switch the cooker to high.

2 Spread the slices of bread with the butter, then cut them in half diagonally. Arrange the triangles in the dish in neat layers, overlapping the slices, with the buttered side facing up. Sprinkle the currants and berries over the bread and between the slices.

3 Place the eggs and caster sugar in a large mixing bowl and briefly beat together. Gradually whisk in the milk, vanilla extract and a large pinch of freshly grated nutmeg until well mixed.

4 Place the baking dish in the ceramic cooking pot, then slowly pour the egg and milk mixture over the bread, pushing the bread slices down to submerge them. Sprinkle the sugar and a little nutmeg over the top, then cover the dish with foil.

5 Pour near-boiling water around the dish, so that the water level comes just over halfway up the sides of the dish. Cover with the lid and cook on high for 3–4 hours, or until a skewer inserted into the centre comes out clean.

6 Carefully remove the dish from the slow cooker and, if you like, briefly brown the top of the pudding under a hot grill (broiler). Cool slightly, then serve with the single cream.

Maple and Pecan Croissant Pudding

Croissants give this tasty, oven-baked dessert a light and fluffy texture.

Serves 4

75g/3oz/generous ½ cup sultanas (golden raisins)
45ml/3 tbsp brandy
50g/2oz/¼ cup butter, plus extra for greasing
4 large croissants
40g/1½oz/⅓ cup pecan nuts, roughly chopped
3 eggs, lightly beaten
300ml/½ pint/1¼ cups milk
150ml/¼ pint/⅔ cup single (light) cream
120ml/4fl oz/½ cup maple syrup
25g/1oz/2 tbsp demerara (raw) sugar
maple syrup and pouring (half-and-half) cream, to serve (optional)

1 Place the sultanas and brandy in a small pan and heat gently, until warm. Leave to stand for 1 hour. Soak a small clay pot in cold water for 15 minutes, then drain. Leave for 2–3 minutes, then lightly grease the base and sides.

2 Cut the croissants into thick slices, and spread with butter on one side. Arrange the slices, butter side up and slightly overlapping, in the soaked clay pot. Sprinkle the brandy-soaked sultanas and the roughly chopped pecan nuts over the buttered croissant slices.

3 In a large bowl, beat the eggs and milk together, then gradually beat in the single cream and maple syrup.

4 Pour the egg custard through a sieve (strainer) over the croissants, fruit and nuts in the dish. Leave the uncooked pudding to stand for 30 minutes, so that some of the egg custard liquid is absorbed by the croissants.

5 Sprinkle the sugar evenly over the top, then cover the dish and place in a cold oven. Set the oven to 180°C/350°F/Gas 4 and bake for 40 minutes. Remove the lid and continue to cook for 20 minutes, or until the custard is set and the top is golden.

6 Leave the pudding to cool for about 15 minutes before serving warm, with extra maple syrup and a little pouring cream, if you like.

Fruity Pudding Energy 405Kcal/1700kJ; Protein 12.6g; Carbohydrate 53.7g, of which sugars 30.7g; Fat 16.9g, of which saturates 8.6g; Cholesterol 202mg; Calcium 234mg; Fibre 2.1g; Sodium 405mg.
Croissant Pudding Energy 731kcal/3056kJ; Protein 15g; Carbohydrate 72.3g, of which sugars 49.4g; Fat 45.6g, of which saturates 19.5g; Cholesterol 226mg; Calcium 217mg; Fibre 1.8g; Sodium 507mg.

Bread and Butter Pudding with Whiskey Sauce

This slowly baked dessert is the ultimate comfort food. The whiskey sauce is heavenly, but the pudding can also be served with chilled cream or vanilla ice cream – the contrast between the hot and cold is utterly mouthwatering.

Serves 6

8 slices of white bread, buttered
115–150g/4–5oz/²⁄₃–³⁄₄ cup sultanas (golden raisins), or mixed dried fruit
2.5ml/¹⁄₂ tsp grated nutmeg

150g/5oz/³⁄₄ cup caster (superfine) sugar
2 large (US extra large) eggs
300ml/¹⁄₂ pint/1¹⁄₄ cups single (light) cream
450ml/³⁄₄ pint/scant 2 cups milk
5ml/1 tsp of vanilla extract
light muscovado (brown) sugar, for sprinkling (optional)

For the whiskey sauce

150g/5oz/10 tbsp butter
115g/4oz/generous ¹⁄₂ cup caster (superfine) sugar
1 egg
45ml/3 tbsp Irish whiskey

1 Preheat the oven to 180°C/350°F/Gas 4. Remove the crusts from the bread and put four slices, buttered side down, in the base of an ovenproof dish. Sprinkle with the fruit, some of the nutmeg and 15ml/1 tbsp sugar.

2 Place the remaining four slices of bread on top, buttered side down, and sprinkle again with nutmeg and 15ml/1 tbsp sugar.

3 Beat the eggs lightly, add the cream, milk, vanilla extract and the remaining sugar, and mix well to make a custard. Pour this mixture over the bread, and sprinkle light muscovado sugar over the top, if you like to have a crispy crust. Bake in the preheated oven for 1 hour, or until all the liquid has been absorbed and the pudding is risen and browned.

4 Meanwhile, make the whiskey sauce. Melt the butter in a heavy pan, add the caster sugar and dissolve over low heat. Remove from the heat and add the egg, whisking vigorously, and then add the whiskey. Serve the pudding on warmed plates, with the whiskey sauce poured over the top.

Apricot Panettone Pudding

Panettone and pecan nuts make a rich addition to this 'no-butter' version of a traditional, oven-baked bread and butter pudding.

Serves 6

sunflower oil, for greasing
350g/12oz panettone, sliced into triangles
25g/1oz/¹⁄₄ cup pecan nuts

75g/3oz/¹⁄₃ cup ready-to-eat dried apricots, chopped
500ml/17fl oz/generous 2 cups full-cream (whole) milk
5ml/1 tsp vanilla extract
1 large (US extra large) egg, beaten
30ml/2 tbsp maple syrup
freshly grated nutmeg
demerara (raw) sugar, for sprinkling

1 Lightly grease a 1 litre/1³⁄₄ pint/4 cup ovenproof earthenware dish. Arrange half of the panettone triangles in the dish, sprinkle over half the pecan nuts and all of the chopped, dried apricots, then add another layer of panettone on top.

2 Heat the milk and vanilla extract in a small pan until the milk just simmers. Put the egg and maple syrup in a large bowl, grate in about 2.5ml/¹⁄₂ tsp nutmeg, then whisk in the hot milk.

3 Preheat the oven to 200°C/400°F/Gas 6. Pour the egg mixture over the panettone, lightly pressing down the bread. Leave the pudding to stand for about 10 minutes, to allow the panettone slices to soak up a little of the liquid.

4 Sprinkle over the reserved pecan nuts and sprinkle a little demerara sugar and freshly grated nutmeg over the top. Bake for 40–45 minutes, until the pudding is risen and golden brown. Serve immediately.

> **Cook's Tip**
> *Panettone is a light fruit cake, originally from northern Italy but now popular all over the world. It is traditionally eaten at festivals such as Christmas or Easter. Panettone is baked in cylindrical moulds, giving it a distinctive shape. You can now find panettone in different flavours.*

Bread Pudding Energy 757kcal/3168kJ; Protein 11.7g; Carbohydrate 82g, of which sugars 65.2g; Fat 40.8g, of which saturates 24.3g; Cholesterol 207mg; Calcium 232mg; Fibre 0.9g; Sodium 472mg.
Apricot Pudding Energy 294kcal/1237kJ; Protein 9.4g; Carbohydrate 43.2g, of which sugars 21.8g; Fat 10.4g, of which saturates 3.7g; Cholesterol 44mg; Calcium 180mg; Fibre 2.3g; Sodium 248mg.

Cherry Batter Pudding

This batter pudding – or 'clafoutis' – originated in the Limousin area of central France, where batters play an important role in the hearty cuisine. Similar fruit and custard desserts are found in Alsace.

Serves 4

450g/1lb ripe cherries
30ml/2 tbsp Kirsch or fruit brandy
    or 15ml/1 tbsp lemon juice
15ml/1 tbsp icing
    (confectioners') sugar
30g/1oz/3 tbsp plain
    (all-purpose) flour
45ml/3 tbsp sugar
175ml/6fl oz/¾ cup milk or
    single (light) cream
2 eggs
grated rind of ½ lemon
pinch of freshly grated nutmeg
1.5ml/¼ tsp vanilla extract

1 Remove the pits from the cherries, if you like, then mix them with the Kirsch, brandy or lemon juice and icing sugar and set aside for 1–2 hours.

2 Preheat the oven to 190°C/375°F/Gas 5. Generously butter a 28cm/11in oval gratin dish or other shallow ovenproof dish.

3 Sift the flour into a bowl, add the sugar and slowly whisk in the milk until smoothly blended.

4 Add the eggs, lemon rind, nutmeg and vanilla extract into the flour mixture and whisk until well combined and smooth.

5 Sprinkle the cherries evenly in the baking dish. Pour over the batter, ensuring it is distributed evenly around the cherries.

6 Bake in the oven for 45 minutes, or until set and puffed around the edges – a knife inserted in the centre should come out clean. Serve warm or at room temperature.

> **Cook's Tip**
> *Serve this dish with whipped double (heavy) cream, custard or vanilla ice cream, if you like.*

Black Cherry Batter Pudding

This version of the traditional French cherry batter pudding is made with slightly tart black cherries. It can be made with cream in place of milk, and is excellent served with ice cream.

Serves 6

450g/1lb/2 cups fresh black
    cherries, pitted
25g/1oz/¼ cup plain
    (all-purpose) flour
50g/2oz/½ cup icing
    (confectioner's) sugar, plus
    extra for dusting
4 eggs, beaten
250ml/8fl oz/1 cup full-cream
    (whole) milk
30ml/2 tbsp cherry liqueur, such
    as Kirsch or maraschino
vanilla ice cream, to serve

1 Preheat the oven to 180°C/350°F/Gas 4. Grease a 1.2 litre/2 pint/5 cup baking dish and add the cherries.

2 Sift the flour and icing sugar into a large mixing bowl, then gradually whisk in the beaten eggs until the mixture is smooth. Whisk in the milk until well blended, then stir in the cherry liqueur.

3 Pour the batter into the baking dish and then stir gently to ensure that the cherries are evenly distributed. Transfer to the oven and bake for about 40 minutes, or until just set and light golden brown. Insert a small knife into the centre of the pudding to test if it is cooked in the middle; the blade should come out clean.

4 Allow the pudding to cool for at least 15 minutes, then dust liberally with icing sugar just before serving, either warm or at room temperature. Vanilla ice cream is a good accompaniment.

> **Variation**
> *Try other fruit or nut liqueurs in this dessert. Almond-flavoured liqueur is delicious teamed with cherries, while hazelnut, raspberry or orange liqueurs will also work well. Other fruits that can be used in this pudding include blackberries, blueberries, plums, peaches, nectarines and apricots.*

Cherry Energy 357kcal/1493kJ; Protein 8.1g; Carbohydrate 39.4g, of which sugars 29.8g; Fat 19.7g, of which saturates 11.4g; Cholesterol 140mg; Calcium 147mg; Fibre 1.4g; Sodium 183mg.
Black Cherry Energy 167kcal/704kJ; Protein 6.7g; Carbohydrate 23.8g, of which sugars 20.6g; Fat 4.5g, of which saturates 1.5g; Cholesterol 129mg; Calcium 89mg; Fibre 0.8g; Sodium 66mg.

Lemon Surprise Pudding

This is a much-loved dessert that many people remember from childhood. The surprise is the unexpected sauce concealed beneath the delectable sponge in this slowly baked dish.

grated rind and juice of 2 lemons
115g/4oz/½ cup caster
 (superfine) sugar
50g/2oz/½ cup self-raising
 (self-rising) flour
2 eggs, separated
300ml/½ pint/1¼ cups milk

Serves 4
50g/2oz/¼ cup butter, plus extra
 for greasing

1 Preheat the oven to 190°C/375°F/Gas 5. Use a little butter to grease a 1.2 litre/2 pint/5 cup baking dish.

2 Beat the lemon rind, remaining butter and caster sugar in a large mixing bowl until pale and fluffy. Sift in the self-raising flour and fold into the creamed butter.

3 Add the egg yolks and beat into the mixture. Gradually whisk in the lemon juice and the milk (don't be alarmed – the mixture will curdle horribly).

4 Place the egg whites in a grease-free bowl and whisk until they form stiff peaks.

5 Fold the egg whites lightly into the lemon mixture using a metal spoon, then pour into the prepared baking dish.

6 Place the dish in a roasting pan and pour in hot water to come halfway up the side of the dish. Bake for 45 minutes, until golden. Serve immediately.

Cook's Tip
Lemons are often waxed before packing. If a recipe uses the rind of the lemons either buy unwaxed lemons or scrub the peel thoroughly to remove the wax.

Apple Pudding

This delectable, oven-baked dessert features tender apples topped with a light, airy sponge.

Serves 4
4 crisp eating apples
a little lemon juice

300ml/½ pint/1¼ cups milk
40g/1½oz/3 tbsp butter
40g/1½oz/⅓ cup plain
 (all-purpose) flour
25g/1oz/2 tbsp caster
 (superfine) sugar
2.5ml/½ tsp vanilla extract
2 eggs, separated

1 Preheat the oven to 200°C/400°F/ Gas 6. Butter an ovenproof dish measuring 20–23cm/8–9in diameter and 5cm/2in deep. Peel, core and slice the apples and place in an even layer in the base of the dish. Pour over the lemon juice.

2 Put the milk, butter and flour in a pan. Stirring continuously with a whisk, cook over medium heat until the sauce thickens and comes to the boil. Let it bubble gently for 1–2 minutes, stirring well to make sure it does not stick and burn on the bottom of the pan. Pour into a bowl, add the sugar and vanilla extract, and then stir in the egg yolks.

3 In a separate bowl, whisk the egg whites until stiff peaks form. With a large metal spoon, fold the egg whites into the custard. Pour the custard mixture evenly over the apple slices in the dish.

4 Put into the hot oven and cook for about 40 minutes, until puffed up, deep golden brown and firm to the touch.

5 Serve the pudding immediately once it comes out of the oven, before the soufflé-like topping begins to fall.

Variation
Stewed fruit, such as cooking apples, plums, rhubarb or gooseberries sweetened with honey or sugar, would also make a good base for this pudding, as would fresh summer berries (blackberries, raspberries, redcurrants and blackcurrants).

Lemon Pudding Energy 319kcal/1341kJ; Protein 7g; Carbohydrate 43.1g, of which sugars 33.8g; Fat 14.5g, of which saturates 8.1g; Cholesterol 126mg; Calcium 166mg; Fibre 0.4g; Sodium 190mg.
Apple Pudding Energy 240kcal/1006kJ; Protein 7g; Carbohydrate 26.8g, of which sugars 19.2g; Fat 12.5g, of which saturates 6.8g; Cholesterol 121mg; Calcium 127mg; Fibre 1.9g; Sodium 131mg.

Steamed Raisin Pudding

This light pudding is slowly steamed in a pan on top of the stove. Use the softest, juiciest raisins you can find.

Serves 6

15–25g/¹⁄₂–1oz/1–2 tbsp
  butter, softened
100g/3¹⁄₂oz/²⁄₃ cup raisins
175g/6oz/3 cups fresh
  white breadcrumbs
75g/3oz/¹⁄₂ cup shredded
  vegetable suet
75g/3oz/6 tbsp soft brown sugar
25g/1oz/¹⁄₄ cup cornflour
  (cornstarch)

finely grated rind of 1 lemon
2 eggs
60ml/4 tbsp orange marmalade
30ml/2 tbsp fresh lemon juice

For the sauce
1 lemon
25g/1oz/¹⁄₄ cup cornflour
  (cornstarch)
300ml/¹⁄₂ pint/1¹⁄₄ cups milk
50g/2oz/¹⁄₄ cup caster
  (superfine) sugar
25g/1oz/2 tbsp butter

1 Smear the butter on the inside of a 1.2 litre/2 pint heatproof bowl and press half the raisins on the buttered surface.

2 Mix together the breadcrumbs, suet, brown sugar, cornflour, lemon rind and the remaining raisins. Beat the eggs with the marmalade and lemon juice and stir into the dry ingredients.

3 Carefully spoon the mixture into the bowl, being careful not to disturb the raisins. Cover the bowl with pleated baking parchment and then a large sheet of foil, also pleated. Tuck the edges under and press tightly to the sides. Steam over a pan of boiling water for 1¾ hours.

4 Pare two or three large strips of lemon rind and put into a pan with 150ml/¹⁄₄ pint/²⁄₃ cup water. Bring to the boil and simmer for 10 minutes. Discard the rind. Blend the cornflour with the milk and stir into the pan. Squeeze the juice from half the lemon and add to the pan with the sugar and butter. Heat until the sauce thickens and comes to the boil.

5 Turn the pudding out on to a warmed serving plate, spooning a little sauce over the top. Serve immediately.

Christmas Pudding

This rich, slowly steamed pudding is a must for any Christmas feast. Serve with a traditional hot white sauce, flavoured with whiskey, brandy or rum, or simply offer a jug of cream liqueur, to be poured over the pudding as a sauce.

**Makes 2 puddings, each
serving 6–8**

275g/10oz/5 cups fresh
  breadcrumbs
225g/8oz/1 cup light muscovado
  (brown) sugar
225g/8oz/1 cup currants
275g/10oz/2 cups raisins
225g/8oz/1¹⁄₃ cups sultanas
  (golden raisins)

50g/2oz/¹⁄₃ cup chopped
  (candied) peel
115g/4oz/¹⁄₂ cup glacé
  (candied) cherries
225g/8oz shredded vegetable
  suet
2.5ml/¹⁄₂ tsp salt
10–20ml/2–4 tsp mixed (apple
  pie) spice
1 carrot, coarsely grated
1 apple, peeled, cored and
  finely chopped
grated rind and juice of
  1 small orange
2 large (US extra large) eggs,
  lightly whisked
450ml/³⁄₄ pint/scant 2 cups stout

1 Mix the breadcrumbs, sugar, dried fruit and peel in a bowl. Add the shredded suet, salt, mixed spice, carrot, apple and orange rind. Mix until well combined. Stir in the orange juice, eggs and stout. Leave the mixture overnight, giving it a stir occasionally, if convenient.

2 Well grease and line two 1.2 litre/2 pint/5 cup heatproof bowls with baking parchment. Stir the mixture and turn into the bowls. Cover with buttered circles of baking parchment, then tie pudding cloths over the top, or tightly cover them with several layers of baking parchment and foil, tied under the rim.

3 Steam for about 6–7 hours. Ensure the puddings do not go off the boil, and top up with more water as needed.

4 When cool, re-cover the puddings with paper or foil and store in a cool, dry place for at least a month. When required, steam for another 2–3 hours. Serve hot, with a traditional white sauce.

Raisin Pudding Energy 456kcal/1922kJ; Protein 7.7g; Carbohydrate 74.4g, of which sugars 43.4g; Fat 16.8g, of which saturates 8.6g; Cholesterol 82mg; Calcium 131mg; Fibre 1.1g; Sodium 304mg.
Christmas Energy 7171kcal/30,432kJ; Protein 38.8g; Carbohydrate 1596.3g, of which sugars 1479.8g; Fat 112.9g, of which saturates 58g; Cholesterol 321mg; Calcium 1071mg; Fibre 13.8g; Sodium 1965mg.

Rich Chocolate Cake

A rich, dense chocolate cake made in the slow cooker.

Serves 8
115g/4oz plain (semisweet)
    chocolate, cut into small pieces
45ml/3 tbsp milk
150g/5oz/10 tbsp butter,
    at room temperature
200g/7oz/scant 1 cup soft light
    brown sugar
3 eggs, lightly beaten
200g/7oz/1¾ cups self-raising
    (self-rising) flour

15ml/1 tbsp unsweetened
    cocoa powder
icing (confectioners') sugar and
    unsweetened cocoa powder,
    for dusting

For the chocolate buttercream
75g/3oz/6 tbsp butter,
    at room temperature
115g/4oz/1 cup icing
    (confectioners') sugar
15ml/1 tbsp (unsweetened)
    cocoa powder
2.5ml/½ tsp vanilla extract

1 Grease and line a deep 18cm/7in cake tin (pan) with baking parchment. Pour about 5cm/2in very hot water into the ceramic cooking pot, then turn the cooker to high. Put the chocolate and milk into a heatproof bowl and place in the pot. Leave for 10 minutes, then stir until smooth. Remove and set aside to cool.

2 Place the butter and sugar in a bowl and beat together until fluffy. Beat in the eggs, then stir in the chocolate mixture. Fold in the flour and cocoa. Spoon into the prepared tin and cover with a piece of foil. Put a saucer in the bottom of the cooking pot, then rest the tin on top. If necessary, pour in more boiling water to come just over halfway up the tin.

3 Cover and cook for 3–3½ hours, or until firm and a skewer comes out clean. Lift the tin out and leave on a wire rack for 10 minutes. Turn out and leave to cool. Remove the lining paper.

4 To make the buttercream, put the butter in a bowl and beat until soft. Sift over the icing sugar and cocoa powder, then stir together. Add the vanilla extract and beat until light and fluffy.

5 Cut the cake in half horizontally and spread a thick layer of the buttercream on one of the halves. Sandwich the cakes back together, then dust with a mix of sugar and cocoa, and serve.

Chocolate Potato Cake

This is a very rich, moist chocolate cake, topped with a thin layer of chocolate icing. Use a good-quality dark chocolate for best results and serve with whipped cream.

Makes a 23cm/9in cake
200g/7oz/1 cup sugar
250g/9oz/1 cup and 2 tbsp butter
4 eggs, separated

275g/10oz dark (bittersweet)
    chocolate
75g/3oz/¾ cup ground almonds
165g/5½oz mashed potato
225g/8oz/2 cups self-raising
    (self-rising) flour
5ml/1 tsp cinnamon
45ml/3 tbsp milk
white and dark (bittersweet)
    chocolate shavings, to garnish
whipped cream, to serve

1 Preheat the oven to 180°C/350°F/Gas 4. Grease and base-line a 23cm/9in round cake tin with a circle of baking parchment. In a large bowl, cream together the sugar and 225g/8oz/1 cup of the butter until light and fluffy. Then beat the egg yolks into the creamed mixture, one at a time, until it is smooth and creamy.

2 Finely chop 175g/6oz of the chocolate and stir it into the creamed mixture with the almonds. Pass the potato through a sieve (strainer) or ricer and stir it into the creamed chocolate mixture. Sift together the flour and cinnamon and fold into the mixture with the milk. Whisk the egg whites until they hold stiff but not dry peaks, and fold into the cake mixture.

3 Spoon into the tin, level the top and make a slight hollow in the middle to keep it level during cooking. Bake for 1¼ hours, until a skewer inserted in the centre comes out clean. Leave to cool slightly in the tin, then turn out and cool on a wire rack.

4 Meanwhile, break the remaining chocolate into a heatproof bowl over a pan of hot water. Add the remaining butter in small pieces and stir until the mixture is smooth and glossy.

5 Peel off the lining paper and trim the top of the cake so that it is level. Smooth over the chocolate icing and allow to set. Decorate with white and dark chocolate shavings and serve with lashings of whipped cream.

Chocolate Cake Energy 564kcal/2363kJ; Protein 6.6g; Carbohydrate 70g, of which sugars 51g; Fat 30.5g, of which saturates 18.2g; Cholesterol 146mg; Calcium 129mg; Fibre 1.5g; Sodium 321mg.
Potato Energy 5707kcal/23853kJ; Protein 82.6g; Carbohydrate 593.8g, of which sugars 393.4g; Fat 350.7g, of which saturates 187g; Cholesterol 1313mg; Calcium 915mg; Fibre 21.1g; Sodium 1878mg.

Frosted Carrot and Parsnip Cake

This slow-cooker cake, decorated with sugared rind, is very light and crumbly.

Serves 8
1 orange or lemon
10ml/2 tsp caster (superfine) sugar
175g/6oz/³/4 cup butter
    or margarine
175g/6oz/³/4 cup soft light
    brown sugar
3 eggs, lightly beaten
175g/6oz carrots and parsnips,
    coarsely grated

50g/2oz/¹/3 cup sultanas
    (golden raisins)
115g/4oz/1 cup self-raising
    (self-rising) flour
50g/2oz/¹/2 cup self-raising
    (self-rising) wholemeal
    (whole-wheat) flour
5ml/1 tsp baking powder

For the topping
50g/2oz/¹/4 cup caster
    (superfine) sugar
1 egg white
pinch of salt

1 Put an upturned saucer or metal pastry cutter in the base of the ceramic cooking pot and pour in about 2.5cm/1in hot water. Turn the slow cooker to high. Lightly grease a deep 18cm/7in round fixed-based cake tin (pan) or soufflé dish with oil and line the base with baking parchment.

2 Finely grate the orange or lemon rind. Selecting the longest shreds, put about half the rind in a bowl and mix with the caster sugar. Arrange the sugar-coated rind on a sheet of baking parchment and leave in a warm place to dry.

3 Put the butter or margarine and brown sugar in a large bowl and beat together until pale and fluffy. Add the eggs a little at a time, beating well after each addition. Stir in the unsugared orange or lemon rind, grated carrots, parsnips and sultanas.

4 Sift the flours and baking powder together, adding any bran left in the sieve (strainer), then gradually fold into the carrot and parsnip mixture. Transfer the mixture to the tin and level the surface. Cover loosely with greased foil, then place in the cooking pot, on top of the saucer or pastry cutter. Pour enough boiling water around the tin to come just over halfway up the sides.

5 Cover the cooker with the lid and cook for 3–5 hours, or until a skewer inserted in the centre of the cake comes out clean. Lift the tin out of the cooker and leave to stand for 5 minutes. Turn the cake out on to a wire rack and leave until cool.

6 To make the topping, place the caster sugar in a bowl over the near-simmering water in the slow cooker. Squeeze the juice from the orange or lemon and add 30ml/2 tbsp of the juice to the sugar. Stir over the heat until the sugar dissolves. Remove from the heat, add the egg white and salt, and whisk for 1 minute with an electric beater.

7 Return the bowl to the heat and whisk for about 6 minutes until the mixture becomes stiff and glossy, holding a good shape. Remove from the heat and allow to cool for about 5 minutes, whisking frequently.

8 Swirl the meringue topping over the cake and leave for about 1 hour to firm up. To serve, sprinkle the cake with the sugared orange or lemon rind.

Pumpkin and Banana Cake

This slow-cooker cake is like a cross between a carrot cake and banana bread.

Serves 12
225g/8oz/2 cups self-raising
    (self-rising) flour
7.5ml/1¹/2 tsp baking powder
2.5ml/¹/2 tsp ground cinnamon
2.5ml/¹/2 tsp ground ginger
pinch of salt
125g/5oz/10 tbsp soft light
    brown sugar
75g/3oz/³/4 cup pecans or
    walnuts, chopped

115g/4oz pumpkin flesh,
    coarsely grated
2 small bananas, mashed
2 eggs, lightly beaten
150ml/¹/4 pint/²/3 cup sunflower oil

For the topping
50g/2oz/¹/4 cup butter,
    at room temperature
150g/5oz/²/3 cup soft cheese
1.5ml/¹/4 tsp vanilla extract
115g/4oz/1 cup icing
    (confectioners') sugar
pecan halves, to decorate

1 Line the base and sides of a deep 20cm/8in round fixed-base cake tin (pan) with baking parchment. Place an upturned saucer in the base of the ceramic cooking pot, then pour in about 2.5cm/1in of very hot water. Switch the slow cooker to high.

2 Sift the flour, baking powder, cinnamon, ginger and salt into a large bowl. Stir in the sugar, chopped pecans or walnuts and grated pumpkin. Make a hollow in the middle. In another bowl, combine the bananas, eggs and oil. Stir into the dry ingredients.

3 Spoon the mixture into the tin. Cover with buttered foil and place in the pot. Pour in boiling water to come just over halfway up the sides of the tin. Cover and cook for 4–4¹/2 hours, or until the cake is firm and a skewer inserted into it comes out clean.

4 Remove the cake from the cooker and stand the tin on a wire rack to cool for 15 minutes. Turn out and leave to cool completely, then peel off the lining paper.

5 To make the topping, put the butter, soft cheese and vanilla extract in a bowl and beat until smooth. Sift in the sugar and beat until creamy. Spread the topping over the top of the cake and decorate with pecan halves. Chill for 1 hour before serving.

Frosted Cake Energy 410kcal/1718kJ; Protein 5.9g; Carbohydrate 53g, of which sugars 38.2g; Fat 20.8g, of which saturates 12.2g; Cholesterol 132mg; Calcium 98mg; Fibre 1.9g; Sodium 290mg.
Pumpkin Cake Energy 374kcal/1567kJ; Protein 5.1g; Carbohydrate 43.2g, of which sugars 28.7g; Fat 21.3g, of which saturates 6.5g; Cholesterol 58mg; Calcium 101.7mg; Fibre 1g; Sodium 203mg.

Light Fruit Cake

This incredibly easy all-in-one fruit cake is made in the slow cooker. It is deliciously light and crumbly, and the combination of wholemeal flour and long cooking ensures that it stays beautifully moist.

Serves 12
2 eggs
130g/4½oz/generous ½ cup butter, at room temperature
225g/8oz/1 cup light muscovado (brown) sugar
150g/5oz/1¼ cups self-raising (self-rising) flour
150g/5oz/1¼ cups wholemeal (whole-wheat) self-raising (self-rising) flour
pinch of salt
5ml/1 tsp mixed (apple pie) spice
450g/1lb/2½ cups luxury mixed dried fruit

1 Line the base and sides of a deep 18cm/7in round or 15cm/6in square fixed-base cake tin (pan) with baking parchment. Place an upturned saucer or metal pastry ring in the base of the ceramic cooking pot, then pour in about 2.5cm/1in of very hot water. Switch the slow cooker to high.

2 Crack the eggs into a large mixing bowl. Add the butter and sugar, then sift over the flours, salt and spice, adding any bran left in the sieve (strainer). Stir together until mixed, then add the dried fruit and beat for 2 minutes until the mixture is smooth and glossy.

3 Spoon the mixture into the prepared cake tin and level the surface. Cover the tin with a piece of buttered foil.

4 Put the tin in the slow cooker and pour in enough boiling water to come just over halfway up the sides of the tin. Cover with the lid and cook for 4–5 hours, or until a skewer inserted into the middle of the cake comes out clean.

5 Remove the cake from the slow cooker and place on a wire rack. Leave the cake to cool in the tin for about 15 minutes, then turn out and leave to cool completely before serving. To store, wrap the cake in baking parchment and then kitchen foil, and keep in a cool, dry place.

Marbled Spice Cake

This slow-cooker cake can be made in a ring-shaped cake mould, called a kugelhupf, or in a plain ring-shaped cake tin. It looks spectacular with smooth, drizzled icing.

Serves 8
75g/3oz/6 tbsp butter, softened, plus extra for greasing
115g/4oz/½ cup soft light brown sugar
2 eggs
few drops of vanilla extract
130g/4½oz/generous 1 cup plain (all-purpose) flour, plus extra for dusting
7.5ml/1½ tsp baking powder
45ml/3 tbsp milk
30ml/2 tbsp malt extract or black treacle (molasses)
5ml/1 tsp mixed (apple pie) spice
2.5ml/½ tsp ground ginger
75g/3oz/¾ cup icing (confectioners') sugar, sifted, to decorate

1 Grease and flour a 1.2 litre/2 pint/5 cup kugelhupf mould or ring-shaped cake tin (pan). Put an upturned saucer in the base of the cooking pot and pour in 5cm/2in hot water. Switch to high.

2 Put the butter and sugar in a bowl and beat until fluffy. In a separate bowl, beat the eggs and vanilla extract, then gradually beat into the butter. Sift together the flour and baking powder, then fold into the butter, adding a little milk between each addition. Spoon one-third of the mixture into a bowl and stir in the malt extract or treacle, mixed spice and ginger.

3 Drop a large spoonful of the light mixture into the cake tin, followed by a spoonful of the dark mixture. Continue in this way until all the mixture has been used. Run a knife or skewer through the mixtures to give a marbled effect.

4 Cover the tin with foil and place in the ceramic cooking pot. Pour boiling water around the tin to come just over halfway up the sides. Cover and cook for 3–4 hours, until a skewer inserted into the cake comes out clean. Lift the cake on to a wire rack and leave in the tin for 10 minutes before turning out to cool.

5 To decorate, place the icing sugar in a bowl and add warm water to make a smooth icing. Drizzle the mixture over the cake, then leave to set before serving in thick slices.

Light Fruit Cake Energy 351kcal/1482kJ; Protein 4.9g; Carbohydrate 63g, of which sugars 46g; Fat 10.6g, of which saturates 6g; Cholesterol 60.8mg; Calcium 78.6mg; Fibre 2.3g; Sodium 148mg.
Marbled Spice Cake Energy 215kcal/902kJ; Protein 2.8g; Carbohydrate 33g, of which sugars 20.3g; Fat 8.8g, of which saturates 5.2g; Cholesterol 49mg; Calcium 84mg; Fibre 0.5g; Sodium 172mg.

Apple Cake

This deliciously fruity cake is perhaps best in autumn, when home-grown apples are in season. It is slowly baked in the oven, which helps to keep the inside lovely and moist, and gives the cake a satisfyingly crunchy top.

Makes 1 cake
225g/8oz/2 cups self-raising
   (self-rising) flour

good pinch of salt
pinch of ground cloves
115g/4oz/1/2 cup butter,
   at room temperature
3 or 4 cooking apples, such as
   Bramley's Seedling
115g/4oz/generous 1/2 cup caster
   (superfine) sugar
2 eggs, beaten
a little milk, to mix
granulated (white) sugar, for
   sprinkling

1 Preheat the oven to 190°C/375°F/Gas 5 and butter a 20cm/8in cake tin (pan).

2 Sift the flour, salt and ground cloves into a bowl. Cut in the butter and, using your fingertips, rub in until the mixture resembles fine breadcrumbs.

3 Peel and core the apples. Slice the flesh thinly and add to the rubbed-in mixture with the caster sugar.

4 Mix in the eggs and enough milk to make a fairly stiff dough, then turn the mixture into the prepared tin and sprinkle with granulated sugar.

5 Bake the cake in the preheated oven for 30–40 minutes, or until springy to the touch and a skewer inserted in the centre of the cake comes out clean. Leave to cool slightly on a wire rack. When cold, turn out and store in an airtight container until ready to serve.

> **Cook's Tip**
> *Serve either cold as a cake or warm, with a spoonful of chilled cream or custard, as a dessert.*

Apple Ring Cake

This attractive fruit and nut cake is slowly baked in a ring-shaped cake tin.

Serves 12
7 eating apples, such as Cox's
   or Granny Smith
350ml/12fl oz/1 1/2 cups
   vegetable oil
450g/1lb/2 1/4 cups caster
   (superfine) sugar
3 eggs

425g/15oz/3 1/2 cups plain
   (all-purpose) flour
5ml/1 tsp salt
5ml/1 tsp bicarbonate of soda
   (baking soda)
5ml/1 tsp ground cinnamon
5ml/1 tsp vanilla extract
115g/4oz/1 cup chopped walnuts
175g/6oz/generous 1 cup raisins
icing (confectioners') sugar,
   for dusting

1 Preheat the oven to 180°C/350°F/Gas 4. Lightly grease a 23cm/9in ring mould.

2 Quarter, peel and core the apples. Thinly slice the apple flesh and place into a bowl. Set aside.

3 With an electric mixer, beat the oil and sugar together in a large mixing bowl until blended. Gradually add the eggs and continue beating until the mixture is creamy.

4 In a separate bowl, sift together the flour, salt, bicarbonate of soda and cinnamon.

5 Fold the flour mixture into the egg mixture, along with the vanilla extract. Stir in the apples, walnuts and raisins.

6 Pour the mixture into the mould and bake until the cake springs back when touched lightly, about 1 1/4 hours. Leave to stand for 15 minutes, then turn out and transfer to a cooling rack. Dust with a layer of icing sugar before serving.

> **Variation**
> *The fruit and nuts in this cake can be varied: use sultanas (golden raisins) glacé cherries, pecans or walnuts, if you prefer.*

Apple Cake Energy 2315kcal/9717kJ; Protein 37g; Carbohydrate 312.5g, of which sugars 145.3g; Fat 110.9g, of which saturates 64.1g; Cholesterol 702mg; Calcium 948mg; Fibre 10.7g; Sodium 1.68g.
Ring Cake Energy 603kcal/2532kJ; Protein 7g; Carbohydrate 83.1g, of which sugars 56g; Fat 29.4g, of which saturates 3.4g; Cholesterol 48mg; Calcium 95mg; Fibre 2.8g; Sodium 32mg.

Spicy Apple Cake

Hundreds of German cakes and desserts include the versatile apple. This moist and spicy *Apfelkuchen* can be found on the menu of Konditoreien, coffee and tea houses, everywhere.

Serves 12
115g/4oz/1 cup plain
  (all-purpose) flour
115g/4oz/1 cup wholemeal
  (whole-wheat) flour
10ml/2 tsp baking powder
5ml/1 tsp cinnamon
2.5ml/¹/₂ tsp mixed (apple pie)
  spice

225g/8oz cooking apple, cored,
  peeled and chopped
75g/3oz/6 tbsp butter
175g/6oz/generous ³/₄ cup soft
  light brown sugar
finely grated rind of 1 small orange
2 eggs, beaten
30ml/2 tbsp milk
whipped cream dusted with
  cinnamon, to serve

For the topping
4 eating apples, cored and sliced
juice of ¹/₂ orange
10ml/2 tsp caster (superfine) sugar
45ml/3 tbsp apricot jam, warmed
  and sieved

1 Preheat the oven to 180°C/350°F/Gas 4. Grease and line a 23cm/9in round loose-bottomed cake tin. Sift the flours, baking powder and spices together in a bowl. Toss the chopped cooking apple in 30ml/2 tbsp of the flour mixture.

2 Cream the butter, brown sugar and orange rind together until light and fluffy. Gradually beat in the eggs, then fold in the flour mixture, the chopped apple and the milk. Spoon the mixture into the cake tin and level the surface.

3 For the topping, toss the apple slices in the orange juice and set them in overlapping circles on top of the cake mixture, pressing down lightly.

4 Sprinkle the caster sugar over the top of the cake and bake for 1–1¹/₄ hours, or until risen and firm. Cover with foil if the apples brown too much.

5 Cool in the tin for 10 minutes, then remove to a wire rack. Glaze the apples with the jam. Cut the cake into wedges and serve with whipped cream, sprinkled with cinnamon.

Tangy Apple Cake

This cake is beautifully firm and moist, with pieces of apple peeking through the top. Using fresh orange juice gives the cake a delicious flavour and the cinnamon is the perfect partner for the apple slices.

Serves 6–8
375g/13oz/3¹/₄ cups self-raising
  (self-rising) flour

3–4 large cooking apples, or
  cooking and eating apples
10ml/2 tsp ground cinnamon
500g/1¹/₄lb/2¹/₂ cups caster
  (superfine) sugar
4 eggs, lightly beaten
250ml/8fl oz/1 cup vegetable oil
120ml/4fl oz/¹/₂ cup
  orange juice
10ml/2 tsp vanilla extract
2.5ml/¹/₂ tsp salt

1 Preheat the oven to 180°C/350°F/Gas 4. Lightly grease a 30 × 38cm/12 × 15in square cake tin (pan) and dust with a little of the flour. Core and thinly slice the apples, but do not peel them.

2 Put the sliced apples in a bowl and mix with the cinnamon and 75ml/5 tbsp of the sugar.

3 In a separate bowl, beat together the eggs, remaining sugar, vegetable oil, orange juice and vanilla extract until well combined. Sift in the remaining flour and salt, then stir into the mixture until combined.

4 Pour two-thirds of the cake mixture into the prepared tin, top with one-third of the apples, then pour over the remaining cake mixture and top with the remaining apples. Bake for about 1 hour, or until golden brown.

5 Leave the cake to cool in the tin to allow the juices to soak in. Serve while still warm, cut into squares.

Cook's Tip
This sturdy little cake is perfect served with with a cup of tea or coffee for an afternoon break.

Spicy Apple Cake Energy 587kcal/2471kJ; Protein 5.5g; Carbohydrate 92g, of which sugars 69.7g; Fat 24.5g, of which saturates 10.6g; Cholesterol 40mg; Calcium 95mg; Fibre 2.5g; Sodium 129mg.
Tangy Apple Cake Energy 653kcal/2751kJ; Protein 7.8g; Carbohydrate 105.4g, of which sugars 70.6g; Fat 25.3g, of which saturates 3.4g; Cholesterol 95mg; Calcium 215mg; Fibre 2.1g; Sodium 210mg.

Citrus Sponge

This light sponge cake is made with matzo and potato flour. The addition of orange juice and citrus rind gives it a wonderful tangy taste.

Serves 6–8

12 eggs, separated
300g/11oz/1½ cups caster (superfine) sugar
120ml/4fl oz/½ cup fresh orange juice
grated rind of 1 orange
grated rind of 1 lemon
50g/2oz/½ cup potato flour, sifted
90g/3½oz/¾ cup fine matzo meal or matzo meal flour, sifted
large pinch of salt
icing (confectioners') sugar, for dusting (optional)
fresh orange or grapefruit pieces, to serve (optional)

1 Preheat the oven to 160°C/325°F/Gas 3. In a large mixing bowl, whisk the egg yolks until they are pale and frothy. Whisk the caster sugar, fresh orange juice, orange rind and lemon rind into the eggs.

2 Fold the two sifted flours into the egg mixture. In a clean, grease-free bowl, whisk the egg whites with the salt until stiff, then fold into the egg yolk mixture.

3 Pour the cake mixture into a deep, ungreased 25cm/10in cake tin (pan) and bake for about 1 hour, or until a cocktail stick (toothpick), inserted in the centre, comes out clean. Leave to cool in the tin.

4 When the cake is cold, turn it out and invert it on to a serving plate. Liberally dust the top of the cake with some icing sugar before serving, if you wish. Serve with pieces of fresh orange or grapefruit, if you like.

> **Cook's Tip**
> When testing to see if the cake is cooked, if you don't have a cocktail stick (toothpick) to hand, use a strand of raw dried spaghetti instead – it will work just as well.

Honey Cake

This cake is sweetened with honey and made with toasted hazelnuts and breadcrumbs instead of flour, which gives it a deliciously rich and moist texture. Bake in a brioche tin to give the cake an attractive shape.

Serves 12

15g/½oz/1 tbsp unsalted butter, melted
115g/4oz/2 cups slightly dry fine white breadcrumbs
175g/6oz/¾ cup set honey, plus extra to serve
50g/2oz/¼ cup soft light brown sugar
4 eggs, separated
115g/4oz/1 cup hazelnuts, chopped and toasted, plus extra to decorate

1 Preheat the oven to 180°C/350°F/Gas 4. Brush a 1.75 litre/3 pint/7½ cup fluted brioche tin (pan) with the melted unsalted butter. Sprinkle the tin with about 15g/½oz/¼ cup of the fine white breadcrumbs.

2 Put the honey in a large heatproof bowl set over a pan of barely simmering water. When the honey melts a little, add the sugar and egg yolks. Whisk until light and frothy. Remove the bowl from the heat.

3 Mix the remaining breadcrumbs with the hazelnuts and fold into the egg yolk and honey mixture. Whisk the egg whites in a separate bowl until stiff, then gently fold in with the other ingredients, half at a time.

4 Spoon the mixture into the prepared tin. Bake in the preheated oven for about 40–45 minutes, until golden brown. Leave to cool in the tin for 5 minutes, then turn out on to a wire rack to cool. Sprinkle over the nuts and drizzle with extra honey to serve.

> **Cook's Tip**
> The cake will rise during cooking and then sink slightly as it cools – this is quite normal.

Citrus Sponge Energy 328kcal/1381kJ; Protein 11.1g; Carbohydrate 53.7g, of which sugars 40.5g; Fat 8.8g, of which saturates 2.3g; Cholesterol 285mg; Calcium 66mg; Fibre 0.4g; Sodium 109mg.
Honey Cake Energy 188kcal/791kJ; Protein 4.6g; Carbohydrate 23.5g, of which sugars 16.1g; Fat 9.1g, of which saturates 1.6g; Cholesterol 66mg; Calcium 39mg; Fibre 0.8g; Sodium 106mg.

Spiced Honey Cake

This classic honey cake is richly spiced, redolent of ginger, cinnamon and other sweet, aromatic scents.

Serves about 8
175g/6oz/1½ cups plain
    (all-purpose) flour
75g/3oz/⅓ cup caster
    (superfine) sugar
2.5ml/½ tsp ground ginger
2.5–5ml/½–1 tsp ground
    cinnamon
5ml/1 tsp mixed (apple pie) spice
5ml/1 tsp bicarbonate of soda
    (baking soda)
225g/8oz/1 cup clear honey
60ml/4 tbsp vegetable or olive oil
grated rind of 1 orange
2 eggs
75ml/5 tbsp orange juice
10ml/2 tsp chopped fresh root
    ginger, or to taste

1 Preheat the oven to 180°C/350°F/Gas 4. Line a rectangular baking tin (pan), measuring 25 × 20 × 5cm/10 × 8 × 2in, with baking parchment. In a large mixing bowl, mix together the flour, sugar, ginger, cinnamon, mixed spice and bicarbonate of soda until well combined.

2 Make a well in the centre of the flour mixture and pour in the clear honey, vegetable or olive oil, orange rind and eggs. Using a wooden spoon or electric whisk, beat until smooth, then add the orange juice. Stir in the chopped ginger.

3 Pour the cake mixture into the prepared tin, then bake for about 50 minutes, or until firm to the touch.

4 Leave the cake to cool in the tin, then turn out and wrap tightly in foil. Store at room temperature for 2–3 days before serving, to allow the flavours of the cake to mature.

Cook's Tip
This honey cake keeps very well. It can be made in two loaf tins (pans), so that one cake can be eaten, while the other can be wrapped in clear film (plastic wrap) and stored or frozen for a later date.

Old-fashioned Treacle Cake

The treacle gives this delicious cake a lovely rich colour and a deep flavour.

Makes a 20cm/8in cake
250g/9oz/2 cups self-raising
    (self-rising) flour
2.5ml/½ tsp mixed
    (apple pie) spice
75g/3oz/6 tbsp butter, cut into
    small cubes
35g/1oz/2 tbsp caster
    (superfine) sugar
150g/5oz/1 cup mixed dried fruit
1 egg
15ml/1 tbsp black treacle
    (molasses)
100ml/3½fl oz/scant ½ cup milk

1 Preheat the oven to 180°C/350°F/Gas 5. Butter a shallow 20–23cm/8–9in ovenproof flan dish or baking tin (pan).

2 Sift the flour and spice into a large mixing bowl. Add the butter and, with your fingertips, rub it into the flour until the mixture resembles fine crumbs. Alternatively, you could do this in a food processor. Stir in the sugar and mixed dried fruit.

3 Beat the egg and, with a small whisk or a fork, stir in the black treacle and then the milk. Stir the liquid into the flour to make a fairly stiff but moist consistency, adding a little extra milk, if necessary.

4 Transfer the cake mixture to the prepared dish or tin with a spoon and level out the surface. Bake the cake in the hot oven and cook for about 1 hour until it has risen, is firm to the touch and fully cooked through. To check if the cake is cooked, insert a small skewer into the centre of the cake – it should come out free of sticky mixture.

5 Leave the cooked treacle cake in the dish or tin to cool completely. Serve it, cut into wedges, straight from the dish.

Cook's Tip
Vary the fruit used in this cake, if you like. Try using chopped ready-to-eat dried apricots and stem ginger, or a packet of luxury dried fruit.

Spiced Honey Cake Energy 264kcal/1115kJ; Protein 3.8g; Carbohydrate 49.1g, of which sugars 32.4g; Fat 7.2g, of which saturates 1.1g; Cholesterol 48mg; Calcium 45mg; Fibre 0.7g; Sodium 23mg.
Treacle Cake Energy 2089kcal/8805kJ; Protein 37.4g; Carbohydrate 343g, of which sugars 152.4g; Fat 72.8g, of which saturates 42.2g; Cholesterol 356mg; Calcium 720mg; Fibre 11.1g; Sodium 676mg.

Moist Golden Ginger Cake

This is the ultimate ginger cake. Because it is made in the slow cooker the cake can be eaten straight away, but the flavour and texture improves if it is wrapped and kept for a day or two.

Serves 10
175g/6oz/generous ¾ cup light muscovado (brown) sugar
115g/4oz/½ cup butter
150g/5oz/⅔ cup golden (light corn) syrup

25g/1oz malt extract
175g/6oz/1½ cups self-raising (self-rising) flour
50g/2oz/½ cup plain (all-purpose) flour
10ml/2 tsp ground ginger
pinch of salt
1 egg, lightly beaten
120ml/4fl oz/½ cup milk, at room temperature
2.5ml/½ tsp bicarbonate of soda (baking soda)

1 Line the base of a deep 18cm/7in round fixed-base cake tin (pan) with baking parchment. Pour 5cm/2in of very hot water into the ceramic cooking pot. Switch to high.

2 Place the sugar, butter, golden syrup and malt extract in a heatproof bowl that will fit inside the slow cooker. Place in the pot and leave for 15 minutes, or until melted.

3 Remove the bowl from the pot and stir until smooth. Place an upturned saucer in the base of the ceramic cooking pot. Sift the flours, ginger and salt into a mixing bowl. Beat into the melted butter mixture until smooth. Mix in the egg.

4 Pour the milk in a jug (pitcher) and stir in the bicarbonate of soda. Pour the mixture into the ginger cake mixture and stir until combined. Pour the mixture into the cake tin, cover with foil and place in the cooking pot. Pour boiling water around the tin or dish to come just over halfway up the sides. Cover with the lid and cook for 5–6 hours, or until firm and a fine skewer inserted into the cake comes out clean.

5 Remove the cake from the slow cooker and place the tin on a wire cooling rack. Leave to cool for 15 minutes, then turn out and leave to cool completely, before serving in slices.

Whiskey Cake

This light, moist cake has the subtle flavours of lemon and cloves, making it seem especially tempting in winter.

Makes one 18cm/7in round cake
225g/8oz/1⅓ cups sultanas (golden raisins)
grated rind of 1 lemon
150ml/¼ pint/⅔ cup Irish whiskey
175g/6oz/¾ cup butter, softened
175g/6oz/¾ cup soft light brown sugar

175g/6oz/1½ cups plain (all-purpose) flour
pinch of salt
1.5ml/¼ tsp ground cloves
5ml/1 tsp baking powder
3 large (US extra large) eggs, separated

For the icing
juice of 1 lemon
225g/8oz/2 cups icing (confectioners') sugar
crystallized lemon slices, to decorate (optional)

1 Put the sultanas and grated lemon rind into a bowl with the whiskey, and leave overnight to soak.

2 Preheat the oven to 180°C/350°F/Gas 4 and grease and base line a loose-based 18cm/7in deep cake tin (pan). Cream the butter and sugar until light and fluffy. Sift the flour, salt, cloves and baking powder together into a bowl.

3 Beat the yolks into the butter and sugar one at a time, adding a little of the flour with each egg and beating well. Gradually blend in the sultana and whiskey mixture, alternating with the remaining flour. Do not overbeat at this stage.

4 Whisk the egg whites until stiff and fold them into the mixture with a metal spoon. Turn the mixture into the prepared tin and bake in the preheated oven for 1½ hours, or until well risen and springy to the touch. Turn out and cool on a rack.

5 Meanwhile, make the icing. Mix the lemon juice with the icing sugar and enough warm water to make a pouring consistency. Lay a plate under the cake rack to catch the drips and pour the icing over the cake a spoonful at a time, letting it dribble down the sides. When the icing has set, it can be decorated with lemon slices, if you like.

Ginger Cake Energy 289kcal/1216kJ; Protein 3.4g; Carbohydrate 48g, of which sugars 31.1g; Fat 10.6g, of which saturates 6.4g; Cholesterol 48mg; Calcium 98mg; Fibre 0.7g; Sodium 211mg.
Whiskey Cake Energy 4691kcal/19,730kJ; Protein 48.1g; Carbohydrate 711.2g, of which sugars 577.8g; Fat 167g, of which saturates 97.1g; Cholesterol 1.06g; Calcium 735mg; Fibre 9.9g; Sodium 1.38g.

Boiled Fruit Cake

The texture of this cake is quite distinctive – moist and plump as a result of boiling the dried fruit with the butter, sugar and milk prior to baking. For special occasions replace some of the milk with sherry or brandy, and arrange cherries and nuts on the surface of the uncooked cake before putting it in the oven. It makes an ideal Christmas cake, too.

Makes a 20cm/8in cake
350g/12oz/2 cups mixed
   dried fruit
225g/8oz/1 cup butter
225g/8oz/1 cup soft dark
   brown sugar
400ml/14fl oz/1²/₃ cup milk
450g/1lb/4 cups self-raising
   (self-rising) flour
5ml/1 tsp bicarbonate of soda
   (baking soda)
5ml/1 tsp mixed (apple pie) spice
2 eggs, beaten

1 Preheat the oven to 160°C/325°F/Gas 3. Lightly grease a 20cm/8in round cake tin (pan) and line it with a piece of baking parchment.

2 Put the mixed dried fruit in a large pan and add the butter and the brown sugar. Bring the mixture slowly to the boil, stirring occasionally.

3 When the butter has melted and the sugar has completely dissolved, bubble the mixture gently for about 2 minutes. Remove from the heat and cool slightly.

4 Sift the flour with the bicarbonate of soda and mixed spice into a bowl. Add this and the eggs to the fruit mixture and mix together well.

5 Pour the cake mixture into the prepared tin and smooth the surface. Bake for about 1½ hours or until firm to the touch and cooked through – a skewer inserted in the centre of the cake should come out free of sticky mixture.

6 Leave the cake in the tin to cool for about 20–30 minutes, then turn out and cool completely on a wire rack before cutting into wedges and serving.

Porter Cake

Porter was a key ingredient in many traditional Irish dishes, adding colour and richness. Stout is a good substitute in recipes like this one.

Makes one 20cm/8in round cake
225g/8oz/1 cup butter,
   at room temperature
225g/8oz/1 cup soft dark
   brown sugar
350g/12oz/3 cups plain
   (all-purpose) flour

pinch of salt
5ml/1 tsp baking powder
5ml/1 tsp mixed (apple pie) spice
3 eggs
450g/1lb/2¹/₃ cups mixed
   dried fruit
115g/4oz/¹/₂ cup glacé
   (candied) cherries
115g/4oz/²/₃ cup mixed
   (candied) peel
50g/2oz/¹/₂ cup chopped
   almonds or walnuts
about 150ml/¹/₄ pint/²/₃ cup
   stout, such as Guinness

1 Preheat the oven to 160°C/325°F/Gas 3. Grease and base line a 20cm/8in round deep cake tin (pan). Cream the butter and sugar in a bowl, until light and fluffy. Sift the flour, salt, baking powder and spice into another bowl.

2 Add the eggs to the butter mixture, one at a time, adding a little of the flour mixture with each egg and beating well. Mix well and blend in any remaining flour. Add the fruit and nuts and enough stout to make quite a soft consistency. Mix well.

3 Turn the mixture into the tin and bake for 1 hour. Reduce the heat to 150°C/300°F/Gas 2 and cook for 1½–2 hours, or until the top is springy to the touch and a skewer pushed into the centre comes out clean. Cool the cake in the tin.

4 When cold, remove the lining paper, wrap in fresh baking parchment and store in an airtight container for at least a week before eating, to give the flavours time to develop.

> **Cook's Tip**
> *Porter cake can be made by many methods, ranging from rubbed-in teabreads to the creaming method, as here.*

Fruit Cake Energy 5150kcal/21689kJ; Protein 72.2g; Carbohydrate 796g, of which sugars 498.8g; Fat 209.1g, of which saturates 125.4g; Cholesterol 884mg; Calcium 2352mg; Fibre 20.1g; Sodium 3297mg.
Porter Cake Energy 6130kcal/25807kJ; Protein 80.2g; Carbohydrate 964.9g, of which sugars 696.9g; Fat 240.2g, of which saturates 125.7g; Cholesterol 1.16g; Calcium 1.42mg; Fibre 31g; Sodium 2.23g.

Caraway Seed Cake

This old-fashioned cake remains popular on farmhouse tea tables.

Makes 1 cake
225g/8oz/2 cups plain
  (all-purpose) flour
115g/4oz/¹⁄₂ cup butter,
  at room temperature
115g/4oz/generous ¹⁄₂ cup caster
  (superfine) sugar
2 large (US extra large) eggs
5ml/1 tsp baking powder
15ml/1 tbsp caraway seeds
30–45ml/2–3 tbsp milk,
  if necessary

1 Preheat the oven to 180°C/350°F/Gas 4. Butter and base line a 18cm/7in deep cake tin (pan) with lightly buttered baking parchment.

2 Sift the flour into a bowl. Cream the butter and sugar together in a separate bowl until fluffy, then add the eggs, a little at a time, with a spoonful of flour with each addition. Add the baking powder and most of the caraway seeds to the remaining flour, reserving a few seeds to sprinkle over the top of the cake.

3 Add the flour and caraway seeds mixture to the butter mixture, and blend in lightly but thoroughly; add a little milk to make a soft mixture if it seems too stiff.

4 Turn the mixture into the tin and sprinkle with the reserved caraway seeds. Put the cake in the preheated oven and bake for 15 minutes. Reduce the temperature to 160°C/325°F/Gas 3 and bake for a further 1 hour, or until the cake is well risen and golden brown.

5 Leave the cake to cool in the tin for about 10 minutes, then remove and finish cooling on a wire rack. When cold, remove the baking parchment and store in an airtight tin.

Cook's Tip
Aromatic caraway seeds come from a herb in the parsley family. They have a mild aniseed flavour and are often used in baking.

Poppy Seed Cake

This plain and simple cake is studded with tiny black poppy seeds that give it a nutty, distinctive taste that is utterly moreish. Serve with a cup of hot tea when you feel like a treat.

Serves about 8
130g/4¹⁄₂oz/generous 1 cup
  self-raising (self-rising) flour
5ml/1 tsp baking powder
2.5ml/¹⁄₂ tsp salt
2 eggs
225g/8oz/generous 1 cup caster
  (superfine) sugar
5–10ml/1–2 tsp vanilla extract
200g/7oz/scant 1¹⁄₂ cups poppy
  seeds, ground
15ml/1 tbsp grated lemon rind
120ml/4fl oz/¹⁄₂ cup milk
130g/4¹⁄₂oz/generous ¹⁄₂ cup
  unsalted butter, melted
  and cooled
30ml/2 tbsp vegetable oil
icing (confectioners') sugar, sifted,
  for dusting

1 Preheat the oven to 180°C/350°F/Gas 4. Grease and base-line a 23cm/9in springform tin (pan). In a large mixing bowl, sift together the flour, baking powder and salt.

2 Using an electric whisk, beat together the eggs, sugar and vanilla extract for 4–5 minutes until pale and fluffy. Stir in the poppy seeds and the lemon rind.

3 Gently fold the sifted ingredients into the egg and poppy seed mixture, working in three batches and alternating with the milk. Gradually fold in the melted butter and vegetable oil until the mixture is well combined.

4 Pour the mixture into the prepared tin and bake for about 40 minutes, or until firm. Cool in the tin for 15 minutes, then invert the cake on to a wire rack to cool completely. Serve cold, dusted with icing sugar.

Variation
To make a poppy seed tart, pour the cake mixture into a par-cooked pastry crust, then bake for 30 minutes, or until the filling is firm and risen.

Caraway Energy 2252kcal/9448kJ; Protein 37.4g; Carbohydrate 295.7g, of which sugars 124.2g; Fat 110.8g, of which saturates 64.1g; Cholesterol 702mg; Calcium 465mg; Fibre 7g; Sodium 879mg.
Poppy Energy 485kcal/2023kJ; Protein 8.3g; Carbohydrate 42.7g, of which sugars 30.5g; Fat 32.4g, of which saturates 11.4g; Cholesterol 83mg; Calcium 267mg; Fibre 2.5g; Sodium 188mg.

Black Bread

This cake has a texture that is similar to pumpernickel and is slowly steamed rather than oven-baked. Empty fruit cans are perfect for producing bread in the traditional round shape.

Makes 2 loaves
50g/2oz/½ cup rye flour
40g/1½ oz/⅓ cup plain
    (all-purpose) flour
4ml/¾ tsp baking powder
2.5ml/½ tsp salt
1.5ml/¼ tsp cinnamon
1.5ml/¼ tsp nutmeg
50g/2oz/⅓ cup fine semolina
60ml/4 tbsp black treacle
    (molasses)
200ml/7fl oz/scant 1 cup
    cultured buttermilk
cherry jam, sour cream or crème
    fraîche and a sprinkling of
    ground allspice, to serve

1 Grease and line 2 × 400g/14oz fruit cans. Sift the flours, baking powder, salt and spices into a large mixing bowl. Stir in the semolina. Add the black treacle and buttermilk and mix until thoroughly combined.

2 Divide the mixture evenly between the two cans, then cover each with a double layer of greased pleated foil.

3 Place the cans on a trivet in a large pan and pour in enough hot water to come halfway up the sides of the cans. Cover the pan tightly and steam for 2 hours, checking the water level occasionally, and topping up if necessary.

4 Carefully remove the cans from the steamer. Turn the bread out on to a wire rack and cool completely. Wrap in foil and use within 1 week.

5 Serve the bread in slices, spread with cherry jam, topped with a spoonful of soured cream or crème fraîche and a sprinkling of allspice.

Cook's Tip
If you cannot get buttermilk, use ordinary milk instead, first soured with 5ml/1 tsp lemon juice.

Christmas Cake

Rich cakes need at least a month to mature, so Christmas cakes are best made by Hallowe'en. This cake may be finished in the traditional way with almond paste and white icing, or glazed with fruit and nuts.

Makes one 20cm/8in round or 18cm/7in square cake
225g/8oz/2 cups plain
    (all-purpose) flour
pinch of salt
7.5ml/1½ tsp mixed
    (apple pie) spice
900g/2lb/5 cups mixed dried fruit
50g/2oz/½ cup slivered almonds
115g/4oz/⅔ cup glacé (candied)
    cherries, halved
115g/4oz/⅔ cup chopped mixed
    (candied) peel
225g/8oz/1 cup butter, at
    room temperature
225g/8oz/1 cup soft dark
    brown sugar
15ml/1 tbsp black treacle
    (molasses)
finely grated rind of 1 orange
5ml/1 tsp vanilla extract
4 large (US extra large) eggs
150ml/¼ pint/⅔ cup Irish whiskey

1 Prepare a 20cm/8in round or an 18cm/7in square loose-based cake tin (pan) by lining it with three layers of greased baking parchment, extending 5cm/2in over the top of the tin. Attach a thick band of folded newspaper or brown paper around the outside of the tin, using string to secure it.

2 Sift the flour, salt and mixed spice in a large mixing bowl. Put the dried fruit in a separate large bowl with the almonds, cherries, mixed peel and 15ml/1 tbsp of flour taken from the measured amount.

3 In another bowl, cream the butter and sugar until light and fluffy, then add the treacle, orange rind and vanilla extract. Beat well. Add the eggs, one at a time, adding a little of the flour mixture with each egg and beating well after each addition. Fold in the fruit mixture and the remaining flour with 30ml/2 tbsp of the whiskey. Mix well.

4 Put the mixture into the prepared tin, smoothing down well with the back of a spoon and leaving a slight hollow in the centre. At this stage, the cake can now be left overnight or until it is convenient to start baking.

5 Preheat the oven to 160°C/325°F/Gas 3. Place the cake in the centre of the oven and bake for about 1½ hours, or until just beginning to brown. Reduce the heat to 150°C/300°F/Gas 2 and continue to bake for another 3 hours, or until cooked. Protect the top of the cake from over-browning by covering loosely with foil or brown paper.

6 When cooked, the top of the cake will feel springy to the touch and a skewer pushed into the centre will come out clean. Leave the cake to cool, then remove the papers and turn upside down.

7 Using a skewer, make small holes all over the base of the cake and pour in the remaining whiskey. Leave the cake to soak up the whiskey. When soaked, wrap the cake in a double layer of baking parchment, followed by a layer of foil. Store the cake in an airtight container in a cool place until about two weeks before Christmas, if you wish to add a topping.

Black Bread Energy 417kcal/1774kJ; Protein 12.3g; Carbohydrate 94g, of which sugars 25.1g; Fat 1.8g, of which saturates 0.3g; Cholesterol 4mg; Calcium 356mg; Fibre 4.7g; Sodium 103mg.
Christmas Cake Energy 9834kcal/41,553kJ; Protein 89.9g; Carbohydrate 1846.1g, of which sugars 1673.2g; Fat 247g, of which saturates 127.3g; Cholesterol 1.39g; Calcium 2.24g; Fibre 46g; Sodium 2.8g.

Barm Brack

The traditional yeasted Hallowe'en barm brack contains all kinds of symbolic tokens, of which the best known is a ring. Serve this version sliced and buttered while still warm.

Makes 2 loaves
450g/1lb/4 cups plain
   (all-purpose) flour
5ml/1 tsp mixed (apple pie)
   spice
2.5ml/½ tsp salt

2 sachets easy-blend (rapid-rise)
   dried yeast
75g/3oz/6 tbsp soft dark
   brown sugar
115g/4oz/½ cup butter, melted
300ml/½ pint/1¼ cups
   tepid milk
1 egg, lightly beaten
375g/13oz/generous 2 cups
   dried mixed fruit
25g/1oz/⅓ cup chopped
   mixed (candied) peel
15ml/1 tbsp caster
   (superfine) sugar

1 Butter two 450g/1lb loaf tins (pans). Mix the flour, spice, salt, yeast and sugar in a large bowl and make a well in the centre.

2 Mix the melted butter with the tepid milk and lightly beaten egg and add to the bowl. Add the mixed fruit and peel to the bowl and mix well.

3 Turn the mixture into the loaf tins. Leave in a warm place for about 30 minutes to rise. Meanwhile, preheat the oven to 200°C/400°F/Gas 6.

4 When the dough has doubled in size, bake in the hot oven for about 45 minutes, or until the loaves begin to shrink slightly from the sides of the tins; when turned out and rapped underneath they should sound hollow.

5 Make a glaze by mixing the caster sugar with 30ml/2 tbsp boiling water. Remove the loaves from the oven and brush over with the glaze.

6 Return the loaves to the oven for about 3 minutes, or until the tops have turned a rich shiny brown. Turn on to a wire rack to cool slightly for 5–10 minutes, before serving in warm slices with plenty of butter.

Bara Brith Teabread

The Welsh spiced loaf known as bara brith is similar to barm brack. Once the fruit has been plumped up by soaking it in tea, this version is easy to make with self-raising flour. Serve sliced, with a little butter, if you like.

Makes 1 large loaf
225g/8oz/1⅓ cups mixed dried
   fruit and chopped mixed
   (candied) peel
225ml/8fl oz/1 cup hot strong
   tea, strained
225g/8oz/2 cups self-raising
   (self-rising) flour
5ml/1 tsp mixed (apple pie) spice
25g/1oz/2 tbsp butter
100g/3¾oz/scant ½ cup soft
   light brown sugar
1 egg, lightly beaten

1 Put the fruit into a heatproof bowl and pour the hot tea over it. Cover and leave to stand at room temperature for several hours or overnight.

2 Preheat the oven to 180°C/350°F/Gas 4. Grease a 900g/2lb loaf tin (pan) and line it with baking parchment.

3 Sift the flour and the mixed spice into a large mixing bowl. Add the butter and, with your fingertips, rub it into the flour until the mixture starts to resemble fine breadcrumbs.

4 Stir in the brown sugar, then add the soaked fruit and its liquid along with the beaten egg. Stir well to make a mixture with a soft consistency.

5 Transfer the mixture to the prepared loaf tin and level the surface. Put into the hot oven and cook for about 1 hour or until a skewer inserted in the centre comes out clean. Turn out on a wire rack and leave to cool completely.

> **Cook's Tip**
> *The flavour of the loaf can be varied subtly by using a variety of teas – try the distinctive perfume of Earl Grey.*

Barm Brack Energy 2019kcal/8524kJ; Protein 34.9g; Carbohydrate 364.6g, of which sugars 193.2g; Fat 57g, of which saturates 32.8g; Cholesterol 246mg; Calcium 704mg; Fibre 11.7g; Sodium 590mg.
Bara Brith Energy 2024kcal/8588kJ; Protein 33.2g; Carbohydrate 432.7g, of which sugars 261.3g; Fat 29.9g, of which saturates 15g; Cholesterol 244mg; Calcium 565mg; Fibre 11.9g; Sodium 342mg.

Fruit Slice

A dried fruit filling is packed between shortcrust pastry and then baked in the oven in this tasty treat.

Makes 24 slices

8 slices of stale bread, or plain cake
75g/3oz/²⁄₃ cup plain (all-purpose) flour
pinch of salt
2.5ml/½ tsp baking powder
10ml/2 tsp mixed (apple pie) spice
115g/4oz/generous ½ cup sugar, plus extra for sprinkling
175g/6oz/¾ cup currants or mixed dried fruit
50g/2oz/¼ cup butter, melted
1 egg, lightly beaten
milk, to mix

For the shortcrust pastry
225g/8oz/2 cups plain (all-purpose) flour
2.5ml/½ tsp salt
115g/4oz/½ cup butter

1 To make the shortcrust pastry, mix together the flour, salt and the butter in a large bowl. Using the fingertips, rub the mixture until it resembles fine breadcrumbs. Mix in 30–45ml/ 2–3 tbsp cold water and knead lightly to form a firm dough. Wrap in clear film (plastic wrap) and chill for 30 minutes.

2 Preheat the oven to 190°C/375°F/Gas 5 and grease and flour a square baking tin (pan).

3 Remove the crusts from the bread and make the remainder into crumbs, or make the cake into crumbs. Put the crumbs into a mixing bowl with the flour, salt, baking powder, mixed spice, sugar and dried fruit. Mix well to combine.

4 Add the butter and egg to the dry ingredients with enough milk to make a fairly stiff, spreadable mixture.

5 Roll out the pastry and, using the baking tin as a guide, cut out one piece to make the lid. Use the rest, re-rolled as necessary, to line the base of the tin. Spread the pastry with the mixture, then cover with the pastry lid.

6 Make diagonal slashes across the top. Bake in the oven for 50–60 minutes, or until golden. Sprinkle with sugar and leave to cool in the tin. Cut into slices.

Classic Cheesecake

This popular cake has many variations but it is hard to beat this simple and plain version. A crushed biscuit base is topped with cream cheese, before being slowly baked in the oven.

Serves 8

50g/2oz/1 cup digestive biscuits (graham crackers), crushed
900g/2lb/4 cups cream cheese, at room temperature
240g/8¾oz/scant 1¼ cups caster (superfine) sugar
grated rind of 1 lemon
45ml/3 tbsp lemon juice
5ml/1 tsp vanilla extract
4 eggs, at room temperature

1 Preheat the oven to 160°C/325°F/Gas 3. Grease a 20cm/8in springform cake tin (pan). Place the tin on a round of foil 10–13cm/4–5in larger than the diameter of the tin. Press it up the sides to seal tightly.

2 Sprinkle the crushed digestive biscuits in the base of the tin. Press down gently to form an even layer.

3 In a large bowl, beat the cream cheese with a wooden spoon or an electric mixer until smooth.

4 Add the sugar, lemon rind and juice, and vanilla extract to the cream cheese, and beat until blended.

5 Beat the eggs into the cheese mixture, one at a time. Beat the mixture just enough to blend thoroughly, being careful not to overmix.

6 Pour the mixture into the prepared tin. Set the tin in a roasting pan and pour enough hot water into the roasting pan to come 2.5cm/1in up the side of the cake tin. Place in the oven.

7 Bake for about 1½ hours, or until the top of the cake is golden brown. Leave to cool in the tin.

8 Run a knife around the edge to loosen, then remove the rim of the tin. Chill for at least 4 hours before serving.

Fruit Slice Energy 156kcal/656kJ; Protein 2.4g; Carbohydrate 24.2g, of which sugars 10.5g; Fat 6.2g, of which saturates 3.7g; Cholesterol 23mg; Calcium 43mg; Fibre 0.8g; Sodium 128mg.
Cheesecake Energy 668kcal/2772kJ; Protein 7g; Carbohydrate 34.8g, of which sugars 33.1g; Fat 56.9g, of which saturates 34.5g; Cholesterol 203mg; Calcium 144mg; Fibre 0.1g; Sodium 393mg.

Chocolate Cheesecake Brownies

A very dense chocolate brownie mixture that is made in the slow cooker. It is swirled with creamy cheese to give it an attractive marbled effect.

Makes 9

50g/2oz dark (bittersweet)
  chocolate (minimum
  70 per cent cocoa solids),
  chopped
50g/2oz/¼ cup unsalted butter

65g/2½oz/5 tbsp light muscovado
  (brown) sugar
1 egg, beaten
25g/1oz/¼ cup plain
  (all-purpose) flour

For the cheesecake mixture

115g/4oz/½ cup full-fat
  cream cheese
25g/1oz/2 tbsp caster
  (superfine) sugar
5ml/1 tsp vanilla extract
½ beaten egg

1 Line the base and sides of a 15cm/6in square fixed-base cake tin (pan) with baking parchment. Pour about 5cm/2in of very hot water into the ceramic cooking pot and switch to high. Put the chocolate and butter in a heatproof bowl and place in the slow cooker. Leave to stand for 10 minutes.

2 Meanwhile, make the cheesecake mixture. Put the cream cheese, sugar and vanilla extract in a clean mixing bowl and beat together. Gradually beat in the egg until the mixture is very smooth and creamy. Set aside.

3 Stir the chocolate and butter mixture until completely melted and smooth, then remove the bowl from the slow cooker. Add the muscovado sugar and stir to combine. Place an upturned saucer in the base of the cooking pot.

4 Mix the beaten egg into the melted chocolate mixture a little at a time, then sift over the flour and gently fold in. Spoon the chocolate mixture into the tin. Drop small spoonfuls of the cheesecake mixture on top and swirl the mixtures together.

5 Cover the tin with foil and place in the pot. Pour in more boiling water around the tin to come just over halfway up the sides. Cook for 2 hours, or until just set. Remove the tin from the pot and place on a wire rack to cool. Cut into squares.

Chocolate Chip Walnut Cake

The tangy flavour of orange works well in this chocolate and nut slow-cooker loaf.

Serves 8

115g/4oz/1 cup plain
  (all-purpose) flour
25g/1oz/¼ cup cornflour
  (cornstarch)
5ml/1 tsp baking powder
115g/4oz/½ cup butter,
  at room temperature
115g/4oz/½ cup golden caster
  (superfine) sugar

2 eggs, lightly beaten
75g/3oz/½ cup plain (semisweet),
  milk or white chocolate chips
50g/2oz/½ cup chopped walnuts
finely grated rind of ½ orange

For the topping

115g/4oz/1 cup icing
  (confectioners') sugar, sifted,
  plus 5ml/1 tsp for dusting
20–30ml/4 tsp–2 tbsp freshly
  squeezed orange juice
walnut halves, to decorate

1 Grease and line a 450g/1lb loaf tin (pan) with baking parchment. Place an upturned saucer in the ceramic cooking pot and pour in 2.5cm/1in very hot water. Switch the cooker to high.

2 Sift the flour, cornflour and baking powder together twice, then set aside. Place the butter in a large bowl and beat until creamy. Add the golden sugar and beat until light and fluffy. Beat in the eggs.

3 Fold half of the flour mixture into the bowl, then add the rest with the chocolate chips, walnuts and orange rind. Fold in until just blended. Spoon into the loaf tin and loosely cover with foil. Put the tin on the saucer inside the pot. Pour in enough boiling water to come two-thirds of the way up the sides of the tin.

4 Cover the cooker with the lid and cook for 2½–3 hours, or until a fine skewer inserted into the cake comes out clean. Remove the cake from the cooker and stand it on a wire rack for 10 minutes, then turn out and leave to cool on the rack.

5 To decorate the cake, place 115g/4oz/1 cup icing sugar in a bowl. Stir in 20ml/4 tsp orange juice, adding a little more if needed to make it the consistency of thick cream. Drizzle the mixture over the cake, then decorate with walnut halves dusted with the 5ml/1 tsp icing sugar. Leave to set before serving.

Brownies Energy 174kcal/727kJ; Protein 2.9g; Carbohydrate 16.2g, of which sugars 14g; Fat 11.3g, of which saturates 6.8g; Cholesterol 65mg; Calcium 25mg; Fibre 0.2g; Sodium 86mg.
Chocolate Chip Cake Energy 395kcal/1655kJ; Protein 4.7g; Carbohydrate 51g, of which sugars 36.9g; Fat 20.5g, of which saturates 9.9g; Cholesterol 87mg; Calcium 49mg; Fibre 0.9g; Sodium 171mg.

Mango Chutney

No Indian meal would be complete without this classic chutney, which is ideal for making in the slow cooker. Its gloriously sweet, tangy flavour is the perfect complement to the warm taste of spices.

Makes 450g/1lb
3 firm mangoes
120ml/4fl oz/½ cup cider vinegar
200g/7oz/scant 1 cup light muscovado (brown) sugar
1 small red finger chilli or jalapeño chilli, split
2.5cm/1in piece fresh root ginger, peeled and finely chopped
1 garlic clove, finely chopped
5 cardamom pods, bruised
1 bay leaf
2.5ml/½ tsp salt

1 Peel the mangoes and cut out the stone (pit), then cut the flesh into small chunks or thin wedges.

2 Put the chopped mango in the ceramic cooking pot. Add the cider vinegar, stir briefly to combine, and cover the slow cooker with the lid. Switch to high and cook for about 2 hours, stirring the chutney halfway through the cooking time.

3 Stir the sugar, chilli, ginger, garlic, bruised cardamom pods, bay leaf and salt into the mango mixture, until the sugar has dissolved completely.

4 Cover and cook for 2 hours, then uncover and let the mixture cook for a further 1 hour, or until the chutney is reduced to a thick consistency and no excess liquid remains. Stir the chutney every 15 minutes during the last hour.

5 Remove and discard the bay leaf and the chilli. Spoon the chutney into hot sterilized jars and seal. Store for 1 week before eating and use within 1 year.

Cook's Tip
To make a more fiery chutney, seed and slice two green chillies and stir into the chutney mixture with the other spices.

Butternut, Apricot and Almond Chutney

Coriander seeds and ground turmeric add a deliciously spicy touch to this rich, slow-cooker chutney. It is ideal spooned on to little savoury canapés or with melting cubes of mozzarella cheese; it is also good in sandwiches, helping to spice up a variety of fillings.

Makes about 1.8kg/4lb
1 small butternut squash, weighing about 800g/1¾ lb
400g/14oz/2 cups golden sugar
300ml/½ pint/1¼ cups cider vinegar
2 onions, finely chopped
225g/8oz/1 cup ready-to-eat dried apricots, chopped
finely grated rind and juice of 1 orange
2.5ml/½ tsp turmeric
15ml/1 tbsp coriander seeds
15ml/1 tbsp salt
115g/4oz/1 cup flaked (sliced) almonds

1 Halve the butternut squash and scoop out the seeds. Peel off the skin, then cut the flesh into 1cm/½in cubes.

2 Put the sugar and vinegar in the ceramic cooking pot and switch to high. Heat for 30 minutes, then stir until the sugar has completely dissolved.

3 Add the butternut squash, onions, apricots, orange rind and juice, turmeric, coriander seeds and salt to the slow cooker and stir well.

4 Cover the cooker with the lid and cook for 5–6 hours, stirring occasionally. After about 5 hours the chutney should be a fairly thick consistency with relatively little liquid. If it is still quite runny at this stage, cook uncovered for the final hour. Stir in the flaked almonds.

5 Spoon the chutney into warmed sterilized jars, cover and seal. Store in a cool, dark place and allow to mature for at least 1 month before eating. It should be used within 2 years. Once opened, store jars of the chutney in the refrigerator and use within 2 months.

Sweet and Hot Dried-fruit Chutney

This rich, thick and slightly sticky preserve of spiced dried fruit is simple to make in the slow cooker. It is a wonderful way to enliven cold left-overs from your Christmas or Thanksgiving dinner.

Makes about 1.5kg/3lb 6oz
350g/12oz/1½ cups ready-to-eat dried apricots
225g/8oz/1½ cups dried dates, stoned (pitted)
225g/8oz/1⅓ cups dried figs
50g/2oz/⅓ cup glacé (candied) citrus peel
150g/5oz/1 cup raisins
50g/2oz/½ cup dried cranberries
75ml/2½fl oz/⅓ cup cranberry juice
300ml/½ pint/1¼ cups cider vinegar
225g/8oz/1 cup caster (superfine) sugar
finely grated rind of 1 lemon
5ml/1 tsp mixed (apple pie) spice
5ml/1 tsp ground coriander
5ml/1 tsp cayenne pepper
5ml/1 tsp salt

1 Chop the apricots, dates, figs and citrus peel, and put all the dried fruit in the ceramic cooking pot. Pour over the cranberry juice, stir, then cover the slow cooker and switch to low. Cook for 1 hour, or until the fruit has absorbed most of the juice.

2 Add the cider vinegar and sugar to the pot. Turn the slow cooker up to high and stir until the sugar has dissolved.

3 Re-cover and cook for 2 more hours, or until the fruit is very soft and the chutney fairly thick (it will thicken further as it cools). Stir in the lemon rind, mixed spice, coriander, cayenne pepper and salt. Cook, uncovered, for 30 minutes, until little excess liquid remains.

4 Spoon the chutney into warmed sterilized jars, cover and seal. Store in a cool, dark place. Open within 10 months and, once opened, store in the refrigerator and use within 2 months.

> **Variation**
> *Pitted prunes can be substituted for the dates, and dried sour cherries for the dried cranberries.*

Beetroot, Date and Orange Preserve

With its vibrant red colour and rich earthy flavour, this distinctive slow-cooker chutney is good with salads as well as cheeses, such as mature Cheddar, Stilton or Gorgonzola.

Makes about 1.4kg/3lb
300ml/½ pint/1¼ cups malt vinegar
200g/7oz/1 cup sugar
350g/12oz raw beetroot (beets)
350g/12oz eating apples
225g/8oz red onions, very finely chopped
1 garlic clove, crushed
finely grated rind of 2 oranges
5ml/1 tsp ground allspice
5ml/1 tsp salt
175g/6oz/1 cup chopped dried dates

1 Put the vinegar and sugar in the ceramic cooking pot. Cover the slow cooker and switch to high. Leave until steaming hot.

2 Meanwhile, scrub the beetroot, then cut into 1cm/½in pieces. Peel, quarter and core the apples and cut into a similar size.

3 Stir the vinegar mixture with a wooden spoon until the sugar has dissolved. Add the beetroot, apples, onions, garlic, orange rind, ground allspice and salt. Stir, then re-cover and cook for 4–5 hours, stirring occasionally, until very tender.

4 Stir in the dates and cook for a further hour until the mixture is really thick. Stir once or twice during this time to prevent the chutney from catching on the base of the ceramic cooking pot.

5 Spoon the chutney into warmed sterilized jars, cover and seal. Store in a cool, dark place and open within 5 months of making. Refrigerate after opening and use within 1 month.

> **Cook's Tip**
> *For really speedy preparation and a deliciously fine-textured chutney, put the peeled beetroot through the coarse grating blade of a food processor. Alternatively, you can simply grate the beetroot by hand.*

Sweet Chutney Energy 2873kcal/12248kJ; Protein 32g; Carbohydrate 714.3g, of which sugars 703.5g; Fat 6.8g, of which saturates 0.2g; Cholesterol 0mg; Calcium 1075mg; Fibre 52.1g; Sodium 2358mg.
Beetroot Preserve Energy 1632kcal/6949kJ; Protein 16.8g; Carbohydrate 413.7g, of which sugars 406g; Fat 1.5g, of which saturates 0.2g; Cholesterol 0mg; Calcium 278mg; Fibre 23.1g; Sodium 2241mg.

Apple and Sultana Chutney

Use wine or cider vinegar for this stovetop chutney to give it a subtle and mellow flavour. The chutney is perfect served with farmhouse cheeses and freshly made soda bread.

Makes about 900g/2lb

350g/12oz cooking apples
115g/4oz/²⁄₃ cup sultanas
   (golden raisins)
50g/2oz onion
25g/1oz/¼ cup almonds,
   blanched
5ml/1 tsp white peppercorns
2.5ml/½ tsp coriander seeds
175g/6oz/scant 1 cup sugar
10ml/2 tsp salt
5ml/1 tsp ground ginger
450ml/¾ pint/scant 2 cups
   cider vinegar
1.5ml/¼ tsp cayenne pepper
red chillies (optional)

1 Peel, core and chop the apples. Chop the sultanas, onion and almonds. Tie the peppercorns and coriander seeds in muslin (cheesecloth), using a long piece of string, and then tie to the handle of a preserving pan or stainless steel pan.

2 Put the sugar, salt, ground ginger and vinegar into the pan, with the cayenne pepper to taste. Heat the mixture gently, stirring, until the sugar has completely dissolved.

3 Add the chopped fruit to the pan. Bring the mixture to the boil and then lower the heat. Simmer for about 1½–2 hours, or until most of the liquid has evaporated.

4 Spoon the chutney into warmed sterilized jars and place one whole fresh chilli in each jar, if using. Leave until cold, then cover and seal the jars and attach a label to each one. Store in a cool, dark place. The chutney is best left for a month to mature before use and will keep for at least 6 months, if correctly stored.

Variation
For a mild chutney, add only a little cayenne pepper. For a spicier one, increase the quantity to taste.

Christmas Mincemeat

In many mincemeat recipes, the raw ingredients are simply mixed together. Here, gentle simmering in the slow cooker develops and intensifies the flavours, so that the mincemeat can be used immediately without being left to mature. At the same time, heating it to simmering point helps prevent fermentation, and allows a longer shelf-life.

Makes about 1.75g/4lb

450g/1lb cooking apples
115g/4oz/¾ cup glacé (candied)
   citrus peel
115g/4oz/½ cup glacé
   (candied) cherries
115g/4oz/½ cup ready-to-eat
   dried apricots
115g/4oz/1 cup blanched almonds
150ml/¼ pint/²⁄₃ cup brandy
225g/8oz/1 cup currants
225g/8oz/1⅓ cups sultanas
   (golden raisins)
450g/1lb/3¼ cups seedless raisins
225g/8oz/1 cup soft dark
   brown sugar
225g/8oz/1²⁄₃ cups suet (US
   chilled, grated shortening) or
   vegetarian suet
10ml/2 tsp ground ginger
5ml/1 tsp ground allspice
5ml/1 tsp ground cinnamon
2.5ml/½ tsp grated nutmeg
grated rind and juice of 1 lemon
grated rind and juice of 1 orange

1 Peel, core and chop the apples, then roughly chop the citrus peel, glacé cherries, apricots and blanched almonds.

2 Reserve half the brandy and put the rest into the ceramic cooking pot with all the other ingredients. Stir until well mixed. Cover the ceramic cooking pot with the lid and switch the slow cooker to high. Cook for 1 hour.

3 Stir the mixture well, then re-cover the pot and reduce the temperature to low. Cook for a further 2 hours, stirring halfway through cooking to prevent the mixture from overheating and sticking to the sides of the pot.

4 Remove the lid and leave the mixture to cool completely, stirring occasionally. Stir the reserved brandy into the mincemeat and spoon the mixture into sterilized jars. Cover and store in a cool, dark place for up to 6 months. Once opened, store in the refrigerator and use within 2 weeks.

Apple Chutney Energy 1299kcal/5525kJ; Protein 10.9g; Carbohydrate 299.5g, of which sugars 297.7g; Fat 14.9g, of which saturates 1.1g; Cholesterol 0mg; Calcium 254mg; Fibre 10.4g; Sodium 3.97g.
Mincemeat Energy 7149kcal/30087kJ; Protein 55.6g; Carbohydrate 1114g, of which sugars 1088.3g; Fat 267.7g, of which saturates 106.3g; Cholesterol 0mg; Calcium 1228mg; Fibre 47.3g; Sodium 774mg.

Confit of Slow-cooked Onions

Onions are caramelized in the slow cooker in sweet-sour balsamic vinegar.

Serves 6

30ml/2 tbsp extra virgin olive oil
15g/¹/₂oz/1 tbsp butter
500g/1¹/₄lb onions, thinly sliced
3–5 fresh thyme sprigs
1 bay leaf
30ml/2 tbsp light muscovado (brown) sugar, plus a little extra
30ml/2 tbsp balsamic vinegar, plus a little extra
120ml/4fl oz/¹/₂ cup red wine
50g/2oz/¹/₄ cup ready-to-eat prunes, chopped
salt and ground black pepper

1 Put the oil and butter in the ceramic cooking pot and heat on high for 15 minutes. Add the onions and stir to coat. Cover the cooker, then place a folded dish towel on top. Cook the onions for 5 hours, stirring the mixture occasionally.

2 Season, then add the thyme, bay leaf, sugar, vinegar and wine. Stir until the sugar has dissolved, then stir in the prunes. Re-cover and cook for 1¹/₂–2 hours, until thickened. Adjust the seasoning, adding sugar and/or vinegar to taste. Store in the refrigerator.

Shallots in Balsamic Vinegar

These whole shallots, slowly simmered in balsamic vinegar and herbs, are a modern variation on pickled onions, but with a gentler, smoother flavour. Bay leaves and thyme are used here, but rosemary or oregano work just as well.

Serves 6

30ml/2 tbsp muscovado (molasses) sugar
several bay leaves and a few fresh thyme sprigs
300ml/¹/₂ pint/1¹/₄ cups balsamic vinegar
500g/1¹/₄lb shallots, peeled

1 Put the sugar, bay leaves, thyme and vinegar in a pan. Bring to the boil. Add the shallots, cover and simmer for 40 minutes.

2 Transfer the mixture to a sterilized jar, seal and label, then store in a cool, dark place. Alternatively, drain and transfer to a serving dish. Leave to cool, then chill until ready to serve.

Blushing Pears

As this slow-cooker pickle matures, the fruits absorb the colour of the vinegar, giving them a glorious pink hue. Their deliciously spicy, sweet-and-sour flavour is especially good with cold Christmas dishes, or with well-flavoured cheese.

Makes about 1.3kg/3lb

1 small lemon
450g/1lb/2¹/₄ cups golden sugar
475ml/16fl oz/2 cups raspberry vinegar
7.5cm/3in cinnamon stick
6 whole cloves
6 allspice berries
150ml/¹/₄ pint/²/₃ cup water
900g/2lb firm pears

1 Using a sharp knife, thinly pare a few strips of rind from the lemon. Squeeze out the juice and add to the ceramic cooking pot with the strips of rind.

2 Add the sugar, raspberry vinegar, spices and water, and switch the slow cooker to high. Cover the cooker and leave to heat for about 30 minutes, then stir gently until the sugar has completely dissolved. Re-cover the cooker with the lid and heat for a further 30 minutes.

3 Meanwhile, prepare the pears. Peel and halve the pears, then scoop out the cores using a melon baller or small teaspoon. If the pears are particularly large, cut them into quarters rather than into halves.

4 Add the pears to the slow cooker, cover and cook for 1¹/₂–2 hours, turning them occasionally to coat them in the syrup. Check the pears frequently; they should be tender and translucent but still retain their shape.

5 Using a slotted spoon, remove the pears from the slow cooker and pack them into hot sterilized jars, adding the spices and strips of lemon rind.

6 Remove any scum from the surface of the syrup remaining in the ceramic cooking pot, then ladle it over the pears in the jars. Cover and seal. Store for a few days before eating, and use within 2 weeks.

Confit of Onions Energy 133kcal/556kJ; Protein 1.2g; Carbohydrate 16.5g, of which sugars 14.6g; Fat 5.9g, of which saturates 1.8g; Cholesterol 5mg; Calcium 26mg; Fibre 1.6g; Sodium 20mg.
Shallots in Balsamic Vinegar Energy 50kcal/209kJ; Protein 1g; Carbohydrate 11.8g, of which sugars 9.9g; Fat 0.2g, of which saturates 0g; Cholesterol 0mg; Calcium 24mg; Fibre 1.2g; Sodium 3mg.
Blushing Pears Energy 2133kcal/9086kJ; Protein 5g; Carbohydrate 560.3g, of which sugars 560.3g; Fat 0.9g, of which saturates 0g; Cholesterol 0mg; Calcium 230mg; Fibre 19.8g; Sodium 50mg.

Red Hot Relish

Make this tangy, stovetop relish during the summer months when tomatoes and peppers are plentiful. It enhances simple, plain dishes, such as a cheese or mushroom omelette.

Makes about 1.3kg/3lb

800g/1³/₄lb ripe tomatoes, skinned and quartered
450g/1lb red onions, chopped
3 red (bell) peppers, seeded and chopped
3 fresh red chillies, seeded and finely sliced
200g/7oz/1 cup sugar
200ml/7fl oz/scant 1 cup red wine vinegar
30ml/2 tbsp mustard seeds
10ml/2 tsp celery seeds
15ml/1 tbsp paprika
5ml/1 tsp salt

1 Put the chopped tomatoes, onions, peppers and chillies in a preserving pan, cover with a tight-fitting lid and simmer over very low heat for about 10 minutes, stirring once or twice, until the tomato juices start to run.

2 Add the sugar and vinegar to the tomato mixture and slowly bring to the boil, stirring occasionally until the sugar has dissolved completely. Add the mustard seeds, celery seeds, paprika and salt, and stir well to combine.

3 Increase the heat under the pan slightly and cook the relish, uncovered, for about 30 minutes, or until most of the liquid has evaporated and the mixture has a thick, but moist consistency. Stir frequently towards the end of the cooking time to prevent the mixture sticking to the pan.

4 Spoon the relish into warmed sterilized jars, cover and seal. Store the jars in a cool, dark place and leave to mature for at least 2 weeks before eating. Use the relish within 1 year of making.

Cook's Tip
Once opened, store jars of the relish in the refrigerator and consume within 2 months.

Carrot and Almond Relish

This Middle Eastern classic, usually made with long fine strands of carrot, is available from many supermarkets. This version, using coarsely grated carrots and gently simmered in the slow cooker, tastes much better.

Makes about 675g/1¹/₂lb

15ml/1 tbsp coriander seeds
500g/1¹/₄lb carrots, grated
50g/2oz fresh root ginger, finely shredded
200g/7oz/1 cup caster (superfine) sugar
120ml/4fl oz/¹/₂ cup white wine vinegar
30ml/2 tbsp clear honey
7.5ml/1¹/₂ tsp salt
finely grated rind of 1 lemon
50g/2oz/¹/₂ cup flaked (sliced) almonds

1 Crush the coriander seeds using a mortar and pestle. Put them in the ceramic cooking pot with the carrots, ginger and sugar, and mix well.

2 Put the vinegar, honey and salt in a jug (pitcher), and stir until the salt has dissolved completely. Pour the mixture over the carrots. Mix well, cover and leave for 1 hour.

3 Switch the slow cooker to high and cook for about 2 hours, or until the carrots and ginger are almost tender, stirring only if the mixture looks dry around the edges.

4 Stir in the lemon rind and cook for a further 1 hour, until the mixture is thick. Stir once towards the end of the cooking time to prevent the mixture from sticking to the base of the ceramic cooking pot.

5 Put the almonds in a frying pan and toast over low heat until just beginning to colour. Gently stir into the relish, taking care not to break the almonds.

6 Spoon the relish into warmed sterilized jars, cover and seal. Store in a cool, dark place and leave to mature for 1 week. The relish will keep unopened for up to 1 year. However, once the jars have been opened, store them in the refrigerator and use within 2 weeks.

Red Hot Relish Energy 1270kcal/5392kJ; Protein 17.8g; Carbohydrate 306.2g, of which sugars 294.1g; Fat 5.6g, of which saturates 1.4g; Cholesterol 0mg; Calcium 320mg; Fibre 23.5g; Sodium 121mg.
Carrot Relish Energy 1407kcal/5947kJ; Protein 13.7g; Carbohydrate 289.6g, of which sugars 285.8g; Fat 29.4g, of which saturates 2.7g; Cholesterol 0mg; Calcium 268mg; Fibre 15.7g; Sodium 2898mg.

Papaya and Lemon Relish

This chunky relish is best made with a firm, unripe papaya. The long, gentle simmering in the slow cooker allows plenty of time for all the flavours to mellow. Serve the relish with roasted vegetables, or cheese and crackers.

Makes 450g/1lb
1 large unripe papaya
1 onion, very thinly sliced

175ml/6fl oz/generous ¾ cup
  red wine vinegar
juice of 2 lemons
165g/5½oz/¾ cup golden caster
  (superfine) sugar
1 cinnamon stick
1 bay leaf
2.5ml/½ tsp hot paprika
2.5ml/½ tsp salt
150g/5oz/1 cup sultanas
  (golden raisins)

1 Peel the papaya and cut it in half lengthways. Remove the seeds and discard, then cut the flesh into small chunks of a roughly similar size.

2 Place the papaya chunks in the ceramic cooking pot, add the onion slices and stir in the red wine vinegar. Switch the slow cooker to the high setting, cover with the lid and cook for 2 hours.

3 Add the lemon juice, golden caster sugar, cinnamon stick, bay leaf, paprika, salt and sultanas to the ceramic cooking pot. Gently stir the mixture thoroughly until all of the sugar has completely dissolved.

4 Cook the chutney for a further 1 hour. Leave the cover of the slow cooker off to allow some of the liquid to evaporate and the mixture to reduce slightly. The relish should be fairly thick and syrupy.

5 Ladle the chutney into hot sterilized jars. Seal the jars and store the chutney for 1 week before using to allow it to mature a little and for the flavours to further develop. The chutney should be used within 1 year of making it. However, once a jar has been opened, the chutney should be stored in the refrigerator and consumed within 2 weeks.

Fresh Lemon Curd

This classic tangy, creamy curd is still one of the most popular of all the curds, and it is simple to make in the slow cooker. Delicious spread thickly over freshly baked bread or served with pancakes, it also makes a wonderfully rich, zesty sauce for fresh fruit tarts.

Makes about 450g/1lb
finely grated rind and juice of
  3 lemons (preferably unwaxed
  or organic)
200g/7oz/1 cup caster
  (superfine) sugar
115g/4oz/½ cup unsalted
  butter, diced
2 large (US extra large) eggs
2 large (US extra large) egg yolks

1 Pour about 5cm/2in very hot water into the ceramic cooking pot. Switch the cooker to high. Put the lemon rind and juice, sugar and butter in the largest heatproof bowl that will fit inside the slow cooker.

2 Put the bowl into the cooking pot, then pour near-boiling water around it to come just over halfway up the sides. Leave for 15 minutes, stirring occasionally, until the sugar has dissolved. Remove to cool for a few minutes. Turn the slow cooker to low.

3 Put the eggs and yolks in a bowl and beat together with a fork. Strain the eggs into the lemon mixture, and whisk well until combined. Cover the bowl with foil, then return it to the cooker.

4 Cook the lemon curd on low for 1–2 hours, stirring every 15 minutes, until thick enough to lightly coat the back of a wooden spoon.

5 Pour the curd into small warmed sterilized jars. Cover and seal. Store in a cool, dark place, ideally in the refrigerator, and use within 3 months. Once opened, store in the refrigerator.

Cook's Tip
To make sharp, tangy lime curd, replace the lemons with the grated zest and juice of 4 large ripe, juicy limes. Lime curd has a lovely pale greenish hue.

Papaya Relish Energy 1294kcal/5511kJ; Protein 8.4g; Carbohydrate 332.7g, of which sugars 332.7g; Fat 1.4g, of which saturates 0g; Cholesterol 0mg; Calcium 272mg; Fibre 16.1g; Sodium 1111mg.
Lemon Curd Energy 1968kcal/8224kJ; Protein 22.4g; Carbohydrate 215.3g, of which sugars 215.3g; Fat 118.9g, of which saturates 66.9g; Cholesterol 1102mg; Calcium 277mg; Fibre 0g; Sodium 895mg.

Fine Lime Shred Marmalade

There is something about lime marmalade that really captures the flavour and essence of the fruit. It is important to cut the slices very finely though, because lime skins tend to be tougher than those on any other citrus fruit and can result in a chewy marmalade if cut too thickly.

Makes about 2.25kg/5lb
12 limes
4 kaffir lime leaves
1.2 litres/2 pints/5 cups water
1.3kg/3lb/6½ cups sugar, warmed

1 Halve the limes lengthways, then slice thinly, reserving any pips (seeds). Tie the pips and lime leaves in a muslin (cheesecloth) bag and place the bag in a large pan with the sliced fruit.

2 Add the water to the pan and bring to the boil. Cover and simmer gently for 1½–2 hours, or until the rind is very soft. Remove the muslin bag, leave to cool, then squeeze it over the pan to release any juice and pectin.

3 Add the sugar to the pan, and stir over low heat until the sugar has dissolved. Bring to the boil, then boil rapidly for 15 minutes, stirring occasionally, until setting point is reached (105°C/220°F).

4 Remove the pan from the heat and skim off any scum. Leave to cool for 5 minutes, stir, then pour into warmed sterilized jars. Seal, then label when cold. Store in a cool, dark place.

Cook's Tips
• *To check for setting, spoon a little marmalade on to a chilled saucer and chill for 2 minutes. Push the surface with your finger; if wrinkles form, the marmalade is ready to bottle.*
• *Stirring marmalade after standing and before potting distributes the fruit rind evenly as the preserve begins to set.*

Whiskey Marmalade

Home-made marmalade is easy to make – it only needs slow simmering on the stove. It tastes delicious and flavouring it with whiskey makes it a special treat.

Makes 3.6–4.5kg/8–10lb
1.3kg/3lb Seville oranges
juice of 2 large lemons
2.75kg/6lb/13½ cups sugar, warmed
about 300ml/½ pint/1¼ cups Irish whiskey

1 Scrub the oranges, using a nylon brush, and pick off the disc at the stalk end. Cut in half and squeeze the juice, retaining the pips (seeds). Quarter the peel, cut away and reserve any thick white pith, and shred the peel – thickly or thinly depending on how you prefer the finished marmalade.

2 Cut up the reserved pith roughly and tie it up with the pips in a square of muslin (cheesecloth), using a long piece of string. Tie the bag loosely and hang it from the handle of the pan.

3 Add the cut peel, strained juices and 3.5 litres/6 pints/15 cups water to the pan. Bring to the boil and simmer for 1½–2 hours, or until the peel is very tender.

4 Lift up the bag of pith and pips and squeeze it out well over the pan to extract as much pectin as possible. Add the sugar to the pan and stir over low heat until it has completely dissolved.

5 Bring to the boil, and then boil hard for 15–20 minutes or until setting point is reached. To test, put a spoonful of marmalade on to a cold saucer. Allow to cool slightly, and then push the surface of the marmalade with your finger. Setting point has been reached if a skin has formed. If not, boil a little longer and keep testing until it sets.

6 Skim, if necessary, and leave to cool for 15 minutes, then stir to redistribute the peel. Divide the whiskey among eight to ten warmed, sterilized jars and swill it around. Pour in the marmalade.

7 Cover and seal the jars while the marmalade is still hot. Label when cold, and store in a cool, dark place until required. The marmalade will keep well for 6 months.

Lime Marmalade Energy 5250kcal/22386kJ; Protein 13.3g; Carbohydrate 1380.1g, of which sugars 1380.1g; Fat 2g, of which saturates 0.7g; Cholesterol 0mg; Calcium 1263mg; Fibre 0g; Sodium 112mg.
Whiskey Marmalade Energy 10,736kcal/45,734kJ; Protein 22.8g; Carbohydrate 2657.8g, of which sugars 2657.8g; Fat 1.3g, of which saturates 0g; Cholesterol 0mg; Calcium 1.74g; Fibre 15.6g; Sodium 187mg.

Rowan Jelly

This astringent jelly is made from the orange fruit of mountain ash trees, which flourish in areas where deer run wild.

Makes about 2.25kg/5lb
1.3kg/3lb/12 cups rowan berries
450g/1lb crab apples, or windfall
cooking apples
450g/1lb/2¼ cups sugar
per 600ml/1 pint/2½ cups
juice, warmed

1 Cut the rowan berries off their stalks, rinse them in a colander and put them into a preserving pan. Remove any damaged parts from the apples before weighing them, then cut them up roughly without peeling or coring. Add the apples to the pan with 1.2 litres/2 pints/5 cups water, which should cover the fruit.

2 Bring to the boil and simmer for about 45 minutes, until the fruit is soft, stirring occasionally and crushing the fruit with a wooden spoon to extract the pectin. Strain the fruit through a jelly bag or a fine sieve (strainer) into a bowl overnight.

3 Measure the juice and allow 450g/1lb/2¼ cups sugar per 600ml/1 pint/2½ cups juice. Return the juice to the rinsed out preserving pan and add the measured amount of sugar.

4 Stir over low heat until the sugar has dissolved, and then bring to the boil and boil hard for 10 minutes, until setting point is reached. To test, put a spoonful of jam on to a cold saucer. Allow to cool slightly, and then push the surface of the jam with your finger. Setting point has been reached if a skin has formed. If not, boil a little longer and keep testing until it sets.

5 Skim, if necessary, and pour into warmed, sterilized jars. Cover, seal and store in a cool, dark place until needed. The jelly will store well for 6 months.

Cook's Tip
For a less astringent jelly, an equal quantity of apples and berries may be used, such as 900g/2lb of each.

Barley Water

Like lemonade, barley water has long been enjoyed as a refreshing summer drink and, until a generation ago, it would always have been home-made. Barley water is usually served cold, but is also very good when served as a hot drink.

Makes about 10 glasses
50g/2oz/⅓ cup pearl barley
1 lemon
sugar, to taste
ice cubes and fresh mint sprigs,
to serve

1 Wash the pearl barley, then put it into a large stainless steel pan and cover with cold water. Bring to the boil and simmer gently for about 2 minutes, then strain the liquid. Return the barley to the rinsed pan.

2 Wash the lemon and pare the rind from it with a vegetable peeler. Squeeze the juice and set aside.

3 Add the lemon rind and 600ml/1 pint/2½ cups cold water to the pan containing the barley. Bring to the boil over a medium heat, then simmer the mixture very gently for 1½–2 hours, stirring occasionally.

4 Strain the liquid into a jug (pitcher), add the lemon juice, and sweeten to taste with sugar. Mix until well combined. Leave to cool. Pour the liquid into a bottle and keep in the refrigerator to use as required.

5 To serve, dilute the barley water to taste with cold water, and add ice cubes or crushed ice and a sprig of fresh mint, if you like.

Variations
• *The barley water can also be used with milk, in which case omit the lemon juice as it would curdle the milk.*
• *Make up the barley water with hot water to be drunk as a cold remedy.*

Rowan Jelly Energy 2340kcal/9993kJ; Protein 15.8g; Carbohydrate 606.4g, of which sugars 606.4g; Fat 0.5g, of which saturates 0g; Cholesterol 0mg; Calcium 1.03g; Fibre 54g; Sodium 80mg.
Barley Water Energy 37.9kcal/161.6kJ; Protein 0.43g; Carbohydrate 9.44g, of which sugars 5.26g; Fat 0.08g, of which saturates 0g; Cholesterol 0mg; Calcium 3.8mg; Fibre 0g; Sodium 0.5mg.

Cranberry and Apple Punch

When you are throwing a party, it is good to have a non-alcoholic punch available. Here, the slow cooker extracts maximum flavour from fresh ginger and lime peel.

Serves 6

1 lime

5cm/2in piece fresh root ginger, peeled and thinly sliced

50g/2oz/¼ cup caster (superfine) sugar

200ml/7fl oz/scant 1 cup near-boiling water

475ml/16fl oz/2 cups cranberry juice

475ml/16fl oz/2 cups clear apple juice

ice and chilled sparkling mineral water or soda water, to serve (optional)

1 Pare the rind off the lime and place in the ceramic cooking pot with the ginger and sugar. Pour over the water and stir until the sugar dissolves.

2 Cover with the lid and heat on high or auto for 1 hour, then reduce the temperature to low or leave on auto and heat for a further 2 hours. Switch off the slow cooker and leave the syrup to cool completely.

3 When cold, strain the syrup through a fine sieve (strainer) into a large serving jug (pitcher) or punch bowl and discard the lime rind and ginger.

4 Squeeze the juice from the lime and strain through a sieve into the syrup. Stir in the cranberry and apple juices. Cover and chill in the refrigerator for at least 3 hours.

5 To serve, pour or ladle the punch over plenty of ice in tall glasses and add sparkling mineral water or soda water, if using.

> **Cook's Tip**
> *You can now buy all kinds of different apple juices made from specific varieties of apple. They have distinctive flavours, and it is well worth searching them out.*

Hot Spiced Wine

On a cold winter's evening, there is nothing more welcoming than a glass of warm spicy wine. The slow cooker is particularly useful when you are making the wine for guests: you can prepare the spiced wine up to four hours before your guests arrive, and the slow cooker will keep it at the ideal serving temperature until you are ready to serve.

Serves 8

50g/2oz/¼ cup soft light brown sugar

150ml/¼ pint/⅔ cup near-boiling water

2 small oranges, preferably unwaxed

6 whole cloves

1 stick cinnamon

½ whole nutmeg

1½ bottles red wine, such as Bordeaux

150ml/¼ pint/⅔ cup brandy

1 Put the sugar in the ceramic cooking pot and pour in the near-boiling water. Stir until the sugar has dissolved, then switch the slow cooker to high.

2 Rinse the oranges, then press the cloves into one and add it to the slow cooker with the cinnamon stick, nutmeg and red wine. Halve the remaining orange, then slice it and set aside until required.

3 Cover the slow cooker with the lid and cook on high or auto for 1 hour, then reduce to low or leave on auto and heat for 3 hours.

4 Stir the brandy into the spiced wine and add the reserved orange slices. Heat for a further 1 hour.

5 Remove the whole orange and the cinnamon stick from the cooking pot. The wine is now ready to serve and can be kept hot for up to 4 hours. Serve in heatproof glasses.

> **Cook's Tip**
> *Use heatproof glasses with a handle, so that guests can hold the hot wine easily.*

Cranberry and Apple Punch Energy 111kcal/475kJ; Protein 0.1g; Carbohydrate 27.9g, of which sugars 16.5g; Fat 0.1g, of which saturates 0g; Cholesterol 0mg; Calcium 8mg; Fibre 0g; Sodium 2mg.
Hot Spiced Wine Energy 162kcal/675kJ; Protein 0.2g; Carbohydrate 6.8g, of which sugars 6.8g; Fat 0g, of which saturates 0g; Cholesterol 0mg; Calcium 12mg; Fibre 0g; Sodium 10mg.

Spiced Coffee

This slow-cooker recipe combines the sweet-tart flavour of apples and spices to make a delicious, tangy coffee.

Serves 4

475ml/16fl oz/2 cups apple juice
30ml/2 tbsp soft brown sugar,
  to taste
2 oranges, thickly sliced
2 small cinnamon sticks
2 whole cloves
pinch of ground allspice
475ml/16fl oz/2 cups hot, freshly
  brewed strong black coffee
halved cinnamon sticks,
  to serve (optional)

1 Pour the apple juice into the ceramic cooking pot and switch the slow cooker on to high.

2 Add the brown sugar, orange slices, cinnamon sticks, whole cloves and allspice to the pot and stir. Cover the cooker with the lid and heat for about 20 minutes. Gently stir the mixture until the sugar has dissolved completely, then re-cover with the lid and heat for 1 hour.

3 When the juice is hot and infused with the spices, switch the slow cooker to the low setting to keep the juice warm for up to 2 hours.

4 Strain the juice into a bowl, discarding the orange slices and spices. Pour the hot coffee into the juice and stir. Quickly pour into warmed mugs or espresso-style cups, adding a halved cinnamon stick to each, if you like.

Cook's Tips
• *For a good flavour, use strong coffee – espresso or filter-/plunger-brewed at 75g/3 tbsp/scant ½ cup coffee per 1 litre/1¾ pints/4 cups water.*
• *To make an alcoholic version of this drink, replace a quarter of the apple juice with the French apple brandy, Calvados. Stir in the brandy after straining the spice-infused apple juice and removing the spices.*

Mexican Hot Chocolate

Blending or whisking the hot chocolate before serving gives it a wonderfully frothy texture. The slow cooker is particularly good for heating the milk in this recipe, because the gentle heating process allows the cinnamon and cloves to infuse and flavour the hot chocolate with their warm and spicy flavour.

Serves 4

1 litre/1¾ pints/4 cups milk
1 cinnamon stick
2 whole cloves
115g/4oz dark (bittersweet)
  chocolate, chopped into
  small pieces
2–3 drops of almond extract
whipped cream and unsweetened
  cocoa powder or grated
  chocolate, to serve (optional)

1 Pour the milk into the ceramic cooking pot. Add the cinnamon stick and cloves, cover with the lid and switch the slow cooker to high. Leave to heat the milk and infuse the spices for 1 hour, or until the milk is almost boiling.

2 Add the chocolate pieces and almond extract to the milk and stir until melted. Turn off the slow cooker.

3 Strain the mixture into a blender (it may be necessary to do this in a couple of batches) and whizz on high speed for about 30 seconds, until frothy. Alternatively, whisk the mixture in the ceramic cooking pot with a hand-held electric whisk or a manual wire whisk.

4 Pour or ladle the hot chocolate into warmed heatproof glasses. If you like, top each with a little whipped cream and a dusting of unsweetened cocoa powder or grated chocolate. Serve immediately.

Cook's Tip
Traditional Mexican hot chocolate is always warmly spiced. It is a popular breakfast drink, often served with delicious deep-fried churros, which are Mexican sugared doughnuts.

Spiced Coffee Energy 85kcal/363kJ; Protein 0.2g; Carbohydrate 22.2g, of which sugars 22.2g; Fat 0.1g, of which saturates 0g; Cholesterol 0mg; Calcium 11mg; Fibre 0g; Sodium 3mg.
Hot Chocolate Energy 262kcal/1102kJ; Protein 9.9g; Carbohydrate 30g, of which sugars 29.7g; Fat 12.3g, of which saturates 7.6g; Cholesterol 17mg; Calcium 309mg; Fibre 0.7g; Sodium 109mg.

Index